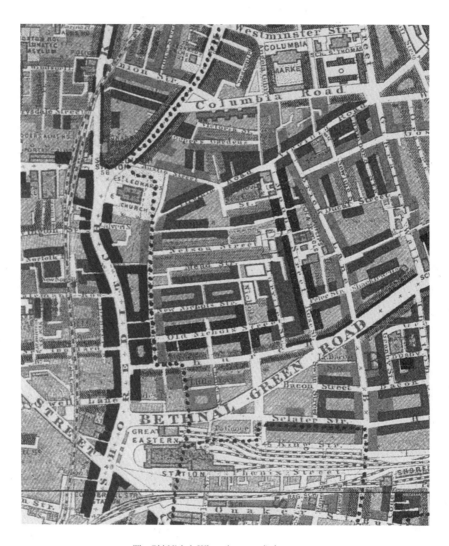

The Old Nichol: Where the streets had two names

Duplications include: Old Castle Street, which was also known as Virginia Road/Row, its continuation; Collingwood Street became Jacob Street; Nelson Street became Fournier Street; Vincent Street became Mead Street; Shearwood Place is Sherwood Place on some maps. There were three Cross Streets: the northernmost one was also known as Jacob Place, the central one was aka Short Street, and Chance Street was the alter ego of the southernmost one. NB Church Street is the main road running east-west at the southern edge of this map; Club Row is running south from it – a continuation of Nichol's Row. Map courtesy of the Museum of London.

The Blackest Streets

The Life and Death of a Victorian Slum

The Blackest Streets

The Life and Death of a Victorian Slum

SARAH WISE

THE BODLEY HEAD
LONDON

Published by The Bodley Head 2008

4 6 8 10 9 7 5 3

First published in Great Britain in 2008 by
The Bodley Head
Random House, 20 Vauxhall Bridge Road,
London SW1V 2SA

www.rbooks.co.uk

Addresses for companies within The Random House Group Limited
can be found at:
www.randomhouse.co.uk/offices.htm

The Random House Group Limited Reg. No. 954009

A CIP catalogue record for this book
is available from the British Library

ISBN 9780224071758

The Random House Group Limited supports The Forest Stewardship
Council (FSC), the leading international forest certification organisation.
All our titles that are printed on Greenpeace approved FSC certified
paper carry the FSC logo. Our paper procurement policy can be found at
www.rbooks.co.uk/environment

Typeset by Palimpsest Book Production Limited,
Grangemouth, Stirlingshire

Printed and bound in Great Britain by
Clays Ltd, St Ives plc

For Anne-Marie Collins

Contents

PART FOUR
Stripeland

'Twas August, and the fierce sun overhead
Smote on the squalid streets of Bethnal Green,
And the pale weaver, through his windows seen
In Spitalfields, looked thrice dispirited.
I met a preacher there I knew, and said:
'Ill and o'erworked, how fare you in this scene?'
'Bravely!' said he; 'for I of late have been
Much cheered with thoughts of Christ, the Living Bread.'...

Matthew Arnold, 'East London'

I thank the Lord for what I've had,
If I had more I should be glad,
But now the times they are so bad,
I must be glad for what I've had.

Grace, as sung by children receiving
charity dinners in the Old Nichol

The poetry of history lies in the quasi-miraculous fact that once, on this earth, once, on this familiar spot of ground, walked other men and women, as actual as we are today, thinking their own thoughts, swayed by their own passions, but now all gone, one generation vanishing into another... The Dead were, and are not. Their place knows them no more, and is ours today. Yet they were once as real as we, and we shall tomorrow be shadows like them.

G.M. Trevelyan

Acknowledgements

Huge thanks are due to Alison Light of the Raphael Samuel History Centre at the University of East London for allowing me to quote extensively the wonderful material that her late husband harvested in his interviews with Arthur Harding; the result of that work, *East End Underworld: Chapters in the Life of Arthur Harding* (1981), is long overdue for a reprint. Thanks also to Annette Day, Senior Curator of the Museum of London's Oral History & Contemporary Collecting Department, for permission to listen to and quote from Samuel's original tape recordings; those quotations appear by kind permission of the Museum and of the trustees of the Raphael Samuel Estate.

Stewart P. Evans, crime historian and indefatigable Ripper-hunter, told me that journalist Donald McCormick was the source of one of the worst libels of the Old Nichol district, and I am extremely grateful to him for his generosity in sharing with me his research on this aspect of Ripper lore.

John Davis of Queen's College, Oxford, has been a great guide to the complicated franchise arrangements of late-Victorian London, and the detailed research that he and colleague Duncan Tanner undertook in the 1980s on the electoral rolls of East London have proved invaluable for my attempts to assess the true level of political engagement of the slums' residents.

Charles Booth's granddaughter, Belinda Norman-Butler, and her nephew, Richard Martineau, kindly granted me permission to quote from the notebooks and papers of the Booth Archives, held at the London School of Economics, and I am grateful to Sue Donnelly and the staff of the Archives, too, for their helpfulness over many visits.

Peter Guillery of English Heritage shared with me his expertise on London's eighteenth-century small buildings. Nicholas Malton of the

NSPCC kindly allowed me to access that organisation's archives and pointed me towards further useful reading; while John Nicholls and Christine Romanowski of the London City Mission generously revealed the treasures in their small archive in Tower Bridge Road.

Thanks also to the helpful and friendly staff of the Library at Lambeth Palace; the London Metropolitan Archives; the British Library's Social Sciences room at St Pancras, and Newspaper Library at Colindale; Malcolm Barr-Hamilton and Christopher Lloyd of Tower Hamlets Local History Library and Archive; the Guildhall Library and Prints Room; Rachel Roberts, archivist of Cheltenham Ladies' College, and Rupert Williams of St Hilda's East, in Old Nichol Street; Jonathan Evans of the Royal London Hospital Archives and Museum; Natalie Hill of the Buildings Team at the National Monuments Record; and Clare Rider and Adrian Blunt at the Library and Archives of Inner Temple. Lucinda Rogers, Leila McAlister and Jean Locker told me what life around the Bandstand is like today.

Thank you to Will Sulkin and Jörg Hensgen, publisher and editor respectively. Prue Jeffreys and Vanessa Taylor – invaluable, wise counsel, as ever. Peter Neish, thanks for everything, once again.

PART ONE

DEAD LETTERS

The Empire of Hunger

At four o'clock in the afternoon of a damp, chilly Saturday in November 1887, two men kept an appointment with each other at Shoreditch railway station. Both were Continental revolutionaries – one, a Communist, wished to reveal to the other, an Anarchist, the very worst face of poverty he had discovered in the East End during his stay in London.

The Communist led the Anarchist into the nearby Hackney Road, then turned south, plunging into the maze-like streets of the area known as the Old Nichol. The bustle of the main road suddenly ceased, and as the two walked southwards the streets grew narrower and darker – canyons of two- and three-storey housing, stretching as far into the distance as the mist and drizzle allowed them to see. The Anarchist soon became disorientated by the repeated left turnings, right turnings, his friend was making, and felt strangely unsettled by the symmetry of the streets, the monotony of the blackened buildings and the repetitive vistas revealed on their convoluted journey. This appeared to him to be a world leached of colour: wherever he looked, all he could discern were various shades of grey. After five minutes of walking, the Communist took the Anarchist down a narrow passage (so narrow they had to turn sideways and move crabwise along) that ran between two houses and into a tiny square surrounded on all sides by tenement buildings. He motioned to a small mound of earth rising between pools of filthy liquid and, as bidden, the Anarchist took his stand upon the mound the better to survey the scene. There was no one in sight, and although they could make out the distant, subdued roar and rumble of the four busy streets that boxed the Old Nichol in, there was no sound nearby. There was not a blade of grass to be seen, but heaps of what looked like rubbish, broken furniture and the like; in one corner lay the carcass of a dog, and here and there a rag of grey linen on a clothesline hung motionless in the cold air. The stone steps leading to the tenement doorways were worn down by generations of feet; every window pane was cracked, some smashed; thin columns of smoke rose from a few of the chimneys and dispersed into the mist. The Anarchist thought that it looked 'as though death had just passed in giant strides through these streets and touched all breathing things with his redeeming hand'. Redeeming: the Anarchist saw death as a blessing in such a place as this.

They returned to the street and walked down the middle of the roadway. They now noted shy, curious eyes following them, and interpreted the gaze as conveying half fear and half hatred, with another quality that they could only define as the look of starvation. They greeted a man kneeling in the gutter hammering at the wheel of a broken cart, and he did not reply; a ragged woman crouching in a doorway started in fright as they neared her, clutched her small, equally ragged child to her breast and rose to her feet as if to defend herself.

The two began to walk faster, feeling as though they were intruders, and guiltily conscious of their own comparatively well-dressed, well-fed appearance. The Anarchist had been shocked by the manifestations of destitution he had just witnessed, and had the sensation, as he later wrote, that he had suddenly stumbled upon 'the secrets of a strange life', with codes of its own not to be understood by outsiders. He privately christened the fifteen acres of the Old Nichol 'The Empire of Hunger'.

The Communist muttered to him that when the Worker State was established, this type of environment would be eradicated. Fear, hate, envy and hunger would disappear. Behaviour would change. The Anarchist did not agree, believing that only when all forms of government were abolished would humanity be able to govern itself, with wisdom and compassion. The reason such a place as the Old Nichol existed, he said, was because the State – parliament, the law – prevented these individuals from running their own lives wisely.[1]

They walked on through the labyrinth until with immense relief they were back out again on a main thoroughfare, Bethnal Green Road, amid the roar of its Saturday market stalls, carts, carriages and cabs.

*   *   *

That was how the streets of the Old Nichol struck strangers on a grey, miserable day; but what was it like indoors? There's no need to knock – in fact, there may well be no front door to knock at, since there is often little else left to burn when you've no money for coals. If the door is still on its hinges, it will no doubt be standing wide open. There's nothing to steal, and no one to fear, and these people have been surveyed and questioned and stared at on such a regular basis for so many years that they're not likely to mind one more set of curious individuals intruding.

Here in Ann's Place, a little court off the western edge of Boundary Street, is a two-roomed tenement that has its own weather: the walls are running with damp, and the meagre fire burning in the grate has drawn some of the moisture out of the plaster, creating a small local fog. Many Nichol rooms feature such indoor mists, caused by the interaction of fires and damp and ill-swept chimneys. This is home to a married couple with six children. There is no bed, and when you ask them how they sleep, the wife replies, 'Oh, we sleep about the room how we can.' Walk through a hole in the wall into the second room and you'll see her husband and two adolescent sons making uppers for boots. They are so busy they don't even look up or gesture; they are haggard and hollow-cheeked. The wife explains that they have to finish their order and deliver it to a local wholesaler by eight o'clock tonight (it's a Saturday), or the family will not be able to eat on Sunday.

Things are not much better at Mrs P——'s home, in New Nichol Street, running east from Boundary Street. Her husband died recently and she supports herself, her children and her aged mother by matchbox-making – a common home industry in the Nichol. Mrs P——'s hands are deformed by rheumatism; nevertheless, she collects the wood, labels and sandpaper (she must pay for her own glue) from a Bryant & May depot in nearby Bacon Street and can earn herself 2 ¼d for every gross (144) she completes. When she gets as good as the best matchbox-makers, and if her family develops the knack too, she will manage to make eight gross a day, bringing in 1s 6d – around one-half of her weekly rent.* The room she and her family occupy is

* See Appendix 1 on p. 277 for a table of late-Victorian East London wages and prices.

filled with drying matchboxes, so there's little space in which to move, and the children are almost always out of doors as a result; sometimes the smaller ones, if they can bear their hunger no longer, will eat her glue.

At 5 Old Nichol Street is another of the many single-room family dwellings in the district. Here, the mother is out at work, having left her seven-year-old daughter and nine-year-old son playing alongside the coffin in which lies their dead father. Along the street at number 53, the Nichol's notorious overcrowding reaches its highest density, with ninety people crammed into one ten-roomed house. But a similar level of tenant-packing is achieved by a room, 7ft 3in by 14ft, in Collingwood Place, which, it is said, is called home by twelve individuals.

At 34 Half Nichol Street, one large family shares its single room with six ducks; the sanitary inspector who has reported this is more used to seeing livestock in the cellars of the Nichol – donkeys, cows, geese and rabbits. Caged songbirds are often to be spotted on windowsills, kept either for the bird-singing competitions in certain Nichol pubs, or for sale in the bird and animal markets of nearby Club Row and Sclater Street. Plant-life abounds in the tenements, and many a foetid Nichol room is to be found packed with the gorgeous blooms of the street flower-sellers. Hawkers of watercress, lavender and herbs also keep their stock in their homes after collecting it from Spitalfields fruit and vegetable market, half a mile to the south. Vile back yards can sometimes be seen filled with cut roses ready for the next day's hawking. In fact, the 730 or so houses of the Nichol adapt themselves very well to various small trades. At 36 Fournier Street Mr Joseph Hyams is one of the area's many smoked-fish purveyors; he has constructed three smoke-holes built of wood, with a tile roof and a large cowl. Nobody minds the smell – it is one of the more pleasant in the neighbourhood. It mingles with another predominant aroma – that of the timber trade. Nearly one-fifth of workers in the Nichol make their living as woodworkers and furniture-makers,* and there are hundreds who live by making cabinets, couches, chairs, mirrors and toys; as sawyers, carvers, french polishers,

* See Appendix 2 on p. 279 for a table of occupations of the inhabitants of the Nichol.

ivory turners, japanners and upholsterers, their tiny homes doubling as makeshift workshops. On weekdays, carts and barrows full of newly sawn planks and freshly turned furniture components sail through the streets, and men and boys laden with tables, chairs, wardrobes, whatnots and tallboys struggle along to the local wholesalers. The Nichol is home to several timber yards, with their large piles of mahogany, rosewood, birch, beech, ash, Italian oak and American walnut.

In a garret in Old Nichol Street, Mr and Mrs Bordon, both in their sixties, are working at two handlooms, a spinning wheel and a wool-winder. The room, for which they pay 3s 3d a week, is in a terrible state of repair but they keep it as clean as they can. The dilapidated ceiling slants down from a height at one end of 7ft 6in to 4ft 6in at the other. They have plenty of work, but the pay is poor and wages are getting lower. This is the notorious 'sweating' system of labour, and one local nickname for the Nichol is 'The Sweaters' Hell', so prevalent here is this type of increasingly unremunerative home-based artisan work. The couple have worked for seventeen years to supply a respected West End furnishings store with woollen upholstery fringing, which retails for a very high price. Working together, they earn 9s a week. They have to be very careful to keep the wool clean and to make sure that the rain that drips through their roof never damages their completed trimming. Once, the husband tried weaving at a small textiles factory but found himself earning 8s a week for a fourteen-hour day, in which he was also expected to act as the factory's porter and errand boy.

Nearby, an eighty-four-year-old former governess to a duke proudly hoards all the crested letters she has received from her noble connections, and elsewhere in the Nichol the brother of a baronet, who has lost all his inheritance through drink, settles to his work of manufacturing billiard balls for a nearby pub.

At 9 New Turville Street, a dog-dealer named James Box has taken over the whole of a former weaver's cottage. His dogs have free run of the three storeys, and Box also stores his offal there, which smells appalling. The ceiling falls in before long, and the rain makes the rotting wood smell so bad that the local sanitary inspector is called in.

In her room around the corner a woman is nursing her young child, who is in bed with a fever. On the floor lies the body of her six-year-old son, who died a few hours earlier. Her husband is a 'chanter' – a singer of street ballads, the sheet music and lyrics of which he sells: 'He's out in the streets singing about the man who was hung on Monday morning. He was cut up when Bobby died in the night, and said he would leave off singing when he had got half a crown, and come home.' When the man does get back, he storms out again when he finds a religious missionary attempting to get his wife to pray.

In a small room in Boundary Street, Charles Mowbray, tailor, is falling behind with his rent. He's secretly rather pleased that this is so, as he has recently co-founded the anti-slum-landlord No-Rent League. In the room that he shares with his wife and four children he has set up a tiny print shop, where he publishes manifestos, posters and pamphlets urging the poor on to revolution. When he finally absconds, Mowbray leaves behind, for his landlord, the paving stone he has been using as an ink slab, with a note stating that the stone is as hard as a slum landlord's heart.[2]

Plenty of people have come to visit Nichol inhabitants such as these, offering practical advice, charitable donations and spiritual guidance – the latter two often interlaced. So thoroughly explored was the Nichol by late 1887, the time of the Anarchist–Communist field trip, that it was becoming a national embarrassment; in fact, in the very month of the foreign revolutionaries' Nichol adventure, commissioners appointed by the Home Secretary were hearing evidence about its sanitary inadequacies at a public inquiry. Added urgency for such an investigation came from the economic crises and subsequent social unrest that were deepening from the mid-1880s.

The Nichol's thirty or so streets and courts of more or less rotten early-nineteenth-century houses were home to around 5,700 people and had a death rate that was almost double that of the rest of Bethnal Green, the very poor East London parish at whose western boundary the Nichol stood. (Six of its streets were in Shoreditch, across the border that gave Boundary Street its name.) The annual mortality rate of the Nichol in the late 1880s was 40 per 1,000 people; Bethnal Green's hovered between 22 and 23 per 1,000 for these years, not much above the London (and, indeed, the national) figure of 19 to 20 per 1,000. (Today, the death rate for England and Wales is 5.95 per 1,000.) One-third of all these London deaths were those of babies and infants. Bethnal Green's death rate for babies under the age of one was in line with the average figure for England and Wales of 150 per 1,000 live births; in the Nichol it was a horrific 252 per 1,000.[3]

Communicable diseases such as whooping cough (which killed more children under five than any other transmissible illness), scarlet fever, diphtheria, measles, smallpox, bronchitis and, above all, tuberculosis proved fatal to twice as many people in the Nichol as in the rest of Bethnal Green, even though the Nichol's contagion rates were not particularly high. Once stricken, however, you were less likely to recover here than elsewhere. Contemporary medical thinking had no hesitation in linking such appalling statistics to environment – to overcrowding; primitive or non-existent sanitary fittings; unconquerable, pervasive damp; and lack of light and wholesome air.

This local scandal was made all the more piquant by rumours that the owners of the freeholds and leaseholds of these death-traps included peers of the realm, churchmen, Bethnal Green vestrymen and several corpses: almost half the properties were managed by solicitors and other trustees to benefit the estates of the long-deceased, and two of the largest Nichol holdings – the Gwatkin Estate and the Woolley Estate, with, between them, 297 houses – were farmed partly on behalf of phantoms. Several other estates, meanwhile, were the subject of long-running Chancery cases, some never to be resolved within the Nichol's lifetime.

One investigator of housing conditions described the mysterious nature of slum-property ownership, writing that many tenants had huge difficulty in finding out who their landlords really were.

> Their rent books contain only the names of the tenants, the amounts and the dates of payment, and the initials of the rent collector. They can . . . only ascertain by chance to whom their houses belong. The collectors are often merely the agents' clerks. Sometimes the persons for whom the collectors act are only farmers of the rents; and they not only bully the tenants, but often take the law into their own hands, and turn the people into the streets without legal warrant of any kind.[4]

A single house could have several interested parties, with the ground landlord, or freeholder, being unaware (if they were alive, that is) of how his or her leaseholder was behaving. Frequently, leaseholders would, in turn, lease out various parts of a house, with the chain of tenure ending in the weekly tenant, who in turn might sublet to lodgers. Lodgers were even known to sublet to other lodgers.

Some 85 per cent of working-class households in London spent one-fifth or more of their income in rent; half of them paid between a quarter and half of their income to their landlords. Per cubic foot, the rents of the Nichol were between four and ten times higher than those of the finest streets and squares of the West End, averaging between 2s 3d to 3s for a single room and around 7s 6d for a three-room lodging. This yielded high returns for speculative property dealers – 'the vampyres of the poor', as another housing-reform campaigner called them.[5] The London evening newspaper the *Pall Mall Gazette* criticised the avidly entrepreneurial house-farmers of London, stating: 'These fever dens are said to be the best-paying property in London, and owners who, if justice were done, would be on the treadmill, are drawing from 50 to 60 per cent on investments in tenement property in the slums.'[6] In fact, the *Gazette* had under-estimated the money that could be made, and profits as large as 150 per cent per annum were not uncommon.[7] The potential for high rental returns was balanced by the higher risks involved in owning and renting slum property. The landlord in the very poorest areas was probably more likely to face the 'moonlight-flitting' tenants who left by night with unpaid arrears, and the squatters and wreckers who might strip a house of its pipework, fireplaces and roof lead to sell on for scrap.

This rotten housing stock was the only type of property that the very poorest could afford to rent, and the surviving Poor Law case histories of the area's inhabitants do indeed show that the Nichol was for many an East Ender a final stopping-off point before entry into the dreaded workhouse, and the less-dreaded death therein. Nichol homes were decrepit, even lethal, but they catered for a vast, desperate section of the London property market. The district was only just outside the City boundary, fifteen minutes' walk from Liverpool Street station, and twenty-five minutes from the Bank, Mansion House and Guildhall, and therefore well situated for those who lived by street selling. It was even closer to Shoreditch's Curtain Road furniture depots and wholesale emporia; and its relative proximity to the London

Docks – consumer of vast amounts of casual, ill-paid labour – further increased the Nichol's desirability to those with the least ability to carve out their own destiny.

With regard to overcrowding, a bad situation had been made significantly worse by the destruction of thousands of homes in the areas immediately adjacent to the Nichol. In the twenty years to 1887, various 'improvement' projects had substituted amenities and commercial premises for dwellings. These included the widening and re-routing through slum streets of Bethnal Green Road in the late 1870s, at the southern edge of the Nichol, which unhoused 800 people; the creation of a large number of warehouses and factories in Shoreditch; and the construction, within the Nichol, of three massive London School Board buildings and a new church in Old Nichol Street. Further pressure on available housing stock resulted from the constant flow of hopeful young migrants from the British countryside, which placed great demands on both living space and employment prospects, as did the influx into East London of Jews from eastern Europe and Russia; by 1890, some 32,000 were estimated to have settled in Whitechapel, Spitalfields and Stepney, districts to the south and east of Bethnal Green. However, the 129,000-strong population of Bethnal Green itself, in the late 1880s, was still racially homogenous, a phenomenon that was at its most noticeable in the Nichol, where second- and third-generation Londoners formed a large majority. While just over a third of London's four million inhabitants had been born outside the metropolis, this figure dipped to an eighth in the Nichol – the lowest figure for any part of London.[8] Although there was a significant number of settled and half-settled Irish gypsy ('didicai') and Romany families, and, to judge by surnames, descendants of the late-seventeenth-century Huguenot settlers, the Nichol was a Cockney enclave.

It was widely alleged that it was a criminal enclave too, with its strange geography assisting a street robber or sneak-thief in his dash to safety. The Nichol had always been a backwater, but in the nineteenth century the vast warehouses along the west side of Boundary Street (punctuated by just two narrow passageways) cut it off from the shops and businesses of Shoreditch High Street. To the north, Virginia Road/Old Castle Street, to the east, Mount Street, and to the south, Church Street/Bethnal Green Road contained few sizeable routes into and out of the maze. 'In the Nichol, there seemed to be a wall enclosing you,' said one resident. 'You got the idea in your head that you were a nation apart, that you were something different.'[9] If you knew which alley connected to which court, which house could be passed right through to bring you out into a different street, which section of fence could be lifted for an escape from one back yard into another, you could easily evade pursuing policemen. Quite how many of the Nichol's inhabitants needed such aids to flight was to be one of the most controversial aspects of its late history.

How to Create a Slum

Its early history was fairly murky too. The lands that became the Nichol are likely to have been a garden, with large barn, belonging to the hospital of St Mary Without Bishopsgate, founded in 1179 a quarter of a mile to the south. Also known as St Mary Spital, the hospital had at the time of its Dissolution in 1538 around 180 beds for the relief of the sick poor. Simcock's (or Sincook's, or Smethecook's) Well, mentioned in 1399, supplied St Mary Spital with water, and may have been the small spring found in Old Nichol Street during building work at the end of the nineteenth century.[1]

It has also been suggested that at the eastern extent of the Nichol there had been buildings and a garden belonging to the nunnery of St John the Baptist at Holywell, founded in 1189 just west of today's Shoreditch High Street. There was a strongly held local belief in the Nichol that there had once been a monastery halfway along Mount Street (which was called Rose Street until the early 1800s), and the eastern part of the Nichol was colloquially known as Friars Mount. Rabidly anti-Catholic writer George Borrow decided in 1874, on very little evidence, that the name Friars Mount was a relic of the days of Popery. In Mount Street, he wrote,

> a set of fellows lived in laziness and luxury on the offerings of foolish and superstitious people . . . The neighbourhood, of course, soon became a resort for vagabonds of every description, for wherever friars are found, rogues and thieves are sure to abound. And about Friars Mount, highwaymen, coiners and Gypsies dwelt in safety under the protection of the ministers of the miraculous image.[2]

But there's a rival explanation. Shoreditch was the meeting point of crucial routes north and east, and during the English Civil War, earthworks, with forts and cannons, were built near the beginning of both Kingsland and Hackney Roads in 1642 – part of the chain of twenty-three fortifications constructed by Parliamentarian London against the expected arrival of 15,000 Royalist troops. Mount Street follows the line of the rampart connecting these Cromwellian redoubts to the next most easterly fort in the chain, halfway along Brick Lane, and some Bethnal Green antiquarians believed that the Nichol's Old Castle Street and Mount Street names commemorated the existence of this rampart.[3] In the 1720s, one James Fryer was farming the field around a small hillock in Mount Street/Rose Street, and it is, alas, far more likely that the 'Friar' part of the name derives from this rather earthbound fact than from Borrow's tales of rollicking monks and Romish debauchery.

Since the tenth century there had been a church of St Leonard's at Shoreditch. The third (and current) St Leonard's, by George Dance the Elder, opened for worship on the north-western corner of the Nichol in 1740, leading to another local nickname for the area – the Back o' St Leonard's.

Upon the Dissolution of the monasteries, the gardens and fields had passed into private hands, and the various parcels of land became known by such names as Preston's Gardens (the southernmost part of the Nichol) and Swan Field (later Mount Street; today's Swanfield Street). At some point, Cock Lane (later Boundary Street and Church Street) was formed, and its curious L-shape, with only tiny alleys connecting it to the wider world, was the original topographical misfortune on which the Nichol's later seclusion would be based.

In the 1670s, central London merchants and lawyers – rather than local men – began buying up the small freeholds behind St Leonard's. Gray's Inn lawyer John Nichol bought 4¾ acres bounded by the two arms of Cock Lane and built seven houses in the fields; in 1680 he leased the land to Jon Richardson, a mason, with permission to dig clay for brick-making, which Richardson did, during London's Restoration era building boom. Richardson then subleased his land to builders to construct houses, and in the 1680s and 1690s Nichol Street (later Old Nichol Street) was developed. Nichol Row and its houses were added by 1703; New Nichol Street between 1705 and 1708, and later

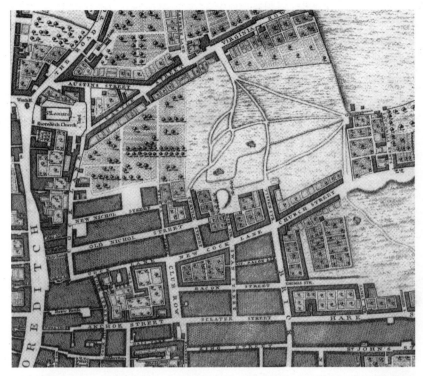

The Nichol in 1746, when the northern part of the area was still a mix of brick-fields and market gardens.

Half Nichol Street.[4] Many of the 25,000 Protestant Huguenot *émigrés* – whose main trade was silk-weaving – who arrived from France in the late 1680s and 1690s, settled in Spitalfields and south Bethnal Green.[5] Many houses in the Nichol featured 'long lights' (also known as 'weavers' windows') – casements that maximised daylight in the upper storey where handloom weavers worked.

Virginia Row/Road and (Old) Castle Street had been built in the 1680s, and Mount/Rose Street existed by 1725. Between these and Half Nichol Street lay fields, until the first decade of the nineteenth century, when the Nichol tragedy really began. Together with a flurry of demolition and rebuilding of the late-seventeenth-century houses, speculative new building saw the creation of Nelson, Vincent, Collingwood, Trafalgar, Mead, Christopher and Sarah Streets, and numerous courts in between. Away from the eyes of surveyors, and in contravention of the Building Acts, an almost instant slum was erected by local

Early-eighteenth-century houses in New Nichol Street, part of the original wave of Nichol development.

builders who had leased the land from owners who did not care what use was made of their acreage so long as it was profitable. Admiral Nelson, his various captains and their victories at Trafalgar and St Vincent had their names commandeered for some of the new streets – a fate their enemies would have relished had they known of it.[6] Later, in the 1870s, the street names of the northern section of the Nichol were changed, in order to protect the admiral's memory from further contamination by association.

Local soap and tallow manufacturer Saunderson Turner Sturtevant bought up land and had mean little houses, some just eight feet in width, constructed in Mount Street between 1804 and 1819. Sturtevant may also have been responsible for one of the most important factors in the swift deterioration of the building fabric of the Nichol. Instead of using traditional mortar, the speculative builders found a cheaper lime-based substance derived from the by-products of soap-making at a local manufactory, possibly Sturtevant's. This 'cement' was known as Billysweet, and quickly became infamous for never thoroughly drying out, and so leading to sagging, unstable walls. Other architectural crimes added to the Nichol's problems. Most of the early-1800s houses had no foundations, their floorboards being laid on to bare earth; cheap timber and half-baked bricks of ash-adulterated clay were used. Roofs were badly pitched, resulting in rotting rafters and plaster-work, with this damp from above joining the damp seeping upwards from the earth to create permanently soggy dwellings.

By 1836 the entire fifteen acres had been built, or rebuilt, upon; but construction didn't stop there. Over the next fifty years, the back yards of Nichol homes and other open spaces would sprout a separate shanty-style development, outrunning surveyors' and cartographers' attempts to keep accurate maps of the Nichol – a parallel world of illegal courts, small houses, workshops, stables, cowsheds and donkey stalls, substantially increasing the already high population density.

The same decades saw the utter failure of a slew of legislation to deal with rotten metropolitan environments and to improve the housing conditions of the nation's working classes. Victorian government, and the Gladstonian Liberalism of 1868–94 in particular, is often identified with *laissez-faire*. The market place made its own rules, and was not to be subject to any governmental interference. Yet non-intervention in commercial matters sat ill with the Evangelicalism and moralism of many who would have considered themselves among *laissez-faire*'s staunchest defenders. And, in fact, the briefest glance at the parliamentary history of the second half of the nineteenth century reveals that far from this being the era of 'Leave it be', it was a period of vast expansion of central government and ceaseless inquiry into the social effects of, among other things, the unfettered market. The conflict between *laissez-faire* and moral/social concern was to result in some very interesting legislative tinkering, nowhere more so than in the field of working-class housing. No fewer than twenty-five Acts, amendments to Acts and consolidations of existing laws were passed by parliament between 1847 and 1885 in the expectation that 'permissive', or 'adoptive', legislation would be all that was necessary to encourage landlords to improve their behaviour and to make it more attractive for private companies – including the so-called Five Per Cent Philanthropists, who needed to make that sum as a minimum profit from working-class housing – to build and let 'model lodgings' for the poor. Surely these moves would make State involvement in the supply or regulation of housing as unnecessary as it was undesirable. The political parties did not significantly differ in their approaches to the housing issue. No matter if legislation had a Liberal or Tory source,

A street in the Nichol, photographed in the 1880s.

the two sacred Victorian cows that were on no account to be slaugh-
tered were the sanctity of private property, and the self-reliance of the
poor. Concern that the poor should not be 'de-moralised' by being
given any help salved the conscience of many who had property rights
that were well worth protecting.

Two early pieces of legislation sought to improve the quality and
stimulate the creation of a greater quantity of low-rent housing. The
1851 Common Lodging Houses Act required the registration and
regular inspection of the hundreds of dosshouses, or 'flop-house kips',
that gave nightly shelter to those with no hope of a more permanent
roof over their heads. In 1883 the Metropolitan Police estimated that
27,000 Londoners slept in common lodging-houses; the Nichol
contained seven dosshouses, accommodating a total of around 150
people. Meanwhile, the Labouring Classes' Lodging Houses Act, also
passed in 1851, hoped to encourage the local authorities of England
and Wales (its vestries) to create new working-class tenements by
permitting them to borrow money for this purpose (using the rates
as loan security) to buy land and build homes, which were then to be
quickly disposed of to the private sector. This Act, extraordinarily

ahead of its time, sanctioning the use of rates money for 'public' housing, was hailed by Charles Dickens as 'the best piece of legislation that ever proceeded from the English parliament'.[7] Nationally, only one vestry ever made use of it.

Another early Act, the 1855 Nuisances Removal Act, allowed vestries to prevent over-crowding in any house that was occupied by more than one family; other nuisances included bad paving, drainage, ventilation and water supply, and the more nebu-lous concepts of cleanliness and state of repair. But the 40s fine the Act permitted held little terror for unscrupulous landlords. Eleven years later, the Sanitary Act gave Whitehall the right to intervene and compel vestries to ensure that nuisances were remedied. Whitehall never did so. Under the same Act, vestries were permitted to register tenement houses let to more than one family and to draw up over-crowding by-laws. But by 1884, of London's thirty-eight vestries, only Chelsea and Hackney had registered their low-rent, multi-occupancy tenements. The Bethnal Green Vestry, the local authority for all but six streets of the Nichol, chose to register not one single house.

Next came two series of Acts that were to be known by the names of the men who introduced them to parliament: William McCullagh Torrens (Liberal MP for the central London seat of Finsbury) and Sir Richard Cross (Tory Home Secretary under Disraeli). The distinction between the Torrens Acts and the Cross Acts is that the former targeted individual unhealthy houses, to be dealt with by vestries, with action funded from the local rates; while the latter were intended to deal with entire areas that were so insanitary as to be fit only for whole-sale demolition and reconstruction by a centralised authority, usually a city council, and paid for by the whole city.[8] One of William Torrens's original intentions, dropped during two and a half years of parlia-mentary wrangling, had been to allow vestries to build, own and rent out housing for the poor. But in the late 1860s, this was felt to be far too radical. The member for Portsmouth, Serjeant S. Gaselee, argued

in the House of Commons that this would be 'monstrous . . . If such
a principle were admitted, they did not know where it could stop. The
next demand made of them [parliament] might be to provide clothing,
if not carriages and horses, for the poor.'[9]

In 1876, the Shoreditch Vestry ordered the demolition, under the
Torrens Act, of a group of houses in Ann's Place, off Boundary Street
(home to the starving bootmaker and his family on p. 5). But the
owner of these tenements successfully appealed to the court of Quarter
Sessions, which allowed him to 'repair' them instead; this despite a
consultant hired by the vestry describing himself as 'nearly poisoned'
by his visit to Ann's Place.[10] The legal case cost the Shoreditch Vestry
the huge sum (to be paid from the rates) of £500, and the medical
officer of health, Dr Henry Gawen Sutton, was convinced that these
repairs would prove to be a superficial patching up, and that within
weeks the conditions at Ann's Place would be as bad as ever. This
experience of trying to implement the Torrens Act had shown the
Shoreditch Vestry good reason why it should shirk its responsibilities.
In addition, the Act had included no workable provision for rehousing
any tenants made homeless as a result of demolition, which was all
the excuse that vestries needed to continue doing nothing at all.
Permission to act was also permission not to act, and so the vast
majority of London's vestries opted for inertia.

In the meantime, the governing councils of Edinburgh, Liverpool
and Glasgow had all obtained powers under local Acts of compulsory
purchase, demolition and reconstruction and were making use of them,
creating the first municipal housing in Britain. London, by contrast,
didn't even have a council. The nearest thing was the Metropolitan
Board of Works, created in 1855 as a supervisory body for London's
sewers, fire brigade, street improvements, highways and parks, as well
as a rag-bag of other matters that included enforcement of animal-
disease regulations, the licensing of dairies, slaughterhouses and baby-
farms; and the sale and storage of petrol and other explosive substances.
The Board oversaw more than 300 separate bodies acting under 250
pieces of legislation; it had no jurisdiction over London's magistrates,
who maintained powers in sanitary matters; nor over the Metropolitan
Police, the London School Board or the Poor Law, and had no medical
officer of health of its own to co-ordinate health and sanitation matters
across the capital. The Board was not directly elected by London

A Nichol court. The photographer did not name the precise location in this shot, but it may have been Ann's Place, off Boundary Street – the site of repeated legal attempts at closure on the grounds of being unfit for human habitation.

ratepayers – the vestries chose its forty-five members – and its major actions (the creation of new streets, for example) each had to be separately sanctioned by Whitehall. Was this any way to run an imperial capital – *the* imperial capital? Many did not think so, but attempts at London government reform failed throughout the 1860s, 70s and 80s.

In 1875 the Metropolitan Board of Works had its administrative portfolio added to with the passing of the Cross Act – the first attempt at comprehensive slum clearance.[11] Henry Gawen Sutton, in Shoreditch, tried, in 1882 and again in 1883, to use the Cross Act to deal with Ann's Place, Boundary Street, since he had failed in his attempt to use the Torrens Act. But when he reported the condition of the tenements to the Metropolitan Board of Works, in the hope that they would demolish the entire court, the Board told him that the Shoreditch Vestry would have to deal with the place under the Torrens Act, at the expense of its own ratepayers. It said that no action could be taken by the Board until it had had further experience in operating the Cross Act. So, nothing new could be tried, because it had not been tried before. Many a medium-sized London slum would be batted back and forth in this way as the vestries and the Board attempted to evade the cost and the controversy of razing private property to make room for new working-class housing.

In proposing his legislation, it had been Richard Cross's intention that 'science', in the form of medico-sanitary professionals, would have the main say in whether or not an area should be condemned and cleared. However, the naïvety of this view quickly became apparent: unfitness for human habitation proved itself to be a subject-ive judgement, not an empirical fact. Appeals by property-owners to higher courts were often successful when medical officers of health were unable to prove beyond all reasonable doubt that a certain house or street could not be lived in without injury to health. Worse, some slum-property-owners (in Shoreditch, the figure was given as nine out of ten such owners) allowed homes to dilapidate, or even speeded up the deterioration process by acts of vandalism, hoping that the vestry could be compelled to make them a cash offer, as the legislation allowed. This loophole – which seemed to reward the very worst slum-lords – would be closed in 1885.

So unworkable did the Torrens and Cross Acts prove to be that a House of Commons Select Committee was convened to consider the source of their failure. Blame was attributed to the complexity and costliness of Cross; and to the slow, tedious nature of proving under Torrens that an individual property was unfit.[12] The Artisans' Dwellings Act of 1882 was passed, which lowered the numbers of people required to be rehoused in a demolition/reconstruction scheme to half the number evicted and further reduced the compensation payable to owners of 'nuisance' property. Some forty acres of London slum were subsequently demolished by the Metropolitan Board of Works, at a cost of almost £1 million, and on these sites twenty-two housing schemes were built by private philanthropic companies and individ-uals (these included George Peabody's blocks, and those of Sidney Waterlow's Improved Industrial Dwellings Company). But there was a net loss of 1,300 homes, and the new buildings had fewer one-room dwellings and so tended to be less affordable to the poorest; so slums like the Nichol, with their proliferation of single-room homes, became even more crowded as the evicted flocked to them. Many of the new 'model dwellings' were constructed with little regard to increasing the levels of light and ventilation within rooms, let alone making any concessions to homeliness or picturesqueness. Home industries were either banned outright or severely restricted. Rules and regulations, and the presence of on-site block superintendents, deterred many independence-loving poor Londoners from even applying for a place in the new buildings.

Joseph Chamberlain – Liberal MP for Birmingham, demagogue and prime mover in the more municipal-minded 'Imperial Liberalism' that would split Gladstone's party – complained bitterly that parliamentary action had been 'tainted and paralysed by the incurable timidity with which Parliament, largely recruited from men of great possessions, is accustomed to deal with the sacred rights of property'.[13] The failure of these Acts had been seized upon by the city's various working-men's Radical associations and clubs, and a body called the Local Rights Association passed a resolution condemning the Acts as total failures in helping the working man to achieve a salubrious home; rent strikes were urged. Detailed evidence of how London's slum tenants themselves felt about their living conditions is not easy to come by at this point, but there are indications of pockets of unrest by the early 1880s. One Bethnal Green vestryman, speaking towards the end of 1883, claimed that in his parish 'the present state of things was creating almost an insurrection like that in Ireland', referring to the agitation among Irish tenant farmers for fair rents and fixity of tenure. The vestryman said that a 'No Rent' movement was forming in the parish, to encourage the poor to withhold their weekly payments for insanitary property.[14] Certainly, as many as 2,000 people at a time would flock to hear anti-landlord speeches being made in Victoria Park, at the eastern end of Bethnal Green, a popular meeting place for demonstrators. Several No-Rent and Fair-Rent associations of various political hues – all acting independently – sprang up throughout Bethnal Green, two of them focused on the Nichol.

By the mid-1880s, three decades of housing legislation had managed to worsen the living conditions of the poor. Various measures passed in the 1860s and 1870s to encourage private philanthropic tenement-building had failed to create the sheer numbers of new homes required to replace the demolished houses; and all the while, the population level was rising, old houses were deteriorating, and central London land prices were soaring. The working-class housing question was like a great blocked drain. But a number of well-informed and articulate individuals were determined to flush it through. They were a hetero-geneous crew – Radicals, Tories, vicars, journalists, philanthropists, Oxford men, magistrates – all pushing to get Progress flowing, and in 1884 a Royal Commission was appointed to consider the crisis afresh.

Dr Bate's Dilemma

The Commission spawned unremarkable new legislation, the 1885 Housing of the Working Classes Act, which trimmed compensation payments to slum-property-owners and removed the requirement of vestries to purchase bad property, should the owner desire them to do so. But it was another dead letter. A more significant outcome of the Commission was the formation, from members of its own committee, of the Mansion House Council on the Dwellings of the Poor – a watchdog with blue blood in its veins, pushing at local level for action on sanitary matters. Prominent among the Mansion House Council's members were the Archbishop of Canterbury; his Catholic opposite number Cardinal Manning, Archbishop of Westminster; the Marquis of Salisbury; the Bishop of Wakefield; the Lord Mayor of London and various of his aldermen.

The Royal Commission recognised how crippled all initiatives had been by the lack of an effective central governing authority for London but also declared that the vestries were to blame because of their inactivity. One member of the Commission said that allowing vestries to appoint their own medical officer of health was like allowing wolves to appoint shepherds.[1] Medical officers were recruited, remunerated and dismissed by vestries, and so for many of them, their working life could be a series of compromises between effective sanitary administration of the parish and keeping their job. Many, perhaps most, London officers proved themselves heroic in very difficult circumstances – in some cases, working themselves to an early death in their zeal to seek out and do battle against metropolitan squalor. Others were more interested in status and pay than in cleaning up the parish. Some were reluctant to condemn bad housing, deciding, for humanitarian reasons, that it was better for people to have a rotten roof over their head than no roof at all. Bethnal Green's medical officer, Dr George Paddock Bate (1844–1925), spent his thirty-seven-year professional life balancing his horror at the notorious uncleanliness of Bethnal Green (with the Nichol as its darkest heart of filth) with his need to ensure that he did not upset his vestry employers: if Bate were to find himself dismissed, and a more compliant doctor hired in his place, the health of the parish would be even more fatally compromised. Like most vestry medical officers, Bate worked only part time for the parish, the vestry being keen not to pay a full salary. (An Act of 1855 compelled vestries to appoint a medical officer; left to make their own choice, many parishes would have had no officer at all.) Bate was a tall, aristocratic-looking man and he lived in a smart town house in King Edward Road, Hackney, from where he ran his private practice; in 1875 he was appointed Bethnal Green's medical officer.[2] His duties included exploring and advising on the parish's water supply, drainage, factories and workshops, food safety, infectious-disease notification, birth and death registration, house disinfections, milk supply, vaccination, refuse collection, dairies and bakehouses, bathhouses, mortuaries, cemeteries and public lavatories. He worked alongside (but was not in charge of) a tiny team of two sanitary inspectors, whose colossal workload also included the inspection of the district's 18,000 or so inhabited houses. Bethnal Green's two-man team, in a parish with a population of 129,000, compared unfavourably with almost every other London parish (Wandsworth, for example, had a population of 210,000 but twelve sanitary inspectors, and six medical officers). The Bethnal Green team's only assistance came from a permanent clerk and a disinfecting man, who appears enigmatically in the records as Meyrick the Flusher.

Bate produced impressive monthly and annual surveys of sanitation, disease and death in Bethnal Green, exhaustive in their data and occasionally powerful enough to silence some of the more parsimonious vestrymen, who challenged every farthing spent in the public good. Bate himself disapproved of the Cross Acts, and was glad that mass clearances had never been used in Bethnal Green: 'To demolish wholesale would no doubt be a very great hardship on the poor people, some of whom might have to go into the workhouse unless their friends consented to take care of them,' he said.[3] In June 1883 Bate forwarded to Whitehall a list of 215 Bethnal Green homes that he

A house in Half Nichol Street with a subterranean passageway; one in ten Nichol houses featured these tunnels.

believed could be dealt with under the Torrens Act – that is to say, as separate, individual dilapidated buildings; almost two-thirds of the houses on Bate's list were in the Nichol. Old Nichol Street itself was described by Bate as being 'in a dangerous condition to health, so as to be unfit for human habitation'. Many houses in the street featured one of the most alarming architectural phenomena Bate had ever come across: the only way to reach the back yard, where the dustbins and lavatory were to be found, was by descending rickety steps, passing through an unlit, unpaved cellar passageway just five feet high, and emerging up another set of steps into the yard. (At number 70 Virginia Road, a dangerously rotten stepladder was found to be giving access to the cellar passage.) Bate discovered in 1883 that some 10 per cent of houses in the Boundary Street area had these subterranean corridors. More worryingly, he found that two cellar rooms in the Nichol were being illegally rented out for accommodation. Since 1855 underground living quarters had to have a window that gave at least 1ft of light at pavement level, a fireplace, drainage and head room of at least 7ft. Bate considered these Nichol cellar rooms highly dangerous to health.

Many of the Nichol houses were revealing the effects of their jerry-building of eighty years earlier. Often, the house lay as much as

A resident emerges into the back yard from the cellar passageway at 13 Old Nichol Street; over the fence a collection of costermongers' barrows can be seen.

eighteen inches below the level of the pavement, and in rainy weather water trickled into the ground floors, some of which were of bare earth with floorboards simply resting upon it; dampness would seep upwards through wainscoting, old plaster and exposed laths. Walls and ceilings were often observed to be bulging, as though pregnant with their inheritance of damp. In December 1885 a coroner's jury would go along to view 58 Old Nichol Street during the post-mortem of Ann Crocomber, fifty-four, who had died of heart disease. Her room was, they later told a newspaper, in 'a shocking condition'; so shocking that part of the ceiling fell in on them during their visit.[4]

Bate also discovered that numbers 42 and 44 Old Nichol Street had each had a house built in their back yards; number 46 had two. In

Half Nichol Street, someone had constructed a vast pigeon loft in a tiny back 'garden'. Like most late-Victorians, Bate was obsessed with ventilation, convinced that fevers festered and spread wherever air ceased to move; and he was particularly alarmed that the 'malposition', as he called it, of the Nichol houses, sheds and workshops was blocking the passage of air. In Sherwood Place, Mount Square, Turville Buildings and George Terrace, Bate also recommended tearing down seven perfectly legally constructed back-to-back houses, as well as a number of high brick walls that turned otherwise passable streets into cul-de-sacs. Bricks and mortar seemed to be asphyxiating the Nichol.[5]

Bate deplored the working-class habit of sealing up all sources of draughts – even if this was probably wise, in order to avoid aches and pains from stiff joints, or rheumatism, especially when, in the winter months, warmth was a luxury. Wherever a pane was missing in a Nichol window, newspaper, rags – even old hats – were to be spotted doing duty for the absent glass. In summer too, windows tended to be kept closed except between midnight and 6 a.m., to keep out the London Blacks – the coal-fire smuts that swept into every room and dirtied everything within.

The Bethnal Green Vestry rejected Bate's request that these murderous houses be dealt with by application of the Torrens Act, and Whitehall made no response at all. So for the next four years, Bate had little choice but to wrestle with the Nuisances Removal Act in order to force improvement or closure upon individual houses. It was usually more cost-effective for landlords to exhaust every legal manoeuvre before carrying out significant repairs. Wheedling with the authorities, and out-and-out fibbing, also helped to delay expenditure. Many of the properties in the Nichol were held on fast-expiring leases, and if the landlord gambled right, s/he would be able to get to the end of the lease without spending any money on improvements. Bate would later reveal the steps in the dance that landlords, unsympathetic magistrates and the supine local authority were able to lead those who wanted to improve working-class housing. The choreography went something like this. A nuisance would be reported (often anonymously, sometimes by former tenants) to the vestry or the medical officer, an inspection would take place and, if action was needed, a notice to ensure the removal of the nuisance was served on the landlord. If this was disregarded, a summons was taken out at the local magistrates' court if the magistrate agreed that a nuisance existed, or had existed and was likely to recur. The magistrate could issue an order for the landlord to make the property safe and habitable within a set time, and could prevent premises being used for human habitation until they had been rendered fit. In certain circumstances the vestry could do the work itself and charge the landlord for it. But only two of the six justices with whom Bate dealt regularly at Worship Street magistrates' court, in Shoreditch, would see things from the medical officer's point of view; some of the magistrates claimed that an Englishman's right to do what he saw fit with his property was under threat, and one went so far as to say that the Bethnal Green Vestry was mounting vindictive prosecutions. Every case the vestry lost, the vestry paid for, both in cash and in the loss to its reputation for probity. Even when a sympathetic JP was sitting, the improvement order he issued was a general one and did not specify what precisely needed to be done in order to make premises safe and habitable. Bate himself did not know, since he was not a surveyor or civil engineer. As he put it, remedial work to tenements was often done 'according to the fancy of the owner, who usually considers a little whitewash and cheap wallpaper all sufficient'.[6]

In June 1886, the Mansion House Council on the Dwellings of the Poor sprang into action in Bethnal Green, sending the vestry 1,601 complaints of insanitary conditions that had been brought to its attention: dirty and dilapidated houses (two-thirds of the first batch to be discovered were in the Nichol), lavatories with no water supply, two illegal cellar dwellings (both in the Nichol; presumably the ones that Dr Bate had found three years earlier), unpaved yards, broken or blocked drains, uncollected refuse, overcrowding and appalling smells. Six months later, the Mansion House Council reported that just 20 per cent of these complaints had been dealt with by the Bethnal Green Vestry; in the meantime, the Council had discovered and notified the vestry of even more 'nuisances'. Dr Bate and the sanitary inspectors buckled under this vast new addition to their workload, and the vestry clerk, Robert Voss, wrote a petulant reply to the Mansion House Council, saying that the vestry 'must decline to act upon all the suggestions of its [the Council's] servants, which are often of a vague, frivolous and inaccurate description'.[7]

Voss had picked a fight with the wrong people. So well organised was the Mansion House Council that it had formed 'Sanitary Aid Committees' in every London parish, which embarked upon letter-writing campaigns to vestries on insanitary conditions. The Bethnal Green Sanitary Aid Committee featured a number of local churchmen, with its chairman, Septimus Hansard, being rector of Bethnal Green's parish church, St Matthew's.[8] Hansard encouraged residents to report bad housing to him, which he would then bring to the vestry's attention. Four other Bethnal Green vicars were local committee members, and the High Church-flavoured Oxford University outreach settlement Oxford House, sited in central Bethnal Green, provided the Committee with eager young (unpaid, amateur) sanitarians and a postal address. The Mansion House Council was a politically conservative body that looked and sounded like a bunch of Radicals; a keenness that the societal status quo should be maintained – landowner, leaseholder, tenant – underlay its insistence that the wealthy do their duty by the poor. *Noblesse* really did have to *oblige*.

In the autumn of 1887, the Mansion House Council successfully lobbied Whitehall into holding a public inquiry into the abysmal sanitary state of Bethnal Green, with the aim of showing the vestry that it already had all the legal powers it needed to clean up the parish. At the inquiry, held at St Matthew's Vestry Hall, Dr Bate was a crucial witness. In a deft performance, he managed to imply that the vestry was only confused about the powers of enforcement that it possessed, rather than wilfully negligent. He prevaricated about just when, or if, action had been taken on individual houses on his original 1883 list of condemnations ('My memory does not serve me so definitely on that matter'). Was the disease rate or the death rate a better indication of a parish's sanitary health? He wasn't really sure any more. In fact, Bate now attributed as much blame to the Nichol residents for the condition of their homes as he did to the vestry and to greedy landlords: 'The habits of the very poor are extremely uncleanly, and whatever sanitary appliances might be supplied, the chances are that they would not be used,' he said. 'The people break up the dustbins, the water-closet doors, and the banisters.'[9] (His description of doorless WCs had the inquiry participants and spectators

Barnum Interviews a Sanitary Inspector.

HE Sanit'ry Inspector friend Willing
    warmly greeted,
And begged both him and Barnum to
    be by all means seated ;
And then, when asked a question,
    began with glibness great,
To rattle off his answer at quite a
    furious rate.

" You are quite right, sir," he commenced by saying ;
" The public certainly is now displaying
The greatest interest in our outcast poor :
And further information to secure,
Specials are going round the courts and all'ys ;
Writers in print are making vigorous sallies ;
Parsons are preaching on this dismal text ;
Tories are jubilant, and Liberals are vext ;
Whilst Radicals indulge in petty snarls,
Because the Marquis was before Sir Charles,
Who now however, with a brand new broom,
Is going round from filthy room to room.

"What's that you say ?—my occupation's gone ?
Bah ! I long since have this conclusion drawn,
That 'tis a nine days' wonder, all this fuss,
And soon will cease, nor do much harm to us.
For we lived before through public agitation,
And know how fleeting is such indignation.
But we, of course, would wish the rookeries down ?
Oh, would we ? You have lately come to town,
Or you would not such ignorance display ;
When Rookeries go, then we have had our day,
For, thanks to their existence, we exist—
They're gold-mines, sir, on which we all subsist.

" You do not follow me ? Well, listen, then :
Say that we know some fearful fever den ;
If we report against it, down it comes,
And scores of souls are rescued from the slums.
But what of that ? That doesn't fill our purse ;
No ! Reformation is our greatest curse ;

For long as ever Fever Alley stands,
A frequent ' tip' to us the owner hands ;
He knows our value, and he takes good care
To pay us well for treating him so fair.
The poor are wretched—that is right enough ;
But as to our protecting them—that's stuff !
Why, they don't tip us, but their landlords do,
And so for landlords we stand up all through.

A TIP-ICAL SONG.

Now, of course, I, as a man,
Try to earn whate'er I can,
And I always stick to those who treat me kind ;
    And if they only pay,
    Why I turn the other way,
And pretend, in my inspection, to be blind.
    I've a sharpish sense of smelling,
    But inside an outcast dwelling
It's astonishing how useless is my nose.
    And to tell me of abuses,
    Not the very slightest use is,
For it all from out my mem'ry quickly goes.
Tip ! tip ! tip ! tip ! once a week, sir !
    Tip ! tip ! tip ! tip ! I don't say no !
Tip ! tip ! tip ! tip ! is what I seek, sir,
    And the poor can go to Jericho.

If an Owner doesn't pay,
Why, I then report away,
And he finds his outcast dwelling quickly down ;
    But another takes the warning,
    And I get the following morning
Quite a lot of extra tips my zeal to crown.
    It is true the wretched poor
    Many hardships must endure,
But I'd rather that they did it far than I ;
    So I go my weekly rounds,
    And where misery abounds
I do my very best to keep it sly.
    Tip ! tip ! tip ! tip ! once a week, sir, &c.

" I think, then, you must see what's my position,
And why I would not change the poor's condition ;
Nor, long as I, and those who work with me,
Can power exert, shall reformation be.
Yes, let the papers rage, and Parliament
Demand returns ; by us it is they're sent ;
And we'll be careful, as you may expect,
That they shall be most grossly incorrect !
Let Harcourt make his new Municipality—
We still shall reign each in his own locality ;
And still, inspired by strong self-preservation,
We'll keep the poor in foulest degradation ;
We'll doom their children to a life of sin ;
We'll let the fever fiend fresh victims win ;
We'll crush out decency, and hope, and health,
Ay, life itself, so we can still make wealth."

In its 1883 Christmas edition, *Truth* magazine lampooned parish vestry sanitary inspection.

loudly guffawing.) Furthermore, said Bate, 'the dilapidated appearance of the unemployed [is] as much the result of drink as of insanitary dwellings'. Bate had shifted his ground, suggesting now that the pig made the sty, rather than the sty making the pig.

The Commissioner of the inquiry had not demanded the presence at the hearings of any of the ground landlords or major leaseholders. They remained, in 1887, largely a mystery. Only one representative of an owner had come forward. Frederick Meakin, surveyor, explained to the inquiry that 'as far as he knew', his employer, the Gwatkin Estate, was the owner of many houses in thirteen streets and courts of the Nichol. Emma Amelia Gwatkin – the name that appeared on any eviction notices served on tenants – was a very old lady, a widow living out the rest of her days in the manor house of the Wiltshire village of Potterne.[10]

When Dr Bate was questioned about the extent to which Bethnal Green vestrymen were also slum-property-owners, his disingenuous reply was, 'I do not know. I prefer not to know.'

But he did know.

The Old Circular Cowpath

The Bethnal Green Vestry was possibly not the laziest and most corrupt in London but it was certainly among the front runners for that distinction (Clerkenwell was a strong contender). The group of small-tradesmen who were 'elected' year in, year out to run the parish knew in what contempt they were held, and as they rallied to defend themselves at the public inquiry of November 1887 a newspaper reporter overheard them muttering that they were quite aware of what was being said about them in London, 'that Bethnal Green was a dirty district, with a toothless, indifferent vestry'.[1] The same local newspaper, which was itself usually far from progressive in its outlook, had earlier editorialised on the extreme parsimony of the Bethnal Green Vestry and how this had led to its falling behind its equally poor neighbours in the provision of amenities and services: 'Our vestry has refused baths and washhouses, stopped tramways, and opposed some other public works; but if more life is not shown, we shall all soon be dead as ditch water.'[2] To be fair, the vestry would not even spend money on its own premises: St Matthew's Vestry Hall was freezing in winter, with curtainless windows so warped they would not close properly, and a badly fed fire was unable to keep the vestrymen and the press reporters warm during the fortnightly vestry meetings. (At the 12 February 1889 meeting, an expanse of dilapidated ceiling plaster 18ft in circumference fell on to the vestrymen, causing one slight injury.)

Most Bethnal Green vestrymen did not live in the parish, but ran their businesses there and so could pass as occupiers; this tended to undermine their noisy indignation at the 'interference' in Bethnal Green affairs by centralised bodies such as the Home Office, the Local Government Board, the Metropolitan Board of Works and the Mansion House Council on the Dwellings of the Poor. A small, self-interested coterie held power in Bethnal Green for around thirty years – with death, extreme old age or illness often being the only reason for an individual's end of tenure; the administration was described by one critic as an 'old circular cowpath that leads to nowhere'.[3] Central government, in the form of the Local Government Board, was exasperated by Bethnal Green's inability or unwillingness to supply data on its income and expenditure; the auditor of this Whitehall department pointed out in August 1888 that 'what St Matthew's Bethnal Green has supplied is no audit at all . . . I would suggest the desirability of the issue of an order for accounts'.[4]

A small number of loud, fiery 'Radicals' were another permanent feature of the vestry, but – with two or three exceptions – these seemingly progressive men sought little more than licence to barrack and make fun of business rivals within Vestry Hall, and, more importantly, within earshot of the several newspaper reporters always present. Vestry meetings in Bethnal Green were often no more than an old pals' act, with vociferous rows and insults traded, only for the evening to end with jocose making-up, rueful back-slapping and very little achieved administratively. (So long were vestry positions held, so intermingled vestrymen's lives, that offspring and godchildren frequently intermarried.) It looked more like theatre than government; but the stage was rarely full – in Bethnal Green, as in the rest of London, vestrymen's attendance ran at about 50 per cent.[5]

The man to whom Dr Bate reported directly, Joseph Jacobs, head of the Vestry Sanitary Committee and a vestryman since 1864, had been running one of the most lucrative pubs in the Nichol – the Victory, at 65 Nelson Street – for forty years. As chairman of the Bethnal Green Licensed Victuallers' Association, Jacobs was a tireless campaigner in the cause of drinkers' and publicans' rights; he spoke passionately at the Victory's club room against parliamentary attempts in 1886 and 1887 to close pubs on Sundays and to ban sales of alcohol to children under thirteen. It was better that children came to the public house to take out beer and spirits than their mothers, who would then be neglecting their domestic duties, Jacobs declared. Our present government, he said, 'was all meddling and muddling', but he wearily acknowledged that, as chairman of the Sanitary Committee, it was his 'unhappy fate to have to put into force penal acts of parliament'.[6] On more than one occasion Jacobs had 'warned' Bate that he must take no housing nuisance case to Worship Street magistrates' court without first consulting him. Jacobs seems to have seen himself as a Falstaffian figure and he liked to refer jovially to the pool from which his clientele was drawn as the Friars Mountaineers, the Men of the Mountain, or the Inhabitants of that Arctic Region. Strangers seemed to him to be intent on interfering with a working man's right to drink whenever he wanted and to live in whatever level of squalor he chose; publicans, property-owners and the working classes, he felt, should unite to oppose the rules and regulations that were closing in on their way of life.

· While Joseph Jacobs merely leased and ran the Victory, Thomas Watson Francis, also a publican and sometime chairman of the Bethnal Green Vestry and of the local Board of Guardians of the Poor, did own Nichol property, and during a sanitary inspection of one of these houses a pie-maker was observed preparing his wares close to a lavatory in the small underground room he rented. Fellow vestryman and Sanitary Committee member Henry Quaintrell, by trade a builder, leased and rented out a large number of Nichol houses, many of them condemned by Bate. Similarly, vestryman and Sanitary Committee member William Walter Burrows, who ran a large cowhouse – the Royal Museum Dairy – in the eastern part of the parish, owned the insanitary 17 and 59 Mead Street. Between 1865 and 1885 Burrows himself had been the Bethnal Green Inspector of Nuisances, but had failed to be self-inspecting (in fact, it was alleged upon his retirement that during most of his career Burrows had placed his inspections in the hands of his son).

But the largest Nichol slumlord to have a seat on the vestry was hardware store/plumbing supplies merchant Henry Collins Gould, vestryman since 1875 and sometime senior churchwarden. He held forty-two houses on lease from the massive Gwatkin Estate, and among his unlovely portfolio was 107 Mount Street, declared a 'dangerous structure' by the parish surveyor. Gould was served with a notice for the insanitary state of his 51 Mount Street and was fined for the conditions at numbers 3 and 49; 9a Sherwood Place was deemed 'obstructive' by Bate, while 7 and 9 Christopher Place were given a closure notice in June 1886 – the same month in which Gould disobeyed magistrates' orders to lay on water to the WCs at his six houses in Jacob Street. In September 1891 Gould's properties would exact their highest

Sherwood Place, part of the unlovely but lucrative property portfolio of Bethnal Green vestryman and churchwarden Henry Collins Gould. Sherwood Place was one of the Nichol's many tiny cul-de-sacs.

toll: six-month-old Joseph Briggs was killed when the ceiling fell down on to the bed he shared with his parents, Selina and Frederick, and his three-year-old brother, at Gould's 55 Mount Street.

Like Joseph Jacobs and Thomas Watson Francis, Gould was a member of the South West Bethnal Green Conservative Association, but elsewhere in the parish, Liberals – from both the Gladstonian and Radical wings of the party – were also implicated in slum-property ownership. In one instance, vestryman and Radical Club member Edwin Dorrell sold an insanitary property just off the Hackney Road to fellow Radical vestryman John Kyffin, who subsequently allowed the house to become even more run-down, resulting in a summons from Worship Street. Dorrell would be the main speaker at a huge demonstration on sanitary matters in Victoria Park in April 1890, at which thousands of East Londoners convened to protest against slumlords and the laxity of legal action against them. Dorrell claimed from his soapbox that many London vestrymen were slumlords; fortunately for him, his listeners didn't know that he was one of them.

Property owned by Gould, Burrows and Quaintrell featured on the

1,601-strong list of insanitary property compiled by the Mansion House Council in June 1886, which forced all three vestrymen to remedy the problems in their houses (though Gould took a few weeks longer to ensure the provision of water in his lavatories). Joseph Norris, who had been on the Vestry Sanitary Committee for fourteen years, explained to the public inquiry in 1887 that the vestry may have seemed slow to act to improve or close insanitary houses, but was, in fact, motivated by 'an indisposition to unduly harass people in peculiar circumstances'.[7] Very recently he had visited Old Nichol Street and had found it to be 'in a very fair condition'. This comment would cause merriment in medical health circles for many years.

The same men who comprised the vestry were also for the main part those who made up the twenty-four-man Bethnal Green Board of Guardians of the Poor, the body that oversaw all parish poor relief, including the workhouse, 'out relief' (cash, food, coals and other necessities granted to the 'deserving' poor, so that they could stay in their own home), and certificates granting free treatment by a local physician or medicine from a dispensary. Each vestry officer had to 'retire' for a year after three consecutive years in his position, but he could be re-elected after the year's enforced absence; in Bethnal Green, as often as not he would spend his time away from the vestry as a guardian. This made sense (to them) since the vestry collected the poor rates on behalf of the guardians but had no say in how this money was spent; other parishes, where the personnel of the two organisations was not identical, endured long battles between vestry and guardians over poor-rate moneys.

The vestry and the guardians were elected in ballots that were highly exclusive. In the 1880s, the local government franchise extended only to those who were the occupiers of property on which at least £40 a year in rates was payable (reducible to £25 for poor districts, such as Bethnal Green). In addition, voters in these local elections had to have paid the poor rate for at least one year in the parish, and these were also the conditions for standing as a candidate for a seat on the vestry or board of guardians. Acceptance of parish poor relief (except, after 1885, a medical order) automatically disenfranchised the receiver. While occupation of a sufficiently highly rated lodging could give a working man the vestry and guardian vote, there were many practical

Victoria Park in Bethnal Green was the East End's major site for open-air meetings and demonstrations in the late-Victorian era. Anti-landlord rallies were a regular occurrence in the park throughout the 1880s.

difficulties in getting and staying on the register, and actually voting. Staying in one parish for one year was not always easy for those with a weekly tenancy; registration had to be applied for in person every year; and for many workers it was difficult to get to the poll during working hours. In 1887 there were 18,493 inhabited houses in Bethnal Green, of which more than 80 per cent were rated below the crucial enfranchising £25 level.[8] Proposals to broaden the franchise for the nation's boards of guardians were described by Lord Salisbury in 1886 as 'rather like leaving the cat in charge of the cream jug'.[9]

Many citizens who were eligible to vote for the vestry and the guardians often had no idea that an election was to take place until it was too late: no more than 24 hours' notice of the vestry elections was required, and this notice took the form of a bill pinned to the church door. Supporters and opponents of the various candidates would then gather at Vestry Hall, and a show of hands decided the winners and losers. For the board of guardians elections, ballot papers were delivered by policemen to the homes of those eligible to vote, and were collected by the police three days later. In 1890, a number of Bethnal Green ratepayers complained that the completed papers had not been collected by a policeman but by a 'stranger', and when the register was checked by the failed Radical candidates, these residents' votes for the guardians were indeed confirmed as having gone missing. Complaints were also made by Radicals that ballot papers often went undelivered, or that collection of completed papers was deliberately made at a time when a householder of known progressive tendencies would not be at home, the insinuation being that certain police officers had been bribed to behave in this way. A number of senior Bethnal Green police officers were members of local Conservative political associations and socialised freely with Tory tradesmen at Masonic lodge meetings, harmonic evenings and other jamborees, including the weekly Metropolitan Police J Division v. Bethnal Green Vestry cricket match in the summer.

Despite such allegiances, party politics tended to play a smaller role in vestry affairs than the jockeying for position of smaller local caucuses and cliques. Towards the end of the 1880s in London, parochial government would begin to coalesce around ideals that connected local political groups to their parties at Westminster.[10] Until then, though, political theory and social ideals rarely had even a walk-on part at vestry meetings, and isolated splinter groups were the outlet for those intent on local reforms. One such body, the East London Advanced Liberal and Parochial Reform Association, held a meeting in Gibraltar Walk, near the Nichol, to pledge its electoral support for four Bethnal Green vestrymen who they believed to be genuine reformers. One of these candidates, Alfred P. Barnard, a local dispensing chemist (and creator of the unlikely concoction 'Barnard's Ipecacuanha Balsam, for Coughs,

Colds, Influenza and Consumption'), had won the Association's approval for his humanitarianism as a Bethnal Green Guardian of the Poor: he had managed to win the right of patients in the workhouse infirmary to be visited by friends or relatives – for one hour on Sundays.

Single issues, like this, dominated debate and these years saw the rapid creation and equally rapid demise of various ratepayers' associations, each formed to contest one or other particular item of vestry expenditure. The tightness or looseness of the parish purse-strings was almost the sole item of concern to Bethnal Green vestrymen.

Can anything be said in defence of the Bethnal Green Vestry? To what extent was its mania for keeping the rates down justifiable? It was certainly true that Bethnal Green householders paid a very high level of rates; in fact, for most of the 1870s and 1880s, Bethnal Green had London's highest rates per individual householder. These local taxes paid for paving, lighting, sewerage and street cleaning, but the highest sum was raised to provide poor relief, which varied according to season, to the economic cycles of various trades and to whatever central government crackdown on pauperism was or was not in operation at the time. (Some £2,123,606 was spent on poor relief in London in the year ending March 1887, 6 per cent less than the year before.) The rates also included contributions to the Metropolitan Board of Works, the Metropolitan Asylums Board and the London School Board, and these fees levied by centralised bodies were particularly resented by ratepayers. Because Bethnal Green was such a poor parish – with an estimated 44.6 per cent of inhabitants classed as 'poor' or 'very poor', and just 4.2 per cent termed 'middle class'[11] – there were comparatively few wealthy householders, who could be highly rated; and precisely because there were so many poor people within its boundaries, Bethnal Green's poor-relief expenditure was high. The wealthiest parish in London, St James's, had a total rateable value per head seven times that of Bethnal Green; but St James's had far fewer paupers to assist.

Some ground had been gained in the battle to end this unfairness. In 1867 the Metropolitan Common Poor Fund had been set up to try to recompense London's poor parishes from the rates of the wealthier, and of the £84,000 that Bethnal Green spent on poor relief in the year 1885, for example, £39,000 had come from the fund. But this still meant that the ratepayers of Bethnal Green had to find an average of 2s 6d

ANOTHER "BITTER CRY."

ALDERMAN. "OH, BUMBLE! JUST TO THINK OF IT!—NO MORE HALDERMEN!!"
BUMBLE. "AR SIR! IT'S WUSS THAN THAT!—NO WESTRIES! NO BEADLES! NO NOTHINK!!"
BOTH (despairingly). "OH, WERDANT 'ARCOURT! WERDANT 'ARCOURT!"——   [They bust into tears.

Punch's satirical take on the opponents of London-government reform, who protested at
Home Secretary Vernon ('Werdant') Harcourt's 1884 attempt to create a single, unified
council for the metropolis. Bumbles, beadles and aldermen had no need to worry, though;
just fifteen MPs on average turned up for the Commons debates on Harcourt's bill, and
he withdrew it rather than face defeat.

in the pound for the poor, in comparison to the London average of
1s 8d. One of the ways in which the vestry tried to make it financially
easier on men like themselves was to under-assess the value of house
property. In order to be able to continue in such a course, expenditure had to be pared to the bone.

The householders of neighbouring, and poor, Shoreditch suffered
similarly high rating, but their vestry differed significantly from that

of Bethnal Green (and, in fact, of most other London parishes) in its readiness to take out loans to pay for long-term improvements to the district.[12] In 1896 Shoreditch would build London's first vestry housing for the working classes – an Arts & Crafts-style apartment block called Municipal Buildings, in Nile Street, just off City Road. The administration in Shoreditch was far from perfect, and three years after the public inquiry into the sanitary condition of Bethnal Green, the Secretary of State would turn his gaze on Shoreditch's failures in this regard. But Shoreditch's capital projects and innovations contrasted with the stagnation in Bethnal Green, where vestrymen showed not the least intention of getting off their circular cowpath. They were delighted at the 1884 parliamentary defeat (through indifference) of Liberal Home Secretary Vernon Harcourt's bill to abolish the vestries and create a new governing council for London.[13] And not one of them raised his voice in support of the Equalisation of the Rates movement, which was ultimately successful, in 1894, in helping to spread the rate burden more fairly across the metropolis. Nor did any of them have the vision to blend their voices with calls for greater financial assistance for London from the Treasury. They preferred to sit tight, to cling grimly to the status quo as the best way of protecting their interests.

Owners

They did so, despite the colossal humiliation of the findings of the public inquiry. The Mansion House Council did not accept that demolition of insanitary property would put an additional burden on the rates, and it found the vestry had been negligent in failing to carry out Dr Bate's original 1883 recommendation to pull down at least half of the Nichol. The Mansion House Council's own inspectors recommended the entire destruction of eight of the Nichol's streets – all of which had been on Bate's original list. The final report of the inquiry found no fault with Bate, and it was strongly urged that he be made head of the sanitary inspectorate, and that three more inspectors should be employed to assist him.

The vestry harrumphed over the results of the inquiry for many months, before deciding that they would neither consolidate Bate's role nor employ any more inspectors. And who was going to make them? Local government was best left to local men, and no intruders were going to dictate otherwise. In the Mansion House Council's 1890 follow-up report on Bethnal Green the wish was expressed that the parish be governed by a mix of working men and 'gentlemen of courage and independence, willing to take part in the management of local affairs'. The Council laid the blame for the Nichol houses having become 'fruitful hotbeds of disease and death' on the lower-middle-class tradesmen who dominated the vestry.[1]

Yet people from every social group were implicated in the lethal squalor that had developed over the decades. One way in which a slum-dweller who had done well in business, or who had had a piece of luck, could capitalise on this was to acquire an interest in a slum property. This was the case, for example, with Susan Morgan, the Romany queen of the Nichol's second-hand clothes traders who clustered together at the top of Mount Street and Turk Street (at that time Brick Lane's name at its northern stretch). 'Mother Morgan' did very well in her trade and used her money to acquire and let out furnished rooms as a sort of pension for herself, and she ran a common lodging-house next to a pub in Turk Street. (She also invested in gold, which she wore in the form of rings on every finger, and multiple earrings.) Mary Ryan, described by a local vicar as a 'virago' – with a long history of street brawling and spells in prison – earned enough money through 'general dealing' and renting out barrows to costermongers to be able to obtain the short leases left on 50 and 51 Old Nichol Street and sublet them for a healthy return. Mrs Ryan and Mother Morgan shared this nose for good profits with the Church of England's property division, the Ecclesiastical Commissioners. The Commissioners owned Calvert Street, a crescent of insalubrious tenements at the north-west corner of the Nichol, on the Shoreditch side of the boundary. The Church was a large freeholder of London land and property, and controversy about the poor condition of many of its estates had been growing in the press in the 1880s. When it eventually became public, this link to the Nichol provided yet more evidence of what a prolific slumlord the Ecclesiastical Commissioners had become.

Flushing out the identities of those who profited most from Nichol properties became the hobby-horse of *Daily Telegraph* reporter Bennet Burleigh, a large, loud-voiced Glaswegian who would go on to become one of that newspaper's most celebrated war correspondents. In the autumn of 1889, Burleigh, writing under the pseudonym 'A Friend of the Poor', mounted a tenacious campaign to unmask some of the East End's most negligent property-owners. Burleigh's original investigation had been into the working conditions of East London's female workers; but it soon became clear to him that the real story was the insanitary condition of the women's homes, since this was where most of their low-paid work was undertaken. Not content with simply reporting his findings, Burleigh assisted in the attempted closure at Worship Street magistrates' court of homes that were unfit for human habitation. In terms of State action, Burleigh wanted to see the imposition of judicial rents in London, to be set by a tribunal, and severe legal penalties for landlords who failed inspection by a medical officer.

His companion in this endeavour was Baroness St Helier, known as

Lady Jeune around the Nichol, where she helped distribute charitable food and clothing donations, and funded and arranged country outings for local children as well as meals for the most famished pupils at the Nichol's three schools, and boots for those who had none. She was married to barrister Francis Henry Jeune, created Baron St Helier, who was president of the Divorce Court; at her weekly soirées at their Wimpole Street home she regularly welcomed Oscar Wilde, Lord and Lady Randolph Churchill, Thomas Hardy, Robert Browning, Henry Irving, Matthew Arnold, Edith Wharton, Ellen Terry and Walter Pater.[2] Jeune was a compelling mixture: she was a formidable thinker, and her 1894 book *Lesser Questions* showed that she had a very firm grip on the economic and social structures that caused the poverty she sought to relieve. In later years, she would go on to be one of the London County Council's first female aldermen, and would prove an effective local politician. At the same time that she was agitating against property-owners in Bethnal Green she was setting up the London Schools' Dinners Association, to pay for the hungriest among the capital's 750,000 schoolchildren to be fed during the school day. But Jeune nevertheless retained a tinge of the condescension and moralism

Lady Mary Jeune – a Society figure who targeted her philanthropic work on the children of the Nichol.

that characterised so much philanthropy at this time. Regarding 'Mrs G.' of 41 New Nichol Street, who had a nearly blind husband, a crippled son and a large family, Jeune asked the local School Board official, 'Would you ask her if she would like one of the smallest boys, the one nearest four or five years old, placed in a home . . . I think the case is a deserving one. Do you know anything against them?'[3]

In his investigative journalism, Bennet Burleigh had come across the notorious Ann's Place, Boundary Street, which the Shoreditch Vestry medical officer of health had twice tried to shut down. The 'model' tenements at Ann's Place had been erected in the 1830s; their thirty-three rooms housed 180 people and a considerably larger number of rats (or 'B Flats', as the locals called them). Burleigh and Jeune had funded and advised three tenants, Timothy O'Brien, Charles Thorpe and Mrs Ellen Simpson, in a Nuisances Removal case at Worship Street. They were lucky to find Montagu Williams, QC presiding that day – another 'friend of the poor', as his obituaries would declare. Despite considering himself a Conservative, Williams was renowned for taking the side of the working classes if any dispute between a poor person and someone, or some entity, wealthier or more powerful came before him. This is the same type of Toryism that inspired the Mansion House Council on the Dwellings of the Poor – a flavour of Conservatism that believed adamantly in privilege, but also in the duties towards the poor that such privilege entailed. (In a particularly cruel winter Williams had white woollen blankets manufactured at his own expense and distributed to the poor, with his 'MW' monogram embroidered in blue, so that they could not be pawned, as he had ordered all the local pawnshops not to accept them as pledges.) Williams listened keenly to the Ann's Place trio's tales of rats, roofs revealing the sky, and lavatories without water; of Mrs Simpson's room being separated from the beasts in the next-door stable by just a thin piece of board. On the other side of the partition the delivery horses of Jeremiah Rotherham's large drapery store and depot – Dolly, Jess, Spot, Punch and Vic – lived in comparative luxury.

Jumping up from the bench, Williams went to see Ann's Place for himself – it was a short carriage drive away. 'Good heavens!' he later recorded in his memoirs. 'The "sanitary" arrangements were much worse than had been described, and we saw some disgusting sights.

When I drew [the rent collector] Mr Revill's attention to certain details, he replied, somewhat heatedly as I thought: "Well sir, if anything is put to rights one day, it is knocked about and destroyed the next."' Williams believed otherwise.

As he drove away, he spotted two pubs close to the alley, and it dawned on him 'how alluring must be those warm and well-lighted public houses to persons living in the filthy holes I had visited'.[4]

The tenants told Williams that although the rent collector's deputy, a man called Akers, was known to them, they had no idea who the owner of Ann's Place was. 'Yes, it is an old dodge of theirs,' said Williams of the way that property-owners hid their identity behind their agents and collectors. Jeune suggested in court that the tenants mount a rent strike as the best means to bring forward the owners, but Burleigh said he would see what he could find out by himself; and within a day he had traced the leaseholders by following a paper trail of rates payments and solicitors' letters. They were discovered to be the National Temperance Land and Building Company, which paid £170 a year to the freeholder, who – Burleigh was able to discover, after one more week of searching – was a fellow journalist. Dr Heinrich Felbermann was the Hungarian-born editor of *Life: A Weekly Journal of Society, Literature, the Fine Arts and Finance*, and resident of Victoria Road, Kensington.

Montagu Williams ordered the immediate closure of the tenements, which, as ever, proved to be a Pyrrhic victory for the tenants: they were now homeless. But the success of the action prompted a few other residents, in other parts of Bethnal Green, to mount cases against landlords, though most other magistrates would prove far less sympathetic than Williams.

Burleigh and like-minded associates soon recognised that suing and withholding rent was, for the most part, culturally alien to the majority of the poor in the Nichol; such action was bound to result not just in the loss of the family home, but in the tenant being branded a trouble-maker and a bad risk to anyone with a room to let. In such a small community as the Nichol, with its scarcity of rental space, such a risk to reputation would be borne only by the foolhardy. And there were not many fools in the Nichol. So Jeune and Burleigh, along with the Bishop of Bedford and a representative of the Women's Trades Union and Provident League, established the Fair Rents for Healthy Homes

Bennet Burleigh was one of the country's most renowned war correspondents; in 1889 he used his *Daily Telegraph* column to reveal the poor housing conditions in the East End. He went on to assist a number of Nichol residents in mounting legal challenges to their landlords.

Montagu Williams was a JP at Worship Street magistrates' court; like Bennet Burleigh, he would be described as 'The Friend of the Poor' in his obituaries. His two volumes of memoirs contain valuable eyewitness accounts of slum life and conditions.

League, which had its inaugural meeting on 7 November 1889 at the Monarch coffee-house in Bethnal Green Road, immediately south of the Nichol, with the aim of threatening owners of filthy property with exposure in the press – taking the battle out of the hands of the tenants themselves.

So it was the *Daily Telegraph*, rather than the Mansion House Council or any other public body, that finally provoked the Bethnal Green Vestry into activity. Within two months of the formation of the Fair Rents for Healthy Homes League, the vestry Sanitary Committee had issued fifty summonses to owners of dirty and dilapidated houses. Burleigh reported gleefully in his December 1889 columns on the flurry of whitewashing, wallpapering, plastering, repointing and roof-mending that was a daily sight in the Nichol, now that the press had

Thirty-eight Nichol properties were owned by Richard Plantagenet Campbell Temple-Nugent-Brydges-Chandos-Grenville – more simply, the third Duke of Buckingham and Chandos.

exposed the negligence of the leaseholders and freeholders. Burleigh wasn't that impressed, though: 'They are but whited sepulchres,' he wrote of the 'improved' rooms.[5]

Back at Worship Street, Montagu Williams was as vigorous as ever, and in closing numbers 1–4 Short Street, twelve houses in Half Nichol Street, and six in New Nichol Street, discovered that the owner was a member of the aristocracy. The man with the longest five-barrelled non-repetitive surname in Great Britain, Richard Plantagenet Campbell Temple-Nugent-Brydges-Chandos-Grenville (more simply, the third Duke of Buckingham and Chandos), owned a plantation in Jamaica and 10,482 acres of Britain, including thirty-eight Nichol properties. He, like some other freeholders, was no longer of this earth, having been carried off in March 1889 by cystitis and prostate complications. He had left his estates to his eldest daughter, Lady Mary Morgan-Grenville, eighth Baroness Kinloss, who, thanks to her gallant lease-holder, one Pearson Goward, and his solicitors, was able to remain masked until 1892, when she had to break cover in order to collect her compulsory-purchase compensation for the houses.[6]

And another! Sir Edward Arthur Colebrooke was Lord of the Manor of Stepney (also known as the Baron Colebrooke of Stebunheath, the ancient name for Stepney). 'Tommy' Colebrooke was a magistrate

Sir Edward Arthur
('Tommy') Colebrooke,
Lord of the Manor of
Stepney, had a large
portfolio of properties
across the Nichol.

and future lord-in-waiting to Edward VII, George V and George VI,
as well as Master of the Robes to Edward VIII. Resident in Abington,
Lanarkshire, he was a High Commissioner to the Church of Scotland
and owned 30,000 acres of Britain, including premises in Boundary
Street, Keeve's Buildings, New Turville Street, Fournier Street, Virginia
Road, Newcastle Street and Jacob's Place. (He left only female heirs,
and so the barony of Stebunheath became extinct upon his death in
1939.)

On 14 November 1889 – at the height of Burleigh's campaign – the
Bethnal Green Vestry held a special meeting on sanitary matters. The
motion was passed sixteen to three to make Dr Bate's post a full-time
one, and to put him in charge of the team of sanitary inspectors,
which was to be enlarged. Vestryman John Valentine Jones claimed
that he hadn't agreed with the Mansion House Council findings two
years earlier but he 'could see now that home and hearth are more
important than considerations of finance'.[7] Now, he said, he felt morti-
fied when he reflected that the Sanitary Committee met only once a
fortnight, and that there was no systematic house visitation in the
parish. Joseph Jacobs defended his twenty-eight-year reign on the
Sanitary Committee. And no, he wasn't taking action now just because
the newspapers were on to him. The Committee had always worked.

hard, and people were always trying to find some fault with it. Yes, said Alfred Ewin (whose son had just made a small fortune by illegally selling on some Metropolitan Board of Works land in Bethnal Green), he himself had pulled down some 300 insanitary properties in the past twenty years. He had nothing to be ashamed of either.

And squabbling and pitying themselves is where we will leave them for now.

PART TWO

THE SECRETS OF A
STRANGE LIFE

Prince Arthur

Between 1973 and 1979, historian Raphael Samuel tape-recorded the reminiscences of a very old man whose memory was still sharp. Arthur Harding had a mordant sense of humour, no self-pity and no urge towards introspection, and his testimony provided unique access to the Nichol just before it passed out of living memory.[1] The tapes that concerned Arthur's childhood and adolescence revealed the codes of behaviour of a certain section – 'the most visible – of the Nichol's population, and their interplay with the Nichol majority. Here were 'the secrets of a strange life' that the Anarchist and Communist intuited on their 1887 visit.

Keeve's Buildings, Arthur's birthplace, stood on Boundary Street between New Turville Street and Half Nichol Street; they were, in Arthur's words, 'a sort-of barracks', three storeys high with twelve rooms let out to twelve families, and a large empty basement where homeless people would come to sleep. The property was owned by Baron Colebrooke. Looking back, Arthur was intrigued by the wood-enness of it all – the wooden staircases, cheap panelled doors, the wainscoting that ran around the rooms to a height of three feet. Arthur's father once, in an uncharacteristic fit of domestic odd-jobbery, attempted to paint the wainscoting in his family's room, infuriat-ing the neighbours because the vermin that lived in the wood and the wallpaper fled the paint fumes and set up home in the adjacent rooms.

Even as a child, Arthur had gained the impression that the courts and alleys of the Nichol were miniaturised. The tiny scale of the place suggested to him the need to pack people in tight so that they could all have a home, as though the builders had somehow been consid-erate in 'congesting the buildings to a small dimension'. It never occurred to him that greed had created the topography of the Nichol – that it was the physical manifestation of Avarice.

Arthur was born on 27 November 1886. There were six in the household: Arthur, his parents, Arthur's older sister 'Mighty' (real name Harriet) and two of Arthur's father's five sons from his previous two marriages. He would be called Prince Arthur, because he was the family's favourite. The room in Keeve's Buildings (cost: 3s a week, dimensions: 12ft by 10ft) was better appointed than the majority of Nichol homes. They had furniture – a table, two armchairs, a chest of drawers, a straw mattress and a small stove. Orange boxes from Spitalfields Market stood in for other items, including Arthur's cot. Over the mantelpiece hung two images – a portrait of Queen Victoria and a brightly coloured picture of the Crucifixion. Arthur showed no interest in his ethnicity, but his mother's maiden name was Milligan, and this, with the Crucifixion picture, suggests that she may have been second-generation Irish Catholic. She attended services of all denominations in the Nichol, though, the better to benefit from the charitable handouts that often accompanied them. The Harding income was derived from many sources, but most of their money at this time was earned from breeding terriers and selling them in the Nichol's pubs. The puppies were kept in cages in the Keeve's Buildings room until they were old enough to be sold.

When an adult, Arthur spoke to other former residents of the Nichol about how his family had been regarded, and many of them told him that the Harding clan had had 'control of the whole place'. They had arrived in London some time in the middle of the century from Helston in Cornwall, migrating to the metropolis as thousands of families did every year. They had lived first in the Borough, just south of London Bridge, and subsequently in Spitalfields and then the Nichol. Arthur's Harding grandparents were established in the trade of basket-weaving, and they had seven children. Of these, Albert became 'respectable', learning the wood trade and becoming an excellent carver, going on to own his own workshop. Uncle Albert was quiet and diligent and kept aloof from his siblings. In fact, so well did Albert and his children do that eventually they were listed in the London telephone directory, which struck Arthur as extraordinarily 'posh'. Albert was the only one of this generation of Hardings who could read and write. Uncle Bill and his wife also considered themselves

a cut above, although they made their money in the filthy, evil-smelling
second-hand clothes trade, with a stall in Turk Street. They chose to
live slightly east of the Nichol, in Chambord Street. Bill died young,
of TB, and all his sons were to die in the Trenches.

The rest of the Harding offspring dug in to Nichol life, tapped into
its needs, and profited. Aunt Liza set herself up as a grocery-store
owner, helped by her brothers 'Lark' and Jim, who also started up the
dog-breeding business, assisted by their brother Jack. Liza's shop stood
on the corner of Fournier and Mount Streets; later, when the business had grown, she moved to a site on Turville Street, facing Old
Nichol Street. As a shopkeeper, Liza was Nichol aristocracy, and even
Arthur was a little scared of her. She considered herself a
Cornishwoman, not a Cockney, and this, together with her unmarried status, made her atypical of Nichol women. The granting or
refusal of credit gave Liza substantial local power; another source of
prestige came from her involvement in theft and the fencing of stolen
goods. Some of her merchandise – usually tea and sugar, but occasionally whisky – was stolen from the London Docks and passed to
her at a knock-down price. Liza always kept the back door of her shop
open, should a thief need to dash in or out of the Nichol to avoid the
police.

Liza's fiancé, whom she never married, ran the Jack Simmons pub
in Church Street, where, on Sunday mornings, the East End élite of
prize-fighters, music hall artistes and racetrack celebrities would mingle
with 'the Swell Mob' – the most successful of the villains, who dressed
flamboyantly in brown double-breasted overcoats and wide black satin
ties. These made-men were known as 'Top Jollies' and were treated
as returning heroes.

Uncle Lark oversaw the running of a number of beershops in the
Nichol, which had dubious licensing status. In fact, Lark's main role
in the Harding empire was to go to prison should anything ever be
proved against the family with regard to licensing. This suited him
because he was very lazy, said Arthur. He once served a six-month
sentence for licence contravention, and on another occasion was fined
the enormous sum of £500.[2]

The local School Board officer, John Reeves, described the Hardings
in his memoirs as 'a family who lent money at high interest – about
5s a week for £1 . . . They also acted as a sort of underground railway

for stolen goods . . . In case of any of the boys "falling down" [being sent to prison] someone would attend the Sessions to get at the witnesses with hush money. In this way they covered themselves and kept up their influence over the criminals.'[3]

Unfortunately for Arthur, his own father, 'Flash Harry' Harding, was falling behind his kinsfolk, becoming far less flash from the early 1880s. He had once run his own pub but, for a reason that Arthur could never fathom, had fallen on hard times. This was when he moved his family to Keeve's Buildings, and the move coincided with a street accident that left Arthur's mother, aged thirty, with a crippled hip that would cause her pain for the rest of her long life (she would die in 1942, aged eighty-six). Flash Harry was now reduced to working on a casual basis in the Jane Shore pub on the west side of Shoreditch High Street ('our Champs Elysées', as Arthur saw it); Harry's pub shifts lasted from six in the morning until midnight for the appalling wage of 2s a day. He also ran errands for Hugo Karamelli, hat-maker to the stars of music hall, whose shop was in Shoreditch High Street. Harry helped with his brothers' dog-breeding, and, in addition, tried his hand at 'slop' cabinet-making, helping to churn out low-quality furniture that was hawked around the wholesalers of Curtain Road. When this too failed to bring in an adequate income, Harry turned to 'cadging' or 'tapping' – the activity for which his son reserved his deepest contempt. During his many trips with his father to plead for food and household goods from shopkeepers and restaurants, Arthur promised himself that he would become anything but a cadger. Anything.

Arthur's mother, meanwhile, had sunk to the least lucrative, most tedious of East London occupations: matchbox-making, for Bryant & May. As deeply as he despised his father, Arthur admired his mother: 'How she was able to carry on the work of a housewife, bring up her children, and make a living is something I can only guess at. Victorian husbands of the working class were very ignorant and brutal in their treatment of their women, and during my early years I often saw the results of a row upon my mother's face.' It would always be a point of honour for Arthur to reserve violence exclusively for use on men.

Arthur's mother, Mary Ann, had come to London in 1875 from Norwich, at the age of eighteen, with her parents and two sisters. They had been agricultural labourers whose wages were so low that the parish had (illegally) subsidised them; when their employer, a local

Arthur as a Barnardo's boy in 1896, aged ten, and towards the end of his life, in the late 1970s.

farmer, discovered this, he lowered the wage. The parents believed that by coming to the city they would be able to earn enough to feed, clothe and house themselves. They were wrong. Although Mary Ann and her sisters were able to make their way in East London, their father and one-eyed mother spent the rest of their lives in and out of the Shoreditch workhouse, where they died. 'I think the poor old chappie died from doing nothing,' said Arthur; 'there was nothing for him in London.' One of Mary Ann's sisters, Caroline, went to the bad, and her children grew up to be notorious Shoreditch tearaways; the other, Harriet, married a policeman and brought up daughters who were educated and found jobs in the new female white-collar world of salesgirls and cashiers, typists and secretaries. Aunt Harriet was 'a steady Christian woman, far superior to my mother', said Arthur, with his unerring eye for social distinctions within his clan. Harriet's daughters would all give Arthur a very wide berth.

Arthur's mother quickly found work in one of the most dangerous and disgusting of East End trades – sorting rags in a rag factory. Exhausted clothing and other knackered textiles were categorised by fabric type before being pulped for paper manufacture, and the sorters risked infection from the lice and fleas that were sometimes found living within the material. Salvation came in the form of Flash Harry, whom Mary Ann met one night in the Bishopsgate pub Dirty Dick's.

The marriage was dead by the late 1880s, with Harry becoming

Arthur's father, 'Flash Harry', in his prime and in his decline.

increasingly elusive (though he visited long enough to father two more children, after Arthur). When he was around, the children kept out of his way, fearing a beating. The step from being an object of terror to an object of pity (or, for Arthur, of indifference) was a short one. Flash Harry had become a charity case by the time Arthur was ten.

The patterns of mutual support, and its denial, in Arthur's family were similar to many among the poor in these years: on the one hand, help was expected and granted; on the other, it was possible to escape the scrum of family interdependence. Those who would not find work could 'sponge' off the more enterprising family members, with varying degrees of tolerance shown towards this parasitism. Aunt Liza's generosity kept her two lazy brothers, Lark and Jim, from ever having to test themselves in London's viciously competitive job market; Lark repaid her by doing spells in prison, but Jim did not seem to repay at all. Arthur's mother constantly wheedled free merchandise from Liza:

Arthur's mother, Mary Ann, photographed in 1928, with one of Arthur's sons on her lap, and ten years later, in Gibraltar Gardens, just east of the Nichol.

'As a family, we was entitled to help,' was Arthur's belief, even though he despised cadgers. Liza also gave freely of her time and expertise in helping Arthur's older sister, Mighty, to become a successful East End small-tradeswoman in her own right. By 1906, Mighty had her own little fruit'n'veg, drapery and money-lending empire, but she would always hand over all her earnings to her mother.[4] Mighty was eventually able to lease a house in Roman Road, further east in Bethnal Green, and she took in Flash Harry when Arthur had thrown him out of the family home for good. Harry often walked down to Brixton to tap money from one of his sons from a previous marriage, music-hall comedian Harry Rich, who was earning very well indeed – £18 to £19 a week. But Flash Harry must have managed to alienate Mighty and Rich too, because his last few years were spent in the Mile End workhouse, where he died in 1930, aged eighty-five.

The aloofness of several of the Hardings and Milligans shows, though, that the achievement of 'respectability' as often as not brought with it the right to withdraw from one's blood relations. Uncle Albert, the master wood-carver, slipped further and further east in Bethnal Green before making his escape with his wife and sons to Gipsy Hill, a salubrious south London suburb. As already noted, Aunt Harriet Milligan and her daughters kept the Hardings at arm's length. Arthur's own children would go on to become select, losing their East End accent, and wanting nothing to do with 'the Bethnal Green crowd'. Arthur showed little bitterness about those who felt that blood was not thicker than water; he simply accepted that when certain individuals became 'big-class people' they no longer wanted to associate with their relatives. (The process worked in reverse, too, and Arthur himself would later say of one of his oldest friends, 'He became an honest man, so I "forgot" him.')

A hard-working and naturally able woman, who managed to keep out of the pub and work diligently in the comfortless surroundings of her tenement room, was often the key to a family's destiny. Arthur's memories reveal the energy and self-possession of many working-class women of the Nichol in fending for themselves and often flourishing, establishing and developing small businesses. Frequently seen by philanthropists and early social scientists as the most hopelessly downtrodden, utterly irredeemable of the East London poor, many Nichol women in fact superseded their menfolk in the struggle to survive and thrive. The woman every young Nichol man who was inclined to idleness hoped to attract and ensnare into marriage was the french polisher. This was one of the many skilled furniture-finishing trades at which women tended to excel, working from home and earning good wages, with no need for a long, formal training or an apprenticeship. There were 250 female french polishers in Bethnal Green and Shoreditch, and some went on to run their own workshops. 'Some of the hooligans married french polishers because they knew they would make good money,' said Arthur.

Arthur's mother, failing to feed her family with her matchbox-making, was a particular favourite of female philanthropists active in the Nichol: she was a cripple, semi-deserted by a feckless husband, and her children were kept scrupulously clean in person and in dress. Clean and crippled and a loving mother was just about perfect in the moral account

There was a large trade in second-hand clothing and footwear in the Nichol, with sellers and stalls clustered around the very northern extent of Brick Lane.

book of many of the givers. Arthur's view of the benevolent West End women's activities was that 'it was a pastime. Queen Victoria encouraged it . . . They'd question the girls, especially the girls, to find out, y'know, all about them.'⁵ (This may have been Arthur's delicate way of approaching the concern about incest in the slums – see pp.119–22 – which had been given publicity throughout the late 1880s and early 1890s.) Mary Ann Harding received many items of clothing from the various charitable sources, and in true entrepreneurial style she took them straight round to Mother Morgan in Turk Street, who would pay Mary Ann as much as 5s for a good pair of trousers. Later on, Mary Ann graduated to stealing from church jumble sales – her thinking was that the sale had been organised to raise funds for the poor, so why not cut out the jumble sale middleman and capitalise directly on the clothes by striking her own deals with the Turk Street clothes-sellers?

While he was still a very little boy, Arthur used to help his mother steal the clothing. The independent spirit that he discerned in some of the adults around him was something Arthur greatly admired. As he would later say, 'You have to be your own master. So, you pick something where you have to depend on your wits. It's a precarious sort of living, but you are not under a foreman.' He was referring here to his time as a bona fide second-hand clothes dealer much later in his life, but he might just as well have been describing his thieving career. Shoreditch High Street was the hunting ground for Arthur and his childhood friends: for the necessities of life, plus booty to exchange for cash. The smaller you were, the more nimbly you could dodge under and around and in and out of the stalls that lined the western side of the High Street. Little gangs of boys and girls would emerge from the two narrow alleys leading between the Nichol and the High Street: Boundary Passage and Hare Alley, the latter known locally as Bonnet Box Court, after the hat shop on its corner. There was a strong sense that they were off their territory now – that there was a physical and social barrier between the Nichol and the Shoreditch Champs Elysées: 'Some people would have liked to build a wall right round it [the Nichol], so that we wouldn't have to come out,' Arthur felt. 'They put everything that was needed inside [the schools, a mission hall, a tiny voluntary hospital] so the kids wouldn't have to come out and be a nuisance.' They had a sense of being untouchable. Arthur claimed that no London shopkeeper or stallkeeper would pursue a child thief, since Londoners would always take the child's side. (The police were rarely informed of these petty thefts.) 'A Cockney's a very sensible person. What's he going to run after a kid for? To give him a slap? Everybody would be setting about him if he did.'

In the winter months, breakfast of bread and milk was supplied by the evangelical London City Mission at the Old Nichol Street Ragged School mission hall to the 120 local children deemed to be most in need, in return for their attendance, twice a day, at Sunday School. 'Everybody in the Nichol went to Sunday School. Morning and afternoon. The hymns didn't make much impression on me, but the Bible did. "Jesus loved little children." They was all very kindly people, the

SKETCHES AT THE NICHOL-STREET RAGGED SCHOOLS, SHOREDITCH: FEEDING THE HUNGRY.

This drawing of the Nichol Street Ragged School appeared in the 17 April 1886 issue of the *Illustrated London News*. The artist appears to be torn between pathos and disgust: large-eyed waifs sit alongside diabolical, simian urchins.

teachers, men and women. When I look back I wonder why they done it – there must have been something in it for them.'

But this Ragged School meal would be, for many of the children of the Nichol, the only certain nourishment of the day: 'You had to trust to luck for your meals,' said Arthur. 'Many people had more empty days than dinner days.' Thieving was making your own luck happen. The stolen food would be eaten back inside the Nichol, and any that was left over was given to family members; if it had been a very large, or exotic, haul, the produce would be sold cheap to the neighbours.

The shopkeepers of Church Street were from time to time another source of cheap, or even free, food. Many visitors to the Nichol were struck by the sight of children's behaviour around food – pinched, pale faces pressed against the steamed-up windows of cookshops, the sticky mouths and fingers of children hanging around sweetshop entrances. Butcher's, the corner shop in Church Street, discounted much of its bakery produce for hungry locals, and Arthur recalled the large bags of broken biscuits that could be bought for a ha'penny, and cake from Clamtree's pudding shop at the knockdown price of 2d a pound. One observer declared that 'the sweet-shop . . . is the child's public house. It abounds in all poor neighbourhoods, and serves as an excellent training in those habits of heedless self-indulgence which are the root of half the misery of the slums.'[6] Regardless of the shop-keepers' real line of business, many shops had sweet foodstuffs – confectionery, small open tarts, sugar butties, a suet and plum pudding called Baby's Head – on display in the windows to tempt children in; small cheap toys were also deployed in this way, as they were in many pubs. There was, in some instances, the sinister purpose of luring children in with a view to encouraging them to pilfer for the shopkeeper, who would fence the stolen goods. Arthur claimed that all the Church Street shopkeepers were 'crooked' and would encourage local kids in their raids on the High Street retailers, offering them cash payments or food for stolen items. Grabbing packages from a courier or delivery boy could reap rewards in this way, and Hill's the large tobacconist store in the High Street, for example, saw many a parcel being ferried away into the Nichol on fast little legs.

Arthur and his friends also pickpocketed and stole women's bags in the High Street. Billy Warner, from a large Nichol didicai family, was adept at this, working alone and feeling no need of a lookout or

Shoreditch High Street in 1896 – 'our Champs Elysées', according to Nichol resident Arthur Harding. This view looks north from the junction with Bethnal Green Road, and the Nichol lay behind the row of buildings on the right in this picture; two tiny alley-ways provided the only connection between these two very different East End worlds. Jeremiah Rotherham's drapery empire threw shadow across the Nichol; beyond it are the towers of the London Music Hall.

accomplice. Wally Shepherd also worked alone, and was especially talented at 'sneak-thieving' – getting his hand in a till was a speciality. Tommy and Patsy Lauchlin of Old Nichol Street were great 'whizzers' (pickpockets). All would die on the Somme, except Tommy, who went down with the warship on which he served. (Arthur recalled watching them train with their regiment, the Royal Fusiliers, City of London, at Columbia Market just north of the Nichol. He saw them setting off for Waterloo station, many of them drunk. 'This was the only time in their short lives that the country needed them.' Locals commemorated those killed with unofficial plaques – 'little wayside shrines', as Arthur put it – but these disappeared in the bombing raids of the next world war.)

It was the opinion of the School Board officer John Reeves that the lives of the children of the Nichol were 'a constant round of sunless drudgery'.[7] Arthur's sister Mighty was what Arthur called 'a grown child' at the age of four: 'they was born older than they are now', he said.[8] She was cooking for the family and doing housework at the age of six so that her mother wouldn't lose time working on the matchboxes. Arthur, meanwhile, believed that he became 'a man' at the age of nine. But Reeves was mistaken – they were quite capable of play. Their favourite playground was the 'backs' behind Prince's Court and Satchwell Rents, just east of the Nichol; this was a former burial ground that had never been built on – local rumour claimed that it was a plague pit – and the police turned a blind eye when local children lit their Guy Fawkes bonfires there.

A travelling Romany sideshow man would set up a hand-drawn six-seater roundabout in the middle of Boundary Street, charging a ha'penny for a five-minute ride; if the child's mother had no money, he would give the child a free ride. His name was White Nob.

And Mighty would treat Arthur to trips to the music hall – the gallery seats at the Standard in Shoreditch High Street and the Britannia in Hoxton Street were only 3*d*. Arthur particularly enjoyed the melo-dramas of George Sims, which 'gave you an idea of how the other half lived'. Villains were loudly hooted and booed, and plenty of fisticuffs was expected in the entertainment. The audience would mill round the stage door and follow the actors as they left, trying to be near them and commenting to them on the action and the charac-ters, just as though it had been real life. The Bryant & May match-girls would walk their favourite performer, Jenny Granger, home down the Mile End Road.

Whenever an organ grinder, or even just a man with a mouth organ, passed through the district, spontaneous dancing would begin. Arthur recalled that as soon as music was heard in the streets, locals would dance in couples or form a large 'all-together business, holdin' hands and goin' round and round'.[9] Arthur said that it wasn't uncommon to see as many as a hundred people dancing in one of the broader streets of the Nichol, young and old – 'It was part of their everyday life.' It was a phenomenon also noted by social investigator Charles Booth, who witnessed street dancing to an itinerant barrel organ in the East End, with men, women, adolescents and children grabbing each other to do a sudden valse, with men dancing together if there were no other available partner. 'A couple of ragged, perhaps even bare-footed, children, dancing conscientiously the step of the latest trois-temps, are a pleasant sight to see,' wrote Booth.[10]

The cheap seats of the East End music halls could cost as little as 3*d*.

As they grew bigger, Arthur and his contemporaries began 'van-dragging'. With lookouts posted along the street, a boy would jump on to the tailgate of a horse-drawn delivery cart, seize some goods and dash into the Nichol. Coal carts were particularly vulnerable to attack, especially during a cold winter: 'It was something which made a mother happy, when a child brought something home. Instead of a bashing they'd get an extra lump of pudding at dinner.' Jeremiah Rotherham's Shoreditch High Street drapery concern was so huge that it towered over Boundary Street, on its west side, blocking out light. Such wealth in the midst of destitution outraged Arthur's mother, who believed 'they shouldn't be allowed to have a place like that down there'. Arthur and co returned some justice to the world, stealing prolifically from Rotherham's vans as they came and went in Boundary Street.

As the boys grew older, violence became an option. But Nichol chums Billy Warner, Wally Shepherd and sneak-thief Wally Saunders (who would die in prison) were – thieving aside – generally quiet boys and not given to physical aggression. The same would not be true of Arthur.

To Arthur, thieving was work – and work was good; cadging was bad, and so was idleness. The rougher the child, said Arthur, the keener he or she was to get out into the world of work and to earn. They had the souls of shopkeepers and would scrape together a few pennies, buy in bulk and sell on at a profit. One trick was to cheat a fruit and vegetable wholesaler at Spitalfields Market, buying a bag of produce, finding some 'specky' (damaged) items discarded on the ground, putting them in the bag at the top and returning for a discount or full refund.

At twelve, Arthur was hawking German-manufactured toys around the twenty-two pubs in the half-mile stretch between St Leonard's, Shoreditch, and Liverpool Street station. Access to a broom could also bring in a few pennies, with children sweeping the pathways and steps of 'decent, respectable people'. Girls from the Nichol were able to make money on Saturdays by being a 'Jew's poker' – lighting fires and doing other housework for Jewish people who were unwilling to break their Sabbath. Near the Nichol, 'Jews' Island', a three-storey tenement block between Ducal and Chambord Streets, built by a Jewish builder to house Jewish immigrants, brought plenty of opportunities for this sort of work. The use of the word 'island' in the local nickname is revealing. The influx of Jewish refugees had transformed the streets of Whitechapel, Spitalfields and Stepney. Jewish families and businesses were starting to move up Brick Lane by the mid-1890s to the southern edges of Bethnal Green, and Jewish woodworkers were appearing in the workshops of Virginia Road. But for the most part Bethnal Green remained over-whelmingly gentile, with just pockets of Jewish inhabitants.

It was Arthur's perception that Jews had not reached Boundary Street when he was a child: 'In the Nichol there was a few Didicais and Irish, but you never saw a Jew. All that you knew about them was what you learned in the Mission. I don't think I ever saw a Jew until we moved to Bacon Street' (just two streets south of the Nichol). The Nichol, in Arthur's view, was hard terrain for any kind of stranger, especially those who looked different: 'It was a close-knit community and everybody knew everybody.' But in fact – and even generously supposing that it was possible for 5,700 people to know each other – a scan of the local newspapers and of Charles Booth's *Life and Labour* survey reveals that some Jews did live in the Nichol, as this sad story shows. In January 1889 Polish Jew Ezra Potier, a basket-maker, committed suicide in his room in Mitchell's Court, off Old Nichol Street. His landlady, Emma Sands, told a coroner's inquest that he had

" I brings up little dogs for fancy men, and takes in sick 'uns to nurse."

A dog-breeder in the
Nichol receiving a
pastoral visit from
a London City
Mission preacher.
Arthur Harding's
family bred terriers
in their one-room
Nichol home.

been out of work for five weeks and went out every day looking for
a job, coming home at six o'clock. She found Potier in his room at
8 p.m. on 31 January, suspended by his coloured woollen scarf from
a hook in the wall.[11]

Arthur seems to have been similarly blind to the presence of old
people in the Nichol: 'It was a rare sight to see an elderly person in
the Nichol, unless they were in the workhouse uniform.' But surviving
Poor Law records and newspapers reveal that old age – in itself a huge
factor in becoming impoverished – was very well represented in the
Nichol. Arthur believed the typical Nichol dweller was young, illiterate, enterprising, had been in trouble with the law and was hard-
working – whether or not the occupation was legal. But that description
fitted only a section of the population – the one to which he belonged,
the most high-profile and attention-worthy, those who were out and
about in the streets, not those who stayed indoors, working. The 'quiet
poor'[12] formed the majority. Arthur rather gives this away with his

comment, 'The predominant idea was paying the rent. That was the first and last duty of everybody, to pay that rent, 'cos you knew how damned hard it was to find another room.' That is hardly the defining characteristic of a wild and feckless community.

Monday was rent day, and so was called 'Black Monday'; it was often a time of panic in the poorest parts of the East End. Early on Monday mornings, women would form queues outside the local pawnshops, carrying bundles of belongings they hoped to 'pop' in order to be able to pay off the house agent for the week to come. The house agents were, according to Arthur, 'the cloth-cap-wearing, pipe-chomping fraternity – I mean, every third word out of their mouth was a swear word'.[13] Particularly vulnerable were families with more than one child who were part of 'the one-room lark'. Such families often lied to be able to obtain a room and 'when they tumbled you had two or three children, out you had to go. They just tipped you out.' Legislation was passed in 1888 to try to stop the worst abuses of bailiffs' 'distraining' goods in lieu of rental arrears, but aggressive and precipitate evictions continued in poor areas.

Because of pulling a one-room lark, Arthur's parents eventually lost their Nichol room, and, with three of their children, settled down for the night under the Wheler Street viaduct – a gloomy road tunnel that led down into Whitechapel from just south of the Nichol. It was January. Mary Ann was nine months pregnant. One side of Wheler Street was, as usual, filled with people sleeping as best they could under old clothes and newspapers, leaving the other pavement free for the police to patrol. Arthur didn't know why the Harding clan had not been appealed to for help; perhaps Flash Harry had got on everyone's nerves once too often. Arthur remembered that at about 5 a.m. the dockers and cabmen began to pass on their way to work, and, seeing pregnant Mary Ann, alongside Mighty, fourteen, Arthur, nine, and Mary, four, threw money down to them. One of them, Big Patsy Connors, told Flash Harry about a room he knew that was available to rent. Then Patsy handed over his lunch.

Help

Arthur's parents had pondered applying for the Board of Guardians' assistance that was supposed, as a last resort, to come between the impoverished individual and starvation or homelessness. But they were told that if the family were to receive any help, Arthur would have to be sent to live at the parish's children's home in suburban Leytonstone. Unwilling to lose Prince Arthur, the Hardings decided to do without.

Arthur, in telling his life story, rarely mentioned the supposed safety nets that existed for the very neediest. His omission is a telling one. The 1834 Poor Law Amendment Act (the 'New Poor Law') had been framed to make parish relief for the able-bodied as unpalatable as possible, in order to slash the nation's soaring poor rates: contemporary estimates suggested that almost 9 per cent of the population of England and Wales received parish relief of some kind in 1834, and by 1850 this figure had fallen by nearly one-third.[1]

In framing the New Poor Law, the principal intent had been that the situation of the pauper should not be made 'really or apparently so *eligible* as the situation of the independent labourer of the lowest class' – eligible meaning desirable, worth choosing. One by-product of the New Poor Law was to keep the wages of the labouring classes down,[2] so that they would see any job, at any pay, as preferable to throwing oneself on the parish.

Under the new regime, no outdoor relief was to be made available to the able-bodied: the only safety net for these men (females are barely mentioned in the 1834 Act, except as the mothers of illegitimate children) and their dependants was to be the workhouse. In 1834, all over the country, a building programme of these 'bastilles of the poor' began, and by 1850 London had thirty workhouses.

The year 1834 marked the triumph of those who believed that poverty was caused by moral failure – that the system of parish assistance dating back to the reign of Elizabeth I had encouraged dependency and had caused a population explosion among the very class of people least able to afford to care for their children. If they were incarcerated in gender-segregated workhouses, the birth rates of the poor would be lowered. 'Overpopulation', not under-employment, was understood by New Poor Law advocates to be the problem. (In *Oliver Twist*, Charles Dickens acidly named those with such beliefs 'Experimental Philosophers . . . whose blood is ice, whose heart is iron'.)

In the 1880s, an average of forty-five Londoners starved to death each year, or had their deaths 'accelerated by privation', as the government enumerators phrased it. Some of these cases were to be found among the 200 or so people found dead in the capital's streets every year (the majority in the East End); but most starvation went on quietly within the home. More often than not, it was those who had been successfully terrified into not seeking Poor Law assistance who paid the ultimate price.

The coroner's court of Bethnal Green regularly heard cases of death from starvation of those who had refused to go into the House, or who had managed to exact some outdoor relief or charitable help that had proved inadequate to keep them alive. The juries at the coroner's hearings found it hard to listen to such cases: 'These horrible deaths from starvation were a disgrace to all . . . It was a pity that no system of help could be devised to meet the cases of poor persons,' said the jury foreman at the January 1886 inquiry into the death of Sophia Nation, described as a 'former lady', aged forty-six, who worked from home as a lace-maker; she finally went along to the Bethnal Green workhouse infirmary ward but it was too late for her to be saved from the effects of malnutrition. Nation had in fact been receiving outdoor relief from the local Board of Guardians, although the sum was not known; but it had clearly not been enough to feed her. In the same week, seventy-eight-year-old stay-maker Annie Maria Rogers died at home of 'heart disease accelerated by want of proper and sufficient nourishment'. At another such hearing, the widow of an old man who had starved to death told the coroner that her husband had been too proud to go into the House, and was also aware that since no accommodation was provided there for married couples, the pair would have to be separated. She said he foresaw little likelihood of them ever re-establishing an independent life for themselves if they went in, and wanted to try to continue subsisting on their outdoor relief of two shillings a week and two loaves.[3]

Like Sophia Nation, many people waited too long before seeking parish medical assistance; and others failed to obtain the help they had requested, with fatal consequences. The confusing shambles of the Nichol's streets claimed a victim in January 1888. Charles Stringfellow, aged sixty-nine, a brass-worker of 22 Collingwood Street, fell ill with bronchitis on New Year's Eve. The next day, his twenty-two-year-old daughter, Maria, obtained a parish order for free medical help for him at home, but the doctor, along with the Nichol's board of guardians relieving officer, Christopher Forrest, wandered up and down the street on 2 January unable to find number 22; number 22 was in fact also number 83, and the door had both numbers chalked on it. After twenty minutes, the doctor and Forrest gave up and left the Nichol. Stringfellow's elderly and emaciated wife would not leave her husband's bedside to find out why the doctor had not arrived, and Maria could not take time off from her job to call at the surgery during practice hours. By the time the doctor had figured out the house-numbering problem, on the 4th, Stringfellow was dead. The numbers confusion was reported to the vestry, but the coroner said the vestrymen were not to blame, and nor was the doctor. What Bethnal Green needed, he said, was a 'glorious fire' to spread through it, cleansing as it destroyed.[4]

A year later, William Williams, aged sixty-three, a hawker, of 5 Nichol's Row, was granted a parish order for admission to the House for medical treatment in its infirmary ward; he had had a bad cough and a chest infection for many weeks. Unable to afford a cab, Williams and his wife Sarah set out to walk to the House, which was at the eastern end of the parish. They made it as far as the workhouse wall, where Williams collapsed, crying, 'Oh! I'm going.' Some men working nearby carried him into the House, where he died shortly afterwards.

John Judd, a fifty-five-year-old unemployed stablehand, too ill to walk, was wheeled to the House in a barrow by his friend John Nixon, of 38 Half Nichol Street, in February 1890. Judd died half an hour after admission, and the Board of Guardians were very angry – Judd wasn't a Bethnal Green man, and Nixon had supplied his own Half Nichol Street address in order to secure Judd's admission. This proved, they said, that strangers were taking advantage of Bethnal Green's generosity.

Far from being generous, Bethnal Green regularly reneged on its Poor Law responsibilities and passed many people on to neighbouring Mile End, Poplar and Whitechapel to be dealt with. Bethnal Green had failed, as required by law, to construct a 'Casual Ward', where people in sudden emergencies (vagrants, for example, known as 'In-And-Outs') could stay for just one night, in return for completing a task of work (usually rock-breaking or oakum-picking) in the morning. Sir Charles Warren himself, Chief Commissioner of the Metropolitan Police, wrote to the Bethnal Green guardians to tell them that he had heard of casuals being turned away from their House because no Casual Ward existed. Warren wanted the guardians to adopt the practice piloted in the Strand Poor Law Union of issuing 4d tickets for one night's accommodation in a common lodging-house to paupers seeking shelter.[5] The 4d tickets were pre-paid by a new charity set up to help tackle the city's homelessness problem. In 1887 there had been 141,733 in-and-out admissions in London's casual wards, but the destitute preferred to make use of the hundreds of 'fourpenny kip-houses' across the capital, despite their notorious dirt and reputation for vice and drunken violence. In 1887, homelessness levels had become embarrassingly acute – the year of the Golden Jubilee had exposed to many a visiting foreign eye a city filled with a vagrant population, and during the extremely hot summer many of the metropolitan poor had made open-air bedrooms of the royal parks and open spaces of the West End.

The Bethnal Green guardians made no response to the Chief Commissioner's 4d ticket idea, just as they continued to ignore Whitehall's demand that they construct a Casual Ward. They did, however, rouse themselves to make public their disapproval of the Salvation Army's attempt to compensate for the lack of parish resources for the poor with the creation of a rough-sleepers' shelter (known as 'The Anchor') in Green Street, in central Bethnal Green, and 'The Dredge' in Whitechapel Road. 'Well, we must lay in plenty of flea powder,' jested vestryman Joseph Jacobs, on hearing of the opening of the Anchor. When the Anchor proved 'successful', the

Bethnal Green guardians complained that it was bringing large numbers of the destitute into the parish; they were perhaps piqued by the publication of various newspaper interviews with the Anchor's sleepers, who told them of the inadequate levels of relief and casual accommodation in Bethnal Green.

The 1834 New Poor Law had been intended to make poor relief uniform across the country, replacing long-established local systems of assistance – decided by the parish and the magistrate – with a standardised, national approach to relief. It created large administrative 'unions' of Guardians of the Poor, elected by local ratepayers but directed in policy by a new central governmental body, the Poor Law Commissioners (later, the Local Government Board). The traditions of paternalism ('wanton parochial profusion', is how the 1834 Report from the Poor Law Commissioners described it)[6] within many small, established communities had resulted in over-generosity to the undeserving, the reformers believed, and from now on, discretion was to be abolished. But in practice, local custom and behaviour were not to be so easily eradicated, and many anomalies remained, which vexed those who took a hard line on pauperism.

From 1871, the Local Government Board attempted the task of evaluating the performance of the 600 or so Poor Law Unions in England and Wales, in an attempt to find out where discrepancies existed in parish help. Bethnal Green had characteristically got itself into a terrible mess in its Poor Law administration and also had the distinction of being the only London parish by 1887 not to have built, or made preparations to build, the separate infirmary required by law. While it had got as far as siphoning off its 450 pauper children to the residential school in Leytonstone, Bethnal Green continued to herd its sick poor into two wards of the workhouse building, siting them alongside the Lunatic Ward and the Imbeciles Ward. This filled the workhouse with people who could have been better cared for elsewhere, and also led to severe overcrowding: while the House was certificated to hold 1,168 inmates, an average of 250 above that number were found there in the mid- and late 1880s. As with so many of the parish's penny-pinching activities, this intransigence would prove a bigger burden on the ratepayers in the longer term: the Metropolitan Common Poor Fund, created in 1867 to help spread the burden of poor-relief spending across London's parishes, reimbursed local guardians at a rate of 5d per House inmate per week, but would not pay out money for any paupers in the House above the permitted 1,168. One observer calculated that in this way, the Bethnal Green Board of Guardians was losing £6,749 7s 6d each year by its failure to make its Poor Law institutions comply with government directives.[7]

The Metropolitan Common Poor Fund also refunded boards of guardians for any money they spent in employing the parish poor to do public works. By early 1887 many London parishes had fallen in with this, one of Whitehall's brighter ideas (which had, in fact, been suggested to the government by a working-men's delegation), and had recruited unemployed local men to undertake various parish tasks for subsistence wages. The great snowstorm of Boxing Day 1886 saw many Bethnal Green jobless men come forward to ask the local guardians that they be allowed to help clear the streets, which had been made impassable by huge drifts. (Six hundred people across London died during this cold snap; the storm had sent the parapet of Dr Bate's Bethnal Green Road surgery crashing down into the street, while in nearby Bacon Street a man would be found dead at the bottom of a deep snowfall, lying where he had fallen when the blizzard came on.) The guardians of the neighbouring parish of Hackney had already set up a public works agreement, and paid its jobless men to shovel the snow, but Bethnal Green's guardians would not – and so the streets of Hackney were passable within two days, while Bethnal Green remained locked in its ice age until the thaw came.

The Local Government Board's London inspector, Robert Hedley, issued complaint after complaint about the Bethnal Green guardians, and would make unannounced visits with his inspectorate to the House, which infuriated the guardians, who saw it as central inter-ference in local matters. The Bethnal Green workhouse was 'home' to very few who could otherwise fend for themselves; the institu-tion was used predominantly by the old, the ill, those with children to keep from starvation, and those who were – for whatever reason – indifferent to their fate. This was in line with Hedley's findings across the capital. Writing at the end of 1886, Hedley reported that 'it would have been difficult to find in any metropolitan workhouse a man whom a railway contractor would have thought of employing, or whom a recruiting sergeant would have thought worthy of a shilling'.[8]

The Bethnal Green workhouse, also known locally as the Waterloo Road workhouse, shortly before its demolition in 1935.

Every workhouse in the nation generated its own horror stories, and Bethnal Green's was no exception. The Local Government Board itself declared it to be filthy and ill-lit. Ward temperatures were reported in a local newspaper to plunge as low as 44 degrees at night-time, and were said to have contributed to the death of two inmates in the bitter January of 1886. Staff were said to run a system of extortion, demanding money from inmates in return for small services that they were salaried to perform, and the elderly were alleged to be particularly subjected to this 'thumbscrewing' and suffered neglect if they did not pay up. The tale of Robert Hunt swept through the parish in the summer of 1890, evoking fear and wonder. Hunt was taken from the workhouse infirmary ward to Guy's Hospital and strapped down by medical students who proceeded to drill a hole in his skull to try to diagnose the illness he had been suffering. Hunt died, and the hospital and the House told his protesting relatives that no consent had been required to undertake this diagnostic operation.[9]

Fatal falls down stairs, mysterious defenestrations in the Imbeciles Ward, louse infestations a certainty for anyone passing through the reception rooms, physical assaults upon lunatics, children dying in fires because they had been locked into their dormitory – it all helped the Bethnal Green very-poor, of whom there were an estimated 25,000, to make the decision to chance their luck elsewhere.

The detailed annual reports that the Local Government Board produced reveal that throughout the 1880s an average 3 per cent of the 28 million population of England and Wales were reliant on parish poor relief of one kind or another, with winter months showing higher figures than summertime. These figures did not reflect the true levels of poverty and privation, since they recorded only those who had come forward to ask for help and had received it. The majority of the desperate coped in other ways – by self-help (pawning, theft, prostitution); mutual assistance (giving, even when you had little to give); charitable assistance; simply enduring the unendurable.

The Local Government Board asked the nation's Poor Law officials to undertake a head count of its relief recipients on 1 January each year. The national data* shows that one-third of the recipients of parish

* See Appendix 3, p. 280.

relief were elderly, while one-fifth were families with no adult male wage earner; the ill and the disabled – whether temporarily invalid or permanently so – also figured large in the statistics, since workhouse infirmaries were used as hospitals by those unable to secure treatment elsewhere. The alternative was to use the voluntary, charity-subscription-funded hospitals, such as the tiny Mildmay, within the Nichol (which was largely for the use of women and children); but these were difficult for the very-poor to access, requiring a personal recommendation from a 'respectable' member of society, and with admissions days often restricted to two a week.

London Poor Law figures compared fairly favourably to those of most other regions,[10] largely because the capital had been the target of a governmental crackdown on outdoor relief. But London also differed from the rest of the country in that the city's guardians could reclaim much of the money they spent on the workhouse poor from the Metropolitan Common Poor Fund, rather than the local poor rates, and this gave even greater incentive to the guardians to offer relief applicants only the House. London had additionally pioneered the provision of specialist, non-workhouse (and largely centrally funded) institutions – insane asylums, homes for the blind, fever hospitals, and schools for 'imbeciles', 'sane epileptics', 'cripples' and a range of other bumptiously categorised individuals.

The South-West of England, Wales and East Anglia showed the highest rates of Poor Law reliance as a prolonged agricultural depression impoverished rural populations. The inward migration that this depression stimulated added to the problems of the London-born poor, as government inspector Hedley noted on 18 February 1888: 'The countryman is physically a better man than the born Londoner, and will be apt to displace him in the labour market. The Londoner becomes a dock or casual labourer, and from that to the status of a pauper, the descent is short'.[11] Countrymen tended to be considered more reliable and trustworthy than the Londoner, and the brawn that developed from farm labouring was also prized by employers. The vast majority of country people made their move to the towns when they were between the ages of fifteen and twenty-five; those who waited any longer than twenty-five to migrate were far less likely to succeed in the London job market. But London took a heavy toll on its workers: an estimated three-quarters of the rural immigrants to

London who ended up applying for parish relief had spent just five years in the capital before falling on hard times.[12] The sickening physical and mental deterioration wrought upon the adult working-class male by his experiences in the city was noted by Maud Corbett, a philanthropic worker in Bethnal Green in the 1890s. Corbett saw that London wives and offspring often had to become the family's main wage earners because the man of the house was soon deemed by employers to be too old for work: 'And this, perhaps, strikes one as being one of the saddest phases of life down here. It seems like saying, "Get all you can out of a man – after that, leave him . . ." There seems so little thought or consideration for the individual,' she wrote.[13] It was well known that East End labouring men of a certain age who were short-sighted would never wear their spectacles at work, while many would also take to tinting their greying hair with bootblack in order to appear more vigorous in the workplace.

From its creation in 1871, the Local Government Board intended to reduce drastically the availability of out-relief, which was felt to be costing the nation too dear – in money and morals. Parish relieving officers – the men to whom the poor applied in the first instance – were to make it clear to claimants that the House was to be their only option. The Board's campaign had been highly successful in London, slashing outdoor relief in the capital from 116,555 cases in 1871 to 44,750 in 1887.

It was the able-bodied who were the focus of anxiety about relief. These were the men and women (but particularly the men) who should have been able to support themselves by working but who were not doing so. The dominant – but increasingly outmoded – view among the governing classes and those whose support they enjoyed was that the availability of relief had created a large 'residuum' (a term first coined in 1867 during a parliamentary debate on enlarging the franchise), whose naturally weak natures had been further corrupted by being able to choose not to work; out-relief, by means of which the indignities and privations of the workhouse were sidestepped, was singled out as having had the most insidious impact on the character of thousands of working men. Others, though, were beginning to seek and find evidence that suggested that only a small minority of able-bodied claimants were idle and thriftless. Bethnal Green South West member of parliament Edward Pickersgill, in whose constituency lay the Nichol, acknowledged the problem posed by the provision of out-relief: 'How to help the industrious poor without feeding the cancer of pauperism is the riddle which the sphinx of modern civilisation forces us to solve.'[14] He offered no solutions.

In Bethnal Green, the years 1885 to 1889 represented a crisis in the operation of the Poor Law. The failure to modernise the parish's institutions had led to overcrowding at the House; yet the Guardians of the Poor were obliged by Whitehall to offer outdoor relief only as a last resort. While national outdoor relief figures had been static since 1878, despite several bad harvests and an economic depression since 1881, and London's outdoor relief numbers had fallen, Bethnal Green's had risen. By October 1887, a record 881 people were receiving outdoor relief – the majority of them elderly – costing ratepayers £99 a week, a rise from £52 a week in 1880.

Bethnal Green was divided into four Poor Law districts. The district in which the Nichol lay was the second most reliant on relief. Christopher Forrest, by trade a builder, had been its relieving officer since 1879. For twenty years, the guardians had been urged to appoint a fifth relieving officer, but had repeatedly voted not to increase staffing levels, even when Whitehall weighed in demanding that they do so. In 1889, eighty ratepayers came together to form the Bethnal Green Ratepayers' Protection Society, specifically to oppose such a move. However, a few months later, George Thurgood, the son of a long-standing vestryman and guardian, was elected Bethnal Green's fifth relieving officer, amid widespread jeering in the parish about such blatant nepotism. Within weeks Thurgood Junior faced an investigation from Whitehall into a mishandled Poor Law case in which an ill, out-of-work man and his family almost starved to death and had been insulted by two guardians in their own home.

At the coldest point of the winter of 1885–86 Bethnal Green's guardians were having to turn away around a hundred relief applicants at a time, including able-bodied unemployed family men who implored to be allowed to do parish work for a few shillings and some loaves for their children. The guardians and vestrymen attempted to paper over the results of their failures in planning, and at crisis points they felt strongly that they must be seen to be assisting the needy. They had failed in their public office of relieving the poor, and turned instead to the practice of private charity. Men like these

Enduring the unendurable: no matter how foul their living conditions, most of the destitute preferred not to go into the workhouse. This illustration, by Frederick Barnard, is from George Sims's 1883 book *How the Poor Live*.

appeared to hold in their mind two opposing impulses: a desire to ameliorate the very worst suffering of the poor; and the equally strong urge to continue to profit from the most submerged strata of society as slumlords and shopkeepers. We call it hypocrisy, but perhaps the Orwellian concept of 'doublethink' gets closer to the truth of this striking phenomenon of Victorian public life. Taking a reporter from the *Eastern Argus* along with them, the guardians went to visit a starving silk weaver, bringing him gifts of mutton, bread and tea. The editorial duly noted that 'this is exactly how a guardian should behave'.[15] Vestryman Joseph Jacobs and the guardians descended on the Bethnal Green workhouse to appear in an evening's entertainment for the inmates organised by the evangelical temperance charity, the Christian Community Abstinence Society. Comic sketches and songs were performed, and at the end, the oldest members of the audience were each presented with a bun and two oranges. A parishioner had paid for issues of *Titbits* to be delivered to the House, and assistant workhouse master Mr Williams played his violin in the Imbeciles Ward.

⋆   ⋆   ⋆

The retrenchment in out-relief faced powerful challenges in 1886 and 1887 and was one of the factors behind the 'West End Riots' of these years, when for a few weeks it looked as though revolution could be imminent (discussed in more detail on pp.143–5). The violence in the West End had put the wind up Joseph Jacobs. The vestry received a letter from the Bethnal Green branch of the Marxist-leaning Social Democratic Federation (SDF) asking if the vestrymen and guardians would be prepared to meet and address a delegation of out-of-work local men who were organising a meeting on open ground in nearby Mile End, to be followed by a demonstration. This request put Jacobs and co into a spin. They said at the vestry meeting that they would not meet the local SDF, and spoke of 'panic' and calling in the police; Jacobs declared the likelihood that his Victory pub in the Nichol would be torched by a 'mob' if this meeting went ahead. In the event, the march passed off peacefully.

One of the outcomes of these months of metropolitan unrest was a boom in charitable giving. Surely if the poor could see how much they were cherished, they would stop being so very angry? One (unconfirmable) estimate of the time suggested that, in London alone, charitable donations in the mid-1880s were larger than the national expenditure on the Navy. Charity was a glorious free market, and absolutely anyone was entitled to set themselves up as a philanthropist. It was a highly competitive field, in which rivals would try to undercut each other by producing the best pamphlets, the most heart-felt pleas, the classiest list of donors and patrons; and fundraisers were not above smearing the opposition, either overtly or by insinuation. So eager were Britons to help their fellow man in these dangerous days that the Charity Organisation Society (COS) – formed in 1869 by concerned volunteers in an attempt to systematise benevolence – came into its own. The poor who sought charitable assistance were supposed to turn up at the COS's local branches and give an account of themselves, just as they had to do if they wanted help from their local relieving officers. The COS would decide who was deserving and who was not; who could be assisted on the path back to self-help, and who was to be institutionalised within the strict interpretation of the Poor Law. For those were to be the only choices. The COS sought a return to the fundamental values that had led to the drafting of the New Poor Law all those decades ago. The Society was keen to use 'science' and modern investigative methods, house-to-house visiting and the construction of case notes for individual claimants to prop up an 1834 view of poverty – that indigence was largely the result of personal moral shortcomings; that overpopulation, not under-employment, was the chief cause of distress.

Unhappily for the COS, however, many of its most diligent and indefatigable researchers discovered during their fieldwork evidence that supported a wholly different point of view. A picture began to emerge of a systemic problem, with low wages, casual labour and poor housing interacting with alcoholism to create chronic poverty. The widely held view, and the one held by the COS, was that heavy drinking was usually a factor in determining whether or not one could live on one's income. But investigation appeared to suggest that, in fact, many people took to drink in order to make their poverty bearable: drink could substitute for food and warmth; it helped you forget, it enhanced confidence, it aided companionship and conviviality – it made up for so much that was otherwise lacking. The interplay of poverty and drink in such crimes as marital violence, suicide, child neglect and abuse, and street stabbings was now becoming the subject of informed debate.[16]

But the COS didn't want complexity: the problem was a simple one – either moral failing or a bout of bad luck caused poverty – and its solution was simple too. This dogged adherence to a pessimistic view of human nature would eventually lead many of the COS's leading lights to part company with the Society in search of more imaginative and comprehensive solutions to the poverty problem, and some – notably Sidney Webb and his wife-to-be, Beatrice Potter – would drift on to the fringes of the various newly emerging Socialist organisations, in particular the Fabian Society.

The head of the Bethnal Green COS branch, W.A. Bailward, was stung by repeated criticisms of his lack of humanity, and claimed in a letter to the *Eastern Argus* of 11 February 1888 that of the 766 cases brought before him in the year to 1 October 1887, he had relieved 386 paupers: 149 had been given sickness assistance, and the others 'helped back into helping themselves'. The vast majority whom he had turned away were, he claimed, Poor Law cases and therefore the local guardians' responsibility. Bailward had come to Bethnal Green from Balliol College, Oxford, in order to put into action his high ideals of character-building among the poor by preventing indiscriminate relief. He was particularly furious at the 'pampering and pauperising' activities of the various Anglican churches of the parish.[17] Bailward also got himself elected to the Bethnal Green Board of Guardians, despite being a resident of Victoria Street, Westminster, and thus was able to practise his soul-saving parsimony in two arenas.

Its many enemies nicknamed the COS the Charity Assassination Society, and one Bethnal Green vicar attacked it as 'a kind of spy on everybody' who was involved in relieving distress.[18] But in streamlining charitable assistance, the COS failed utterly. The Nichol was awash with charity, with some fifteen to twenty separate bodies elbowing each other out of the way in the rush to alleviate suffering – all sincere, and many of their helpers risking their health, even their lives, by working among contagion, vermin and damp. But their offerings, while tiding over a number of individuals, could not begin to address the problems of the 5,700 inhabitants of the Nichol. The benefits of such charity work accrued more to the givers – in self-esteem, a sense of usefulness, a broadening of experience, and a liberation from the constrictions of conventional middle-class life – than to the receivers. For the poor, ignorance of the charitable assistance available and the pride that made accepting charity impossible were their contribution to the overall failure of the various agencies. A cultural chasm between the giver and the given-to made many of the poorest unwilling to ask for help: if bread, clothing, boots, medical aid, coal and candles were to be accompanied by a sermon, a lecture, a tract, an intrusive questioning of the applicant's life history – well, perhaps the hunger and cold would be bearable for a little longer. So they continued to fall to their deaths in the crevasses between the Poor Law and philanthropy.

Phantoms in the Fog

Not Arthur, though. We left him, aged nine, with his family, under a railway arch on a freezing night. The room that Patsy Connors had mentioned to his parents was at 37 Bacon Street, just south of the Nichol, and with Patsy's help they secured it the next day. Two days later, Arthur's mother gave birth; and, unable to stand the noise and smell of the baby, and feeling left out, Arthur took to the streets. The Jewish families in the nearby Sclater Street tenements didn't mind him sleeping on their stairway; and certain night-watchmen in the area were happy for him to sleep alongside their braziers and would feed him from time to time. Arthur's mother was stranded three storeys up in Bacon Street with her crippled hip and new baby: 'It wasn't anything out of the ordinary,' Arthur recalled of his time as a child vagrant. 'There were hundreds of kids roaming about the streets. I got very lousy and dirty by myself, but my mother was too ill to trouble.'[1]

Arthur had often had cause to be grateful to the officers of the Kingsland Road police station because when he was very young and had got lost, he would be taken up and made a great fuss of by the policemen at the station house. They'd feed him, let him play with the toys there and then carry him back home. Arthur supposed that they preferred this sort of task to taking in the local drunk-and-disorderlies. This time, after three weeks on the streets, Arthur was picked up by the police and was handed over to Dr Thomas Barnardo, whose East End Juvenile Mission in Stepney Causeway was home to 8,000 orphaned or abandoned children. Dr Barnardo's was one of London's most dynamic and least discriminating of charities, which marked it out for the scorn of its rivals and for persecution, in the late 1870s, led by the Charity Organisation Society. 'Dr Barnardo's seemed to occupy the largest part of my childhood from nine till I was nearly twelve years old,' Arthur recalled. 'We were allowed out on Saturdays, and I went home and stayed a few hours.'

At Barnardo's Arthur became a good reader and writer. He considered himself to be a cut above, because of the education he had received. When he briefly attended the local Board School it was discovered that he was far ahead of the other pupils – the State had nothing to teach him: 'I was a good scholar, and people looked up to me . . . I was a wee bit on the flash side.' The desirable jobs were, he knew, the 'jobs for life' – in the breweries; on the railways; in the local druggist stores; or as a 'shit raker' or 'sparrow starver' – cleaning the Corporation of London's roadways and getting promoted to a better position the longer you stayed.

But Arthur couldn't settle: it was all so dull. Also, he felt keenly the unfairness of doing 'slop' work in the declining furniture-manufacturing trades: 'Too much hard work, slave labour, kids wouldn't stick it.' He lasted three days in a job at a mill in Hoxton that Mighty had found for him. Next, he earned 8s a week at a Shoreditch deckchair manufactory; but he never felt comfortable there after a policeman called on him at work pursuing a charge against him of disorderly conduct, and he left the firm after one month. He tried his hand as a glassblower in a workshop in Hanbury Street, Whitechapel, but suffered burns that hospitalised him for a week. Then he became a general factotum for a cabinet-maker, but soon discovered that the most exciting part of his time there was cheating both the firm and the individual workmen of cash.

He began to hang around Clark's coffee-house, at the corner of Brick Lane and Hare Street (today's Cheshire Street), with One-Eyed Charlie Walker, king of the van-draggers (very violent, and fated to die young, of TB). This was more like it. Arthur started to help out Charlie and his gang, stealing, fencing and menacing the shopkeepers of Brick Lane with up to thirty cohorts, and he didn't get lagged until February 1902. He was given twelve months' hard labour, which he served in Wormwood Scrubs.

Not long after his release, he was sent down again. Arthur's best friend of the time was 'Peaky', who had grown up in the Nichol and whose father had a white-collar job with the Port of London Authority. Peaky had begun truanting from school (he would never be literate) to go hawking and begging, but his ambition was to have a job on the railways. One day in April 1903, Arthur and Peaky set off on a pickpocketing expedition. Arthur removed a watch from the pocket of an apprentice printer and, to Arthur's astonishment, the victim had the temerity to go to the police. Arthur and Peaky were arrested and identified. Arthur was given a twenty-month jail sentence, and Peaky, as his accomplice and lookout, got nine months. Any hopes of a job for life now vanished. Peaky died of blood poisoning a year later. At his wake, standing over his open coffin, Peaky's mother said to Arthur, '"I'd sooner see him in there than he should be like you." For years and years that kept going through my head.'[2]

Borstal had recently been invented, and Arthur passed his time at his Kent borstal in learning carpentry and reading the works of Charles Dickens. The Borstal Association wanted to help Arthur to make a new life for himself – to leave behind his morally contaminating environment and associates. (Many in the area felt that it was Arthur who contaminated his surroundings; the Brick Lane shopkeepers, who had known him since he was a small boy, claimed that they only felt safe when Arthur was 'away'.)[3] On his release, the Association paid his fare to Cardiff, where he was to board a ship bound for Canada, but Arthur changed his mind: 'I walked all the way home. That was the last time I tried to break free of Bethnal Green.'

He was something of a local hero among some of his old pals. 'I was more intelligent than the other boys. I had a reputation for being tough . . . I had no "prospects" but I had supreme confidence in my ability to survive.' He turned to 'snide-pitching' – passing fake coins. His friend Billy Holmes was particularly skilled at making realistic-looking 1862 two-shilling pieces. By now, though, Arthur had more significant pals, and enemies. He was ensconced in the gang warfare that had broken out among some of the former children of the Nichol. Guns first made their appearance among the Brick Lane crowd in 1904, obtainable for just 4–5s each. Potentially lethal vendettas arose; insults, or perceived insults, to you or one of your associates had to be avenged. Everyone was frightened of the Baileys, for instance, who tried to frame Arthur for shooting at the chief of their clan, as part of a five-year feud. Of the Baileys, Arthur said: 'They come out of the Nichol. They wasn't thieves, though one of them turned burglar and done a lot of time for screwing [housebreaking]. They was a vicious family. Alf, the father, was always getting into fights . . . He wasn't a thief but a hooligan – stabbing people and all that sort of thing. He didn't make any money at it, it was just terrorism, the instinct of the savage . . .' Arthur didn't consider himself to be a savage. Although he loved the thrill of violence, he felt that in his case it was always used to further an end that could in some light or other be viewed as honourable.

Arthur was highly articulate, and his fluent tongue before magistrates had thwarted several police attempts to prosecute him. He bought or stole second-hand law books and became a self-taught expert, surprising many in court with his talent for chicanery. There was something plausible about him. In April 1906 Arthur was on trial at the Old Bailey for shooting with intent to cause injury at Daniel Cody, as part of an offshoot vendetta of the Bailey feud. The evidence against Arthur seemed convincing, but when Arthur took the stand, he asserted that it was his friend, Hymie Eisenberg, who had pulled the trigger on that gloomy night in a badly lit street; and the jury chose to believe that it was the Jewish Eisenberg, rather than the Cockney Arthur, who had fired the shots.[4]

In 1908, an unfriendly policeman arrested Arthur under the Prevention of Crimes Act, 1871, because he had failed to give him a credible account of why he had come to Brick Lane one Sunday morning. The Prevention of Crimes Act was known in the Nichol as the Fly-Paper, because once caught, it was very difficult to get off. Again Arthur was given twelve months' hard labour – the mandatory sentence for being a suspected person with two previous convictions. The local CID described Arthur in his early twenties as 'a most slippery and dangerous criminal. He is the leader of a numerous band of thieves by whom he is feared on account of his various acts of violence . . . and a misleader of youth at the critical stage between boyhood and manhood.'[5] Arthur would get his revenge, decades later, with his tape-recorded memoirs, naming the East End CID officers who had been the most talented perjurers, the most physically brutal at the station-house, augmenting their pay with regular backhanders from local extortionists.

Arthur got involved in another fracas. Notorious Spitalfields ponce Darkie the Coon – real name, Isaac Bogard – had fought and triumphed over one of Arthur's friends. Jewish, not black, Bogard described himself as 'a comedian' to court and prison officials but in fact he lived off the earnings of Whitechapel prostitutes and had nine convictions for crimes that included robbery with violence, malicious wounding of a female and assaults upon police officers. He liked to dress as a cowboy – unusual for the East End of these years. Arthur loathed ponces: 'It gives a man a bad name.' He would never drink with a ponce. Wouldn't even speak to a ponce. On the night of 10 September 1911, Arthur, with seven friends, set upon 'the Coon' in the Bluecoat Boy pub, just south of Shoreditch High Street; while one of the gang slashed Bogard's throat, Arthur smashed a beer glass and thrust it into Bogard's face, 'leaving the Coon with a face like the map of England'.

At his subsequent trial for riot, felonious wounding with intent, and assault, Arthur admitted the slashing but said that it had been done in self-defence. The jury did not agree, and Arthur received a sentence of five years.

He spent most of the next decade in prison; most of the 1920s organising muscle to be used to break strikes but also to intimidate blackleg labour and to do the police's behest in disrupting the operations of rival gangs. The 1930s and 1940s were for Arthur a mix of extortion, scrap-metal and second-hand-clothes dealing, and being a family man, with six children, out in the suburb of Leytonstone – going straight by small degrees. He became part of the Mosley crowd (Sir Oswald even called him 'Uncle'), but this was for the violence and because he was paid by both Mosley and by those who wanted to keep tabs on the British Union of Fascists. Arthur also helped Scotland Yard's 'Ghost Squad', investigating the criminal fortunes made in the black markets of World War II. Squeaking to the slits like this was unforgivable,[6] and Arthur was cut adrift by his old Bethnal Green colleagues. Which upset him somewhat: he felt his native district was, everything considered, a better place than Leytonstone and its 'neighbours who don't want to know you'. The East End of his childhood had been a far happier place, he said. He died in August 1981 at the age of ninety-five.

In certain respects, Arthur was an embodiment of the Marxist quasi-theory of the *lumpenproletariat*. For Marx and Engels, the *lumpen* – the 'ragged' – comprised the criminals, vagabonds, beggars, prostitutes, the bohemian, the *demi-monde*, charity cases, and those engaged in 'useless' non-productive labour, such as the hawkers, costers and tinkers. They were, Marx wrote, the 'scum, offal, refuse of all classes'.[7] The *lumpen* of the lower classes lived outside the wage/labour system and were alienated from the proletariat, either because they made a conscious decision to reject traditional employment, or because, as a result of their individual shortcomings, they were rejected by the entire labour market and so had to find other methods of fending for themselves. Arthur couldn't and wouldn't be employed in a regular line of work. As a bright, strong, energetic adolescent with a good basic schooling, he had had certain employment opportunities (not very good ones, it's true, and probably destined to become more precarious the older he became) open to him that were not available to other poor young East End males; and he had by his own behaviour wrecked them. But in any case, he preferred criminality as a mode of making a living. Independence and autonomy were crucial to him, but where others expressed this by trying to become masters of their own trade, Arthur chose to strike out alone by preying on those less well organised than himself.

He fulfilled the definition of *lumpen* in his renegade attitude to his own people, his own class, and for his rampant individualism. For Marx, the *lumpen* were a huge problem for the proletariat, since they would side with the latter's natural enemies – the police, capitalist bosses, the army – when called upon, for their own short-term personal gain. They made great counter-revolutionaries. Their entire lack of class solidarity made them naturally traitorous, thought Marx. Arthur didn't want anything to change: he used his wits and physical force to try to make an unfair system bend to fulfil his needs and desires. His family had come to pre-eminence in the Nichol by profiting from the penury of its citizens – by usury, not mutual assistance; violence, not co-operation. What was wrong with that? The strongest survived. Who but a fool or a foreigner would argue with such a system? But what Arthur had failed to see was that far from making him a Superman, in thrall to no controlling force, his criminal activities robbed him of years of autonomy, rendering him that most dependent and servile of society members – the prisoner.

Arthur did not consider himself a political animal: 'Didn't appeal to me at all . . . For me, it was too much to scheme to live.'[8] But when he did come to consider the matter, he was struck by the fact that all the Hardings had been lifelong Conservative supporters. The Liberals were in favour of Free Trade, and they 'was seen as being for the foreigner'. Arthur, his family and associates hadn't wanted the English working man threatened by cheap imports and cheap labour. (This from a man who took pleasure in his work as a General Strike breaker.) He had believed that the Conservatives were rich, powerful and generous; that the Radicals and Liberals tended to come from a lower social class and so 'were obviously out for themselves'. But in later years Arthur changed his mind, feeling that he had been somewhat duped: 'We wasn't educated, so we believed all the Rule Britannia stuff,' said Arthur, who at fourteen years old had rushed to enlist to fight in the Boer War (he was rejected, his age having been discovered). 'It's a terrible thing to think about, that only in later life did you realise that we was a very, very rich country.'[9] Arthur described himself as 'a Conservative at heart' but voted Labour in the 1970s because he wanted his children 'to grow up in a country where they would have a chance'.[10]

To what extent did Arthur's physical and familial environment create him? Many commentators who took an interest in slum life towards the end of the nineteenth century feared that the worst aspect of a place like the Nichol was the moral contamination of its children. Of Arthur's childhood contemporaries, the majority were killed in World War I, and it is impossible to say whether they would have returned home from the Trenches to a life of crime or to 'respectable' jobs, marriage and suburbanisation. (Darkie the Coon himself went off to war and was decorated for heroism.) Extrapolating from Arthur's memories of those who were children in the Nichol and who did turn out to be violent criminals, it appears that growing up within the established criminal families – the Kings, the Baileys, the Hardings and at least three others – was a more powerful indicator than physical environment and material deprivation of future violent criminality (as opposed to the type of criminality that sought profits from renting out dangerously insanitary property). Arthur spoke of people who were violent for fun, using intimidation that was out of proportion to the financial gain to be made. But his own feeling was that in the Nichol of his childhood there were three predominant criminal activities, none of which posed a threat to any 'outsiders': there was the shoplifting, van-dragging and fencing of stolen goods; faction fighting, which could last for days and was part of a number of long-running feuds that existed between large local clans and their hangers-on; and a broad range of petty street nuisances that the authorities were increasingly keen to clamp down on – street gambling, unlicensed stallholding, out-of-hours drinking, fortune-telling, and simply being a 'Habitual Criminal' under the Prevention of Crimes Act, or a 'Habitual Drunkard' under the 1879 Act of the same name.

The topographical seclusion of the Nichol allowed it to be used by a number of successful thieves and fences, many of them also trading as shopkeepers. Arthur's Aunt Liza was one; another prolific thief in his own right and secreter of other people's booty was fish-shop-owner Charlie Burdett of 18 Boundary Street – 'a lovable old chap', as Arthur recalled. Lovable old Charlie would serve twenty years for firing a gun at a householder during a burglary in Muswell Hill, but in the late 1880s he was a stealer of horses and a fence for other people's stolen nags. He rented stalls in a large stables at the back of the Five Ink Horns pub in New Nichol Street, through which many purloined horses and donkeys passed. Charlie was also a dog-napper, and after he stole a fine rare-breed from a lady's maid in Belgravia, Inspector Abberline (of Jack the Ripper fame) searched his premises and found six beautiful pedigree dogs stolen from their owners. During his various spells in prison, Burdett's wife Sarah kept the business running, and so successful was she that Burdett's went on to become one of that part of London's best known fish and chip shops, relocating to Church Street. Burdett's son, also called Charles, took up his father's trades (combining fish-dealing with thieving), and when plain-clothes officers searched his premises at 8 Jacob Street in January 1891, they found in his back yard two ponies stolen from Chingford; Burdett the Younger was sentenced to five years.

There is further anecdotal evidence that some of the shopkeepers of the Nichol acted as fences. In February 1891 a pawnshop cum general store in Church Street was burgled by two men who were caught in the act by a constable. They had been in the process of making off with the most amazing treasure haul: £259 in gold, silver and copper coin; jewels to the value of £300, and a 5s piece from the reign of Charles II. All this had been kept in an upstairs room in a locked chest that the accused had jemmied open. It is curious that a small shop in such a very poor part of town should be home to such a hoard, and it is likely that these were in fact the proceeds of previous robberies, since pawnshops/general stores were one of the main ways in which stolen property was fenced.

But rather than burglary, it was street robbery and larceny from the person that most concerned the late-Victorians – the safeness, or otherwise, of the street for the 'respectable'. Arthur maintained that the reputation the Nichol had for being a nest of 'cosh-carriers' (today we would call them muggers) was ill deserved: for one thing, he said, people of the Nichol were too stunted to be able to attack their social betters with a cosh. Certainly, the unfortunate victims of the following robberies with violence in or near the Nichol were far from being 'toffs'; they were just ordinary working men who looked as though they might have had something about their person worth stealing. On New Year's Eve 1887, Robert Rattray, an eighteen-year-old coster-monger who lived in Mount Square, off Mount Street, dragged Alfred Wallace, a plasterer of Defoe Road, Stoke Newington, from the Bethnal Green Road and into Little York Place, in the south of the Nichol. Rattray had three accomplices and they took from Wallace £2 15s 8d and his boots. Just as they were demanding his clothes too, Wallace called out 'Murder!' and 'Police!' The gang started to beat and kick him, fracturing his skull before running off. But Rattray ran straight into a police constable. He was tried, found guilty and given fifteen months' hard labour with twenty strokes of 'the cat'. His accomplices were never found.

Close to midnight on Saturday 28 April 1888, shoemaker John Vincent, aged thirty, along with two others, robbed and assaulted a stonemason, John Corfield, in Club Row, stealing Corfield's tobacco box and 9s 6d. Having impressive previous form, Vincent was sentenced to eighteen months in Pentonville Prison, with three years' police supervision to follow.

In July 1889 John Shea, aged twenty, a tailor, and John Collins, twenty-three, an engraver, robbed and half throttled builder Charles Rinnell, who lived in Boundary Street. He was walking home under the Wheler Street arches. The police caught Shea and Collins but not a third attacker.

Charles Major, nineteen, who grew up in Mount Street, robbed

William Hoare, who was drunkenly walking along Mount Street late at night in October 1890. Major was with five others, who joined in the attack on Hoare. Magistrate Montagu Williams told the victim, who had lived in Bethnal Green for just a week: 'It is as certain as the day is long that if you go out to get drunk and have money in your pocket, you will, in this neighbourhood, get robbed.'[11] Yet crimes such as these – with stranger inflicting violence upon stranger – appear in the newspaper and judicial records no more frequently in connection with the Nichol than with anywhere else in Bethnal Green, or Whitechapel, or the Docks area, for the years 1885–95. Although extremely unpleasant in themselves, these incidents, when set against the background of street violence in the East End as a whole, do not support the sense of the Nichol as a particularly dangerous place for outsiders after dark.

The police, too, presented an unremarkable picture of the Nichol, with regard to both the level and the types of crime committed there. In 1890, the police superintendent of J Division, Bethnal Green, compiled a detailed breakdown of arrests made within the Boundary Street area in the year to 31 July 1890. There had been 214 arrests, he reported, in a population of 5,700, with the highest number being for drunk and disorderly (at seventy-two) and the second highest for assaults upon police (thirty-five). There was one arrest for stabbing; one for wounding, and three for indecent assault. The arrest figures continue thus: for assaults on a wife, seven; for assaults on women, nine; attempted suicide, two; burglary, one; desertion of children, one; gambling, thirty-three; pickpocketing, four; receiving stolen property, one; stealing, fourteen; wilful damage, two; unlawful possession, eight; 'other', twenty.[12]

The written record never reflects the true state of crime; and the 'dark figure' that haunts criminal statistics of every age and every place gets a whole lot darker whenever the victims feel they have something to hide, or that the police and the judiciary may be unsympathetic towards them. Nevertheless, the truth of the matter is that drunk-and-disorderlies, fights between man and wife, missing dogs, the ill-treatment of birds for sale in Club Row, parental failure to comply with compulsory child vaccination and school attendance orders, and pub licensing contraventions form the dreary bulk of police and magistrates' records of criminal activity in the Nichol in the 1870s,

1880s and early 1890s. The Nichol looked, smelt and sounded bad, but criminal mayhem was not the norm on its streets. Certainly, the middle and lower-middle classes seemed perfectly happy to go into the Nichol for evening social occasions. For example, each October, the Star Mutual Loan and Investment Society held its annual supper and harmonic evening upstairs at a pub in Half Nichol Street (Joseph Jacobs's rendition of 'Blue-Eyed Nelly' was much admired); while the Gospel Temperance Society held regular do's at the Old Nichol Street Mission Hall, where vestryman James Milbourn revealed he had been dry for forty-eight years and had never felt better, and Mrs Holloway sang 'Bravely Launch the Temperance Lifeboat'. The Royal Rat Club, a Masonic lodge, held celebrations twice a year at the Prince of Wales in Old Nichol Street, with a local vicar, the rates collector and several members of the Bethnal Green shopocracy in attendance. These pillars of the community clearly did not believe that they would be under attack once they entered the maze. Anecdotal evidence provided by a local nurse and by members of a religious brotherhood attests that when they walked the Nichol in their uniform, or habit, they were not even subject to insulting remark, let alone physical assault. Mr J.F. Barnard, the manager of the Nichol Street Penny Bank, a tiny private concern where locals could make small contributions to savings accounts, walked regularly to Shoreditch High Street with all his takings on his person and was robbed not once in twenty-three years of service.[13] And far from being a police no-go area, where even in daylight no officer would walk alone (as East End legend had it), five police officers chose to live in the Nichol.

Dr George Paddock Bate's mortality figures revealed the non-murderous nature of Bethnal Green as a whole. Bate registered around two or three homicides per year in the parish (although suspicion attached to many suffocation deaths of babies, which coroners habit-ually, and increasingly controversially, recorded as accidental). On the streets of Bethnal Green, the concern was less with serious violent assault than with 'rowdyism', jostling, name-calling and the persistent street harassing of women (especially if they were well dressed, or out walking with their sweetheart) of a nature that could swiftly move from the mischievous to the malevolent. Three boys were each jailed for three weeks by a Worship Street magistrate for 'Sunday ruffianism' in the Hackney Road. They would jostle women, and then encircle with their linked arms any who particularly took their fancy, refusing to let them escape, and eventually punching the face of one who struggled to get away. Women would sometimes have their best clothes ruined by a 'Ladies' Teazer' or 'Ladies' Tormentor' – a small contraption like a long-range water-pistol that squirted dirty water, or worse, on to a woman's frock, bonnet or hair; the Teazers sold in their hundreds from Saturday market stalls in Bethnal Green Road. 'The London rough is supreme,' the *Eastern Argus* editorialised in June 1888. 'A lot of filth can be thrown on you if you are decently dressed, and a young girl is insulted with indecent words and pushed into the gutter.'

Women were not just the victims of street violence and harassment, though: the 'lumbering prostitute' was a feature of East End night-life of these years. She would entice a man into a darkened court or alley for a Tuppenny Upright, whereupon a male accomplice would emerge from the gloom, attack and rob the victim. A variation was for a group of prostitutes to drug the drinks of a man in a pub before robbing him. This happened to Thomas Edwards, aged fifty-seven, a hawker who lived in a common lodging-house at the Nichol end of Brick Lane. He arrived home at midnight on Saturday 21 July 1888 with his face covered in blood, and swollen eyes. A fellow lodger helped him to bed, but he became very ill and died three days later of a brain haemorrhage. Mysteriously, the coroner would not allow ten witnesses – with tales of how Edwards had been drugged and robbed and 'given the boot' in the head by a group of Whitechapel women – to address the court, and the jury brought in a verdict of accidental death.[14]

John Sparrow, aged fifty-eight, came up to London from Colchester on business one day in October 1890. He was found in the evening in Club Row, lying on the pavement either drunk or drugged, with injuries to his face, a wound to the back of his head and blood all over his collar. He told the stranger who came to help him that all he remembered was spending part of the evening drinking with some men and women in a pub in the vicinity – though he could not say which – and now discovered that he had 'lost' his watch and chain and £17 in cash. He refused help from the stranger, borrowed a sovereign from a railway worker at Bethnal Green Junction to get home, and died in the night in his bed.

The notion of robbers acting in concert and using disproportionate violence was to inspire a twentieth-century myth about the Nichol, which was first put into circulation by mischievous journalist-turned-Ripperologist Donald McCormick in his 1959 book *The Identity of Jack the Ripper*, and which has been repeated with increasing confidence by various commentators on the Ripper case. McCormick conjured up the Old Nichol Gang, giving a label to a previously unnamed gang of extortionists who were alleged to mistreat East End street prostitutes who could not, or would not, pay them protection money.[15] In the early days of the Whitechapel Murders, which happened just a few streets to the south of the Nichol, one theory that did the rounds as rumour and then as report was that such a gang was responsible for the killings of Emma Smith on 3 April 1888, Martha Turner (or Tabram) on 7 August, and Mary Ann (or Polly) Nichols on 31 August, as the violence of their retribution became ever more ferocious. The *Daily Telegraph*, in its report on the Nichols case, dated 1 September, stated that the most convincing idea about the three murders was that 'one or more of a gang of men who are in the habit of frequenting the streets late at night and levying blackmail on women' were responsible for the deaths of Nichols, Turner and Smith. The report continued by stating that the police were working on the idea 'that a sort of "High Rip" gang exists in the neighbourhood, which, blackmailing women of the same class as the deceased, takes vengeance on those who do not find money for them'.[16] The enterprising journalist who twenty-five days later created the 'Jack the Ripper' *nom de plume* in the infamous hoax letter sent to the Central News Agency may well have been influenced by the 'Rip' in 'High Rip'. Similarly, McCormick may have been half thinking of Nichols, as in Polly Nichols, when he devised his Old Nichol Gang; or perhaps the diabolical homophone 'Old Nick' – 'Old Nichol'. While such packs of juvenile delinquents as the Mare Street Rowdies, Hackney Road Roughs, Columbia Road Larkers and the King Edward Road 'Monkey Parade' feature once or twice in the newspapers of the day, no contemporary reference was ever made to an (or the) Old Nichol Gang; but it has nevertheless swirled into the fog of journalistic misreporting, and plain invention, that has cloaked so much of the Whitechapel Murders case.

McCormick may also have taken inspiration from tales of the notorious faction fights of the 1870s, 1880s and early 1890s in which two or three Nichol clans and their cohorts were involved. These dramatic feuds saw gangs – mostly young and male, but not exclusively so, since one or two Nichol women put in ferociously violent performances – pit themselves against each other, armed with knives and staves, un-molested by the local constabulary unless a serious injury occurred. But the fights were not just between Nichol families: other mobs from this part of central East London included groups from Norfolk Gardens (off Curtain Road, and today called Dereham Gardens); from Columbia Road, just to the north of the Nichol; from Hoxton Market, and from St George's in the East, near Wapping. When clans of the Nichol decided to fight 'outsiders', they named themselves the Lads from the Village. When news of an invading mob broke in the Nichol, one course of action was to clamber on to the roof of a disused building in Old Nichol Street with boiling water and bricks, to mount an attack from above.

Police and magistrates were completely in the dark about the causes of the arguments, and local vicar Arthur Osborne Jay, who came to know some of the gang members, could never get to the bottom of how the rows had started; but Jay was convinced that once a feud had kicked off, it would be handed down the generations and continued long after the original slight or loss of face had disappeared from collective memory. Jay claimed that there had to be 'some Irish element in it to make the thing genuine,'[17] and perhaps the cultural gap between a Church of England vicar and his second- and third-generation London Irish parishioners was simply too wide for him to be able to explore the phenomenon of the internecine punch-up. Jay wrote sardonically,

In this street [Old Nichol Street] there are two great rival families, two different schools of philosophy, two claimants to the homage and honour of the rest. Each family has many members, and each family will sometimes unite with the other in the suppression of newcomers; but then, on the other hand, when that unity is broken, that concordat thrown to the winds, who can describe the excitement and the extent of the faction fight which ensues?[18]

During one fight, a Nichol man known as Pompey was stabbed in the head and hospitalised for two months; his assailant – one of the Hoxton Market Lads – was captured and jailed for six months. In July 1892 a street battle led to the death of Nichol boy Charles Clayton, a seventeen-year-old living in Sherwood Place. Clayton had been one of a gang of thirty to forty young men who had been to Hoxton Fair on a Wednesday night and then marched eastwards to hunt and 'pay back' a gang – no name has come to light – who lived near St Matthew's church, central Bethnal Green. One witness said that the original dispute had been about the fairness or otherwise of a recent boxing match in which rival gang members had taken part. Another claimed that the argument had been about a girl whose affections had been stolen by a member of the rival gang. Battle commenced in Mape Street, half a mile east of the Nichol. 'Nichol, hold tight,' the Lads from the Village called to each other; but during the fray, Clayton was stabbed in the back, groin and arm and died of peritonitis four days later in the London Hospital in Whitechapel. Witnesses were hard to find, and those who did come to give evidence to the coroner's court were vague in their testimony. Even Clayton – in his hospital bed – refused to give the police the names of his assailants. This was, the coroner said, 'a most disgraceful state of affairs'. The culprit was never discovered.

It was Arthur Harding's feeling that as long as crime did not spill out to harm 'innocent' members of the public, the police were happy not to have to become involved; to be largely deaf and blind to brawling amongst drunks and violent assaults within the home, unless officers were called on by an inhabitant to intervene. Police non-intervention also allowed faction fighting to burn itself out, so long as bystanders were not injured and local trade did not suffer. Containment of criminality – rather than its investigation and eradication – was a more realistic goal for a Metropolitan Police force that suffered staff shortages and high rates of absenteeism due to illness and injury, a matter that would be brought to the public's attention during 'The Autumn of Terror', when the Ripper murders were at their peak. Bethnal Green's police chief James Keating could call to mind – when asked during the Autumn of Terror about his own division's experiences in the year 1888 – only one serious incident on his patch: the non-fatal stabbing and bludgeoning of one of his 609 officers while arresting a housebreaker in Mile End. The superintendent's figures were published in the *Eastern Argus* of 13 October 1888, and he left out of his survey the four non-fatal civilian stabbings, two cases of robbery with violence, two attempted robberies with violence, two violent non-sexual attacks on women, one assault by a mother on her child, and the fatal exposure of an unidentified baby that had made their way into the columns of the local newspapers in 1888. It's possible that Keating was deliberately minimising the level of crime in J Division in order to keep in good repute with his superiors, and to reassure a jittery public – and parliament – that the streets of the East End were under the full control of the Metropolitan Police. One of the most interesting matters to arise during the Autumn of Terror (and one that adds to the macabre fascination of the Whitechapel Murders) is the police insistence that the streets were quiet at the time of each killing – that nothing was seen or heard by any officers on their beats.[19] The Whitechapel beats were small – smaller than those of most East London police divisions – and if the officers had, on the nights of the murders, been adhering strictly to their routes and timings, as they all maintained that they did, the killer would sometimes have had just a few minutes in which to accost his victim, kill, perform mutilations and exit the scene.

The adequacy or inadequacy of the policing of the whole of the East End had been a subject of debate in the local newspapers even before the killings had begun. A letter to the *East London Observer*, dated 7 January 1888, from one J.E. Harris of Mile End Road East, complained of the poor street lighting and absence of beat officers throughout the East End, with 'ruffians' being able to rob with impunity from anyone walking after dark. After three Ripper killings, Whitechapel resident Henry Tibbatts wrote to the *Daily News*, on 3 September, about the 'shamefully inadequate' policing of Whitechapel, stating that he had witnessed near-fatal fights in the Osborn Street and Fashion Street area, but that 'never at any of these critical periods are the police to be found' – they were 'conspicuous by their absence'. Oxford and Cambridge men, spending time at the Toynbee Hall University Settlement in the heart of Whitechapel, formed their own vigilante groups at the time of the Ripper killings, patrolling the streets, often alone and unarmed. One of these later recalled his surprise at the *lack* of rowdyism and robbery: 'No Toynbee man was ever molested, and I have always been completely sceptical of the stories of places in London which were not safe to enter at night. I have picked out of the gutter an occasional respectable grocer from the provinces in nothing but shirt and trousers, and in a state of stupor, which suggested drugging, but either drink or love had led to his undoing.'[20]

In a similar way, the head of Whitechapel's H Division, Superintendent Thomas Arnold (who would succeed Keating as chief of the Bethnal Green J Division upon the latter's premature death), argued that the level of crime in the East End was not as bad as the public were being led to believe by press reports. In an internal memo to the Chief Commissioner, James Monro, Arnold stated, 'Brawling and fighting does and will take place amongst the low class of persons to be found in Whitechapel, but not nearly to such an extent as might be expected and is generally believed by persons non resident in the district.'[21] The true state of East End policing and crime levels in these years remains mysterious, with the written record offering contradictory evidence.

The written record also supports two wholly conflicting views of the interaction of the police and the inhabitants of the Nichol; and the only conclusion to be drawn is the rather bland one that some police officers were invaluable assets to the community – humane, brave and effective – while others were corrupt and violent, provoking street fights rather than preventing them. There are plenty of reports which confirm that police officers were called upon to perform a range of tasks within the community that had nothing to do with the prevention or investigation of crime. For instance, in February 1893, William Rollin, a forty-nine-year-old fishmonger of 13 Jacob Street, approached a police officer late at night in Shoreditch High Street and asked him if he would help him to get home, as not only had Rollin been drinking heavily all night but his leg was mysteriously bleeding heavily. The officer half carried Rollin back into the Nichol, with a trail of blood appearing along the pavement behind him. Then the officer went to fetch a doctor, who spotted that some ulcers on Rollin's leg had haemorrhaged, an injury that proved fatal.

Whenever a serious accident within the home occurred, the police were the first point of contact in an age when medical assistance could be hard to secure or prohibitively expensive. Coroners' inquiry reports make it clear that where a doctor defaulted in his duty, it was the police the public would turn to. When seventy-seven-year-old Rebecca Fitt of 21 Old Nichol Street fell ill with bronchitis, and the local physician failed to turn up as requested by Fitt's neighbour and her common-law

husband, it was a police officer they called in off the street on a January
night in 1892, just in time to see Fitt die. The constable was asked
medical questions at the ensuing coroner's inquiry – and was therefore
being expected to stray a long way from his official remit.

However, virtually all commentators who spent any amount of
time in the Nichol reported, with surprise, the fear and dislike many
of its inhabitants felt for the police. Many charity and church workers
and local officials reported that until the Nichol people accepted that
they were not in league with the Met, there would be an utter lack
of trust and an unwillingness to communicate. The Reverend Arthur
Osborne Jay reported that the inhabitants of the Nichol considered
policemen to be 'thoroughly wicked people, whose sole duty was to
swear away a man's life or liberty'.[22] The Nichol was home to a higher
than average number of 'ticket-of-leave' men – prisoners who were
out on parole; there were sixty-four in Old Nichol Street alone. Anyone
who was on the Habitual Criminals and/or Habitual Drunkards
Register could be arrested and landed with a considerable spell in
prison if the 'right' magistrate was on the bench on the day of the
hearing. There was no guarantee that this would happen, though,
since certain justices of the peace disliked the Metropolitan Police as
a centralised imposition on local affairs and distrusted particular officers who showed little understanding of the rights of the individual
and who appeared to persecute those who had previous convictions.
(This is one reason that Arthur Harding saw so many charges against
him dismissed before they reached a higher court.) There were many
allegations by members of the public across London of wrongful
arrest and the unnecessary use of force that would provoke the arrested
person into defending themselves, these defensive movements then
being twisted into a tale of 'resisting arrest' and 'assaulting an officer'.
The rising number of allegations of malicious and/or brutal arrests
would prompt a Royal Commission inquiry in 1906.

In the Nichol, miniature battles could arise following a disputed
arrest; and it is usually hard to deduce from the written record who
was the offending party. An infamous Nichol incident gives a flavour.
On a Sunday afternoon at the end of July 1888, a constable patrolling
the Nichol attempted to arrest a young boy for playing the street-
gambling game Pitch & Toss – one of a host of open-air activities
that were illegal. The boy's enraged father, Richard Leary, attempted

a 'rescue' of the lad. The constable went off for reinforcements and returned to the house in Old Nichol Street where the family lived. Leary Senior claimed – and in this was backed by eyewitnesses, who appeared in court with a range of allegedly police-inflicted cuts and contusions – that the officers set about him with their batons. A small crowd gathered and pelted the officers with stones and bits of brick. One of the neighbours, twenty-two-year-old Mary Hunt, threw a 6lb chunk of masonry from a first-floor window on to the head of the original arresting constable. Leary was given one month's hard labour, and Hunt was fined 10s – the latter a lenient sentence that may suggest the magistrate had some trouble believing the police officers' accounts of events.[23]

(Meanwhile, at a time of stretched resources and staff shortage, prosecutions such as that of Thomas Power, a twenty-eight-year-old hawker with no legs and one arm, were an odd priority: he was charged and fined 5s for being drunk and disorderly in Church Street.)

Another 'attempted rescue' in the Nichol degenerated into a small-scale riot in Mount Street during the May Bank Holiday of 1887. Four Nichol men in their twenties, and one woman, were being arrested by a single police officer for being drunk, and a mêlée of mutual rescuing resulted in fines and spells in gaol when the magistrates' court opened the next morning. This Bank Holiday had brought the 'usual' number of arrests and hearings at Worship Street, according to the presiding magistrate. That number was twenty-nine – hardly excessive for a large stretch of East London, but, equally, not likely to be a realistic figure of actual criminality. To ponder that further, we need to go indoors.

The Cruelty Men

Between 1885 and 1895, just one murder occurred within the Nichol. James Muir, a thirty-nine-year-old shoemaker and prodigious drinker, came back on the evening of 16 December 1891 to the room at 4 Old Nichol Street that he had formerly shared with his common-law wife Abigail Sullivan, and during a row – and in front of neighbour Selina Lewis – drove a knife into Sullivan's chest. She died within seconds.

Various neighbours had intervened to break up the couple during previous drunken rows and to apprehend Muir after the killing. Yet none of the witnesses had been willing to turn up to his committal hearing at the magistrates' court. A sign of Nichol solidarity against the authorities? More likely it was sheer terror lest a violent drunkard should be discharged and come seeking vengeance. In the event, Muir was indicted, and plenty of neighbours came forward at his Old Bailey trial to testify to his drunken threats against Sullivan. Muir was found guilty, and was executed on 1 March 1892.[1]

Selina Lewis had told the court: 'I have heard people threaten to kill others before. It is a common expression in rows down there.' Couples "avin' a jangle' was the most common cause of violently inflicted injuries within the Nichol. While the nation worked itself into a panic as the toll of Ripper victims rose, the most dangerous place for a woman was, as it remains, her home.

The Nichol had a bad reputation for domestic cruelty. Charles Booth concluded that 'for brutality within the circle of family life, perhaps nothing in all London quite equalled the Old Nichol Street neighbourhood', and John Reeves, the London School Board inspector for the Nichol from whom Booth took some of his data, stated that the children of the area 'never played as children play, they never seemed to think as children, they were prematurely old and the victims of awful

"IT'S ALL A MISTAKE, YOUR WUSHIP, ALL A MISTAKE ; HE
DIDN'T DO NUFFING, HE WOULDN'T 'URT A FLY !"

cruelty'.[2] Drink played a major role in the domestic assaults and fights
that are on record. The return of a spouse from a night's drinking
was a time of panic in many households, with women and children
scurrying around to remove from sight anything that could enrage a
drunken paterfamilias. For years, the family of Thomas Jones, aged
fifty, a brass finisher of Half Nichol Street – who had his bench and
lathe at home but made little use of them – had been physically bullied
by him. Beatings were common when he was drunk, and on occasions he had turned his wife Sarah out into the street barely clothed.
Late one night in May 1885 Sarah was hurrying to take down her
drying washing – stretched across the family room – when Thomas
arrived home and broke her nose. Supported by her adolescent
daughter and married son, Sarah found a police officer and had Jones
arrested. The son later told the Worship Street magistrates' court that

"I'LL DO FOR YOU WEN I COME OUT."

his mother had always worked to support them, that both he and his sister had learned a trade and were earning now, so they needed nothing more from their father – who was given three months' hard labour; a judicial separation was granted to Sarah.

Most of the Worship Street magistrates showed a high level of sympathy for the victims of brutal husbands or lovers and often gave the maximum sentences to offenders and granted wives separations – even in cases in which a wife changed her story or tried to back out of the prosecution. During the October 1890 hearing into the felonious wounding of Nichol woman Alice Coulson by her common-law husband William Morris, of Vincent Street, magistrate Montagu Williams said: 'It is remarkable the way people get injured in this district. They run against tables, chairs, knives; fall down and split their heads open upon the stones.'[3] Coulson had failed to turn up to court to prosecute Morris, and Williams was wryly commenting on how allegations of marital violence often changed into tales of accidents when a wife attempted to stop the case and retract her original statement. Williams, in his memoirs, recalled visits he made on Friday and Saturday nights to the London Hospital in Whitechapel, during which he saw women being treated following violent drunken assaults by spouses; his impression was that the majority of these women pleaded with the nurses not to involve the police, claiming that they had probably brought the beating upon themselves – that their husband was a good man, really.[4] In June 1888, James Cannon, a thirty-seven-year-old labourer of Jacob Street, appeared at Worship Street, having kicked his wife Emma in the head. But Emma had to be subpoenaed to appear in court, and when she eventually showed up she told the magistrate, Henry Bushby, that she didn't want to prosecute. 'He is a good husband,' she maintained, in the witness box. Bushby was having none of this, and gave James Cannon six months' hard labour. But Bushby (who had worked as a lawyer in imperial India, and had so interested himself in cruelty to women that he produced a treatise on the practice of suttee) tended towards leniency when the plaintiff was male and the accused female: in May 1885 he merely bound over Catherine M'Mahon of Old Nichol Street for hitting her husband in the eye with a milk jug during a drunken row. She had claimed that her husband had struck the first blow, and Bushby believed her.

Legal redress for domestically inflicted injuries was, of course, only obtainable if the authorities were alerted to it. In the Thomas and Sarah Jones case, it was their children who made the move to end the violence. For women who had no such familial help an organisation had been set up as early as 1843 to encourage the poorest to seek the protection that the law afforded them. This body, the Associate Institute for Improving and Enforcing the Laws for the Protection of Women and Children, was created and staffed by people who were already keen animal-rights, anti-vivisection and temperance activists, keen to extend protection to the higher beasts. (The first animal-cruelty legislation had been passed in 1824 – nineteen iniquitous years before parliament passed the 1853 Act for the Better Prevention and Punishment of Aggravated Assaults upon Women and Children, which put the first ever legal limit on the degree of physical force a husband/father could use.) The Associate Institute's inspectors brought prosecutions and sat alongside the plaintiff in magistrates' courts in an attempt to keep her spirits up and to protect her from any threats from the accused. It helped Ellen Withrington of Boundary Street, among many others, to prosecute her husband Lawrence in 1877 for assault and battery, and he was sentenced to six months' hard labour; the Associate Institute's East London prosecutor sat with Ellen throughout the hearing.

The Associate Institute's work was focused on working-class women: middle-class and aristocratic women were not deemed to be in need of any such protection since it was working-class males who were assumed to be prone to violence within the home – a sure sign of their lack of true manliness and their proximity to the mores of the savage. This view was rarely challenged, although in 1860 Mr J. Walter, MP for Berkshire, told the House of Commons that if the honourable members 'looked to the revelations in the Divorce Court they might well fear that if the secrets of all households were known, these brutal assaults upon women were by no means confined to the lower classes'.[5]

The setting up of the Associate Institute had been a controversial early attempt at intervention in the private lives of the working classes. Until 1894, the police, magistrates and philanthropists had no legal right to enter a domestic space on the suspicion of neglect or assault upon a child, and until 1889 the only body able to mount prosecutions of violent or neglectful parents were the Poor Law Guardians, if such cases had been brought to their attention. Frustration about this was felt in the early 1870s by London City Missioner John Matthias Weylland. As part of his proselytising tours of the neighbourhood, he knocked on a door in Devonshire Place, one of the Nichol's most repulsive courts, and the door was opened by a young girl with part of her face blackened, as if by soot. 'Do your mother and father live here?' asked Weylland. 'What a stunner!' replied the child, "cos I ain't got no mother. She died of cholera. Dusty is my uncle – he took me out of the workus and I earns him lots – ten shills a week . . . Billy Mutton is our guv'nor.'[6] Wanting an explanation, and concerned at how tired and unwell the child looked, Weylland followed her upstairs to the 'sky parlour', where he listened astonished as Uncle Dusty explained how he had taken the girl, Poll, from the Poor Law authorities and turned her into 'Black Poll', touring all over London and at seaside resorts as part of their 'nigger minstrel' shows. As they spoke, Uncle Dusty and his troupe were blacking up in front of a dressing table with two cheap looking-glasses, using burnt corks, tallow and black powder, and gluing on negroid noses. 'When I ain't black I sings "Charming Judy O'Calligan",' Poll explained to Weylland. 'Blackface' music and comedy acts were phenomenally popular (Bethnal Green's own J Division police inspectors blacked up for occasional public performances), and Poll was bringing in 10s a week for her minstrelsy, but she told Weylland that overwork meant that her voice was starting to crack and her feet were painful after hour upon hour of comic dancing. When she could no longer work for them, said Dusty, she would be left with old Mother Dell, down the court. When Weylland objected to her fate, the troupe took up their fiddles and sang an anti-religious song over his protestations.

Legally, there was nothing Weylland could do for Poll beyond informing the Bethnal Green Poor Law authorities, who might, or might not, decide to act. Around the corner he was harangued by 'The Imp Woman', a gin-sodden widow who objected to Weylland's implied criticism of her domestic and business set-up: she rented out her three offspring and other local children to the cheapest types of theatres – the penny gaffs – as imps, goblins, angels, cats, frogs, etc. Her own son was making her a guinea a week as a monkey in a Christmas pantomime. The Imp Woman plied her performers with gin, to try to stop them outgrowing their expensive stage costumes.[7]

The minimum working age was ten (in Europe, only Italy had a lower limit), raised to eleven in 1893, and government estimates of schoolchildren who had jobs put the figure for London at between 6.5 and 8 per cent. Many London School Board inspectors showed great leniency to parents with working children, knowing how crucial their wages could be for the family's survival outside the workhouse. Arthur Harding's sister Mighty, for instance, was allowed by the Nichol's school inspector John Reeves to go to school for just two days a week when she was over the age of ten, since Reeves knew that her mother was an invalid and that Mighty's wages kept the entire family going. Arthur liked the local teachers at the Nichol's Board School, 'educated people' who showed great sympathy with their pupils: 'They knew what a terrible life we were living.'[8]

In practice in the 1870s and 1880s, it was only when a family came forward for poor relief that the State, in the form of the parish, intervened in family life, splitting up couples and isolating them from their children. That was the trade-off – request assistance, and you yield up the sanctity of your domestic relationships. In 1888 the Local Government Board issued a circular reminding the nation's Poor Law guardians of their duty to prosecute where cruelty or neglect was discovered or brought to their attention, and the circular's existence suggests that Whitehall had detected reluctance on the part of guardians to take cases to court. Child-maltreatment prosecutions were difficult for the Poor Law authorities to undertake, since until 1889 husband and wife could not give evidence against each other (except in treason trials, or where spouses accused each other of assault), and children were not deemed to be 'competent witnesses'. Nevertheless, in June 1888 the Bethnal Green guardians – of all people – successfully prosecuted Annie Hooper, a thirty-one-year-old basket-maker of New Nichol Street, for biting and beating her small son James; Hooper was given three months' hard labour, and James was sent to live at the workhouse.

Slowly, legislation and the higher courts had been chipping away at the absolute power that a husband had over his wife; but the relationship between parent and child was considered to be more private, further off-limits for the State, and changes in the law that would alter this relationship were more hotly contested. There was, for instance, no law on incest until 1908 (after four failed attempts at legislation, from 1899 onwards), and indecencies committed within the family had to be prosecuted under the existing rape and sexual assault laws.

In 1885, the passing of the Criminal Law Amendment Act (CLAA) had raised hopes that children could be afforded greater legal protection from a range of sexual crimes. The CLAA was the culmination of years of campaigning by a variety of evangelicals, child-welfare volunteers, feminists, temperance advocates and 'social purity' activists intent on raising the moral tone of Britain (of its cities in particular); but in the end it had taken just one enterprising journalist to turn years of data collection and agitation into an instant brouhaha from which a government reluctant to meddle with the sexual prerogative of adult males could not back away. W.T. Stead, the editor of the *Pall Mall Gazette*, bought thirteen-year-old Eliza Armstrong from her

mother on a London street for £5, just to prove in print that such a thing was possible and that it was time for government to act – to protect young women from sexual predators, but also to criminalise a range of 'deviant' sexual behaviour and indecencies previously outside the scope of legislation. (The infamous Labouchere amendment to the CLAA would also outlaw homosexual acts, even between consenting adult males.) Stead's series of *Gazette* articles, which had the overall heading 'The Maiden Tribute of Modern Babylon', was published in the summer of 1885, and within weeks of its appearance the CLAA was passed, raising the age of consent for females to sixteen (from thirteen), and introducing a range of measures[9] designed to make easier the investigation and prosecution of sexual assaults and enforced sexual slavery in brothels and the trafficking of young women. Stead was nicknamed 'Bed-Stead' by those who deplored his sensationalist journalism, but child-protection campaigners were delighted that he had used whatever means were necessary to shatter the nation's silence on the sexual exploitation of children. The *Pall Mall Gazette's* circulation soared because of the 'Maiden Tribute' series, and Stead's trial, in October 1885, for abduction with intent to commit indecent assault, and his sentence of three months' hard labour, did the sales figures no harm either. (The judge had not accepted as mitigation the fact that Stead had bought Eliza solely in the interests of writing an exposé.)

Stead also co-founded the National Vigilance Association, an unusual and not entirely comfortable amalgam of old-fashioned patriarchal paternalists with thoroughly modern feminists, such as Josephine Butler and Millicent Garrett Fawcett. Its aim was to ensure that the CLAA was enforced throughout the country, and its local branches sought to mount prosecutions for rape, attempted rape, sexual assault, indecent exposure and the sexual harassment of women and girls in the street and in their workplaces. It was intent on making the police and judiciary take such matters seriously, pointing out that whenever the victim of a sexual assault was a young male, sentences against the male predator were significantly longer than in cases where the victim was a girl or young woman. Bethnal Green's own branch, the Vigilance Committee & Purity Association, fully intended to improve the sexual morality of the parish, though it was hampered by its use of euphemism, feeling unable to state clearly the nature of the various acts that dared not speak their names which, the Vigilance Committee claimed, were taking place quite openly in Bethnal Green streets, parks and alleyways. As noted in the previous chapter, women and girls in Bethnal Green ran a high risk of minor physical and verbal abuse in the street, much of it of a sexual nature, and the Vigilance Committee assisted in the prosecution for such offences of several 'ruffians' at Worship Street.

The CLAA had also been framed to attempt to make easier the prosecution of incestuous indecency, under the existing rape and sexual assault laws. Incest was and remains the least discoverable, and therefore most speculated about, of crimes.[10] The domestic life of the working classes – surveyed in its capacity for being a social 'problem' – was subject to an intense scrutiny not enjoyed by wealthier families, and so allegations about the prevalence, or otherwise, of incest rarely reached beyond the slums; and whatever levels may have existed of sexual coercion within 'respectable' families of the Victorian era will never be known. But many philanthropists and campaigners came back from the slums with a strong impression (formed in their minds by the foul language they had heard, and the sight of boys and girls relaxed in each others' company, flirting, mock-fighting, drinking) of sexual laxity and a casualness about carnality that was hard for them to comprehend. This openness and lack of shame, in neighbourhoods where families slept together in one room, led many observers to go on to conclude that single-room living encouraged slum families to prey on each other sexually; at the very least, children observed intercourse between their parents at close quarters and this, it was believed, corrupted them for life.

Arthur Harding was baffling on the subject; on the two occasions on which he referred (*en passant*) to incest, he contradicted himself. Recalling the one-room family, he claimed that unlike the early 1970s, the time of his tape recordings, people did not look at each other with 'an evil mind' – there was no shame in being naked as family members washed in front of each other. 'There was a different mentality,' Arthur said. But later, describing neighbours in Gibraltar Gardens, just east of the Nichol, he recalled a brother and sister who lived as man and wife and had 'barmy kids' together: 'The unfortunate thing about the East End of London and all slum districts is the one-bedroomed house. And no separate accommodation for the girls and boys. In a good many cases the girl and the boy as they grow up together become intimate.'[11]

The most (in)famous and oft-quoted pronouncements on poverty and incest – found in two separate mid-1880s investigations into the housing conditions of the poor – managed to raise dreadful images and anxieties about sex in the slums without substantiating them. No details of actual incidents were ever brought into the light. The shocking and heart-rending pamphlet written by Congregationalist minister Andrew Mearns in 1883, *The Bitter Cry of Outcast London*, stated baldly, 'Incest is common.' No more than that; these three words were quite enough for his readership. And two years later Lord Shaftesbury broached 'this painful subject' at the Royal Commission on the Housing of the Working Classes: 'If you go into these single rooms you may sometimes find two beds, but you will generally find one bed, occupied by the whole family, in many of these cases consisting of father, mother, and son; or of father and daughters; or brothers and sisters. It is impossible to say how fatal the result of that is.'[12] The chaplain of Clerkenwell Prison, a witness at the Royal Commission, claimed that he had made a private study of the causes of criminality and that in every case of incest he had come across, the single room was involved. Which is not the same as saying that all single rooms led to incest. The vicar of Christ Church, Spitalfields, said that he himself was 'positive' from his own 'personal observation' that overcrowding caused incest. Two other vicars questioned by the Commission disagreed, claiming that drunkenness was the cause of any incest they had come across. However, the vicar of St Paul's, Bunhill Row, who had become fascinated by the subject, said, 'I have questioned not only scripture readers, city missionaries and mission women, but also medical men who have been connected with poor parishes for years, and the testimony of all those, without exception, is that they have never known a single case of it.'[13]

The Reverend Alfred T. Fryer, curate at St Philip's, Clerkenwell, stated that he believed that it was precisely because working-class homes were so hugger-mugger that the communities were able to police sexual behaviour with greater vigilance than was possible in middle-class neighbourhoods: 'There is a kind of public feeling in operation,' he said, which 'inhibited wrongdoing and quickly exposed any miscreants to public shame.'[14] Fellow Commission witness

T. Marchant Williams (the London School Board inspector for the City of London and the very poor areas of St Luke's, St Giles and Clerkenwell) agreed, saying that, in his experience, cases of incest had been 'not so frequent as I was led to anticipate, because I found that when a case of that kind came to the knowledge even of the lowest people, there was an outcry in the neighbourhood. For instance, in the case of a father having intercourse with his child, it was known all over the district.' The questioner asked him: 'That was regarded by the people with horror?' 'Invariably,' said Williams.[15]

Fabian Socialist and social researcher Beatrice Webb recalled in her memoirs, published in 1926, that she had had to omit from the reports she had written in the late 1880s of life among the workshop and factory girls of the East End all mention of

> the prevalence of incest in one-roomed tenements. The fact that some of my workmates – young girls, who were in no way mentally defect-ive, who were, on the contrary, just as keen-witted and generous-hearted as my own circle of friends – could chaff each other about having babies by their fathers and brothers, was a gruesome example of the effect of debased social environment on personal character and family life . . . The violation of little children was another not in-frequent result . . . To put it bluntly, sexual promiscuity, and even sexual perversion, are almost unavoidable among men and women of average character and intelligence crowded into the one-roomed tenements of slum areas.[16]

The creation in 1884 of the London Society for the Prevention of Cruelty to Children (becoming 'National' in May 1889, when the country's thirty-one local committees amalgamated) provided a huge stimulus to child-protection measures and kept the incest debate in play, using a comparatively straightforward approach: the subject was too important for coyness. The records of the Society's East London Aid Committee have largely disappeared, but the second and third annual reports have survived and give glimpses of how its East End inspectors dealt with this distressing and shocking issue. In the year to 31 December 1890, 541 incidents of child cruelty or neglect came to the attention of the Society's East London staff, of which 197 were cases of starvation, desertion or 'dangerous neglect'; 89 were 'cruel

exposure to excite sympathy' – that is, the use of pitiful-looking children during parents' begging expeditions; 90 were injurious assault
cases; 107 were unspecified incidents that caused 'unnecessary
suffering', while 58 involved 'gross immorality against girl children'.
The East London NSPCC booklet did not pull its punches in discussing
such cases, and in its review of the year stated:

> In cases of crimes of an unnatural and immoral kind against girl chil-
> dren, the record is a black one . . . with, in many instances, the offenders
> being the fathers or near male relatives of the injured ones, punish-
> ment having been inflicted on the ruffians who committed these
> outrages by terms of imprisonment varying from six months' to eight
> years' penal servitude.[17]

The NSPCC record is entirely silent on incestuous assaults on male
children, possibly indicating the unthinkability to late-nineteenth-
century minds of homosexuality combined with incest; an estimated
93 per cent of plaintiffs in child sexual assault cases were female.[18]

The NSPCC inspectors, known colloquially in the East End as 'the
Cruelty Men', had discovered in their investigations a number of 'child-
mothers' who had been impregnated by family members, and girls
between the ages of four and fifteen 'ruined for life by immoral usage'.
The inspectors were shocked, too, by the precocity about sexual
matters shown by many of the 'rescued' children who had been
'brought up on oaths and curses, and whose language when first they
come into the Society's Shelter is horrible, the evil words sounding
doubly strange when issuing from sweet child-lips'[19] – this phrase
revealing how far short slum children fell from the rather creepy
Victorian ideal of infant innocence cherished by the NSPCC inspectorate. The typical Cruelty Man was thirty-seven years old and had
formerly worked as a policeman, army officer, clerk or School Board
inspector; the Society paid salaries, and so these men were professionals, not volunteers. The majority of them had already been
part of such movements as the temperance and 'social purity'/
'moral vigilance' drives. A significant proportion had also been
animal-cruelty/anti-vivisection campaigners, and some had joined
from other, smaller, child-protection bodies, such as the Church of
England Waifs and Strays Society, the Crutch & Kindness League (for

An NSPCC inspector
delivers a summons to
a slum family, in this
obviously posed photo-
graph from George
Sims's book *Living London*.

'cripples') and the Metropolitan Association for Befriending Young
Servants. But the inspectors were determined to pursue and prosecute
cruel parents across the social spectrum, and partly because of this,
the NSPCC for the main part managed to avoid provoking the hostility
of both the working classes and of *laissez-faire* non-interventionists,
who would otherwise have been able to claim that the child-protection
movement was simply one more attack on lower-class liberties and
modes of living. The relatively sophisticated analysis that the Society
made of its own findings did indeed suggest that while neglect
predominated in poorer homes (with alcoholism interacting with
poverty to result in poorly fed, clothed and shod children), the rates
for violent assaults upon infants were unaffected by either income or
family size. In the provinces especially, the NSPCC prosecuted
churchmen, doctors, civic figures – and their wives – who had set
about their offspring with hot pokers, rubber tubing and whips as well
as their own fists and feet.[20]

In 1887 the NSPCC ran a 'Make Friends with Your Coroner'
campaign. Concern was growing at the high and rising numbers of
deaths of children under one year old from suffocation in bed, which
were routinely dismissed as accidental at coroners' inquest hearings.

Nationally, the rise was from 130 per million live births in 1881 to 174 per million by 1890. In Bethnal Green in 1887, it was reported that around five out of six infant deaths investigated by coroners were found to be suffocation cases in one-room homes in which entire families had to sleep in one bed.[21] These deaths were said to be the result of 'overlaying', with a sleeping parent, or much older child, rolling on top of the smallest and accidentally killing them. It was often noted in press reports that such incidents were more common on Friday nights/Saturday mornings and Saturday nights/Sunday mornings, and that this suggested that heavy drinking was a factor in the fatalities. Others, though, worried that there was a darker explanation. How better to be rid of an unwanted, and probably insured, infant than by murdering in this way, in the knowledge that a coroner and his jury would be highly unlikely to pass any other verdict than that of accidental death? (In fact, an investigation by the Prudential insurance company found that insured children had a lower death rate than standard life tables would predict.) Most poor people were insured for their burial, a pauper grave being considered more shameful and tragic than a pauper life; and 80 per cent of the poor insured their children too,[22] to avoid the stigma of a cheap and shoddy funeral. Mrs Watts, the wife of a shellfish-stall keeper, of 26 Half Nichol Street, was devastated by the fact that 'people made remarks' on the too-brisk and austere funeral provided to her last child; a local undertaker had charged Mrs Watts 30s for a service she considered 'inferior', and she – heavily pregnant and bedridden with bronchitis – angrily announced to a visiting philanthropist that she would be withholding the final 8s in protest.[23]

Many social explorers could not comprehend why parents would jeopardise their outlay on food and shelter in order to be able to meet the weekly insurance policy payment. The Nichol, because of the extremely high density of its population, had above the London average number of overlaying deaths. At the December 1885 inquest into the death of two-month-old Annie Moore of 15 Half Nichol Street, killed when her mother rolled on top of her while asleep, trouble was taken to establish whether or not the baby had been insured. A neighbour confirmed that she had not been, and nor had any of the mother's ten children, half of whom had not survived early infancy. The next month, the Bethnal Green coroner found himself overwhelmed with

overlaying cases and the local newspaper ran out of room in which
to report the court's proceedings. This was proving to be a bitter
winter, and many families heaped on every scrap of textile in their
room to try to keep small children warm, sometimes fatally blocking
their airways. Harriet Evans, a hawker, of 17 Chance Street, in the
Nichol, put her baby Alice to bed wrapped in an adult's shawl and a
bonnet; in the morning she had stopped breathing.[24]

The NSPCC's agitation on infant deaths is likely to have contributed
to the huge rise in inquests on children who died of suffocation,
malnourishment, convulsions, or accidents that had occurred because
the child was either untended or was being looked after by another
child. In April 1889, fourteen-month-old Annie Melton of Old Nichol
Street was being cared for by a five-year-old neighbour while her
parents were out at work, and was scalded by a pan of boiling water
that fell from the fire, causing fatal injuries.

East End coroners and magistrates were often sympathetic in these
tragic episodes in the lives of the very-poor, even when some degree
of culpability was established. On a freezing December day, a labourer
on his way to work in the early morning found a naked newborn girl
in the sleet-filled gutter of Boundary Street. She was taken to the
workhouse infirmary ward but died twelve days later. Her mother,
Caroline Shepherd, twenty-two, an out-of-work maidservant, was
traced, having been given post-partum care by a Columbia Road doctor
who had noted that Shepherd's newborn baby was not on the premises in Brick Lane, where she lodged. Shepherd was given a one-month
gaol sentence for the exposure, since the judge believed that there
were many mitigating circumstances.[25]

In August 1889, the NSPCC succeeded in getting through parliament an Act for the Prevention of Cruelty to Children – informally
known as 'The Children's Charter'. Parliamentary opposition had
concentrated on the likely destruction by such legislation of that
Victorian holy of holies: the family home. Opponents of the bill had
argued that the clause allowing spouse to give evidence against spouse
would rend asunder the closest tie in human society. The Act had
been debated for eight weeks and did not go as far as the NSPCC
had wanted, but it nevertheless gave the State wholly new inroads
into private lives. Among its clauses were measures that defined more
clearly the notion of 'ill-treatment' and specified particular acts as

Two 1887 drawings of Nichol one-room homes, sketched as part of a sanitary inspection. The amount of furniture in the rooms suggests these families were among the better off in the district.

'cruel'; spouses could now testify against each other; magistrates were given various powers to search the home and to make custody provisions for a child once a charge of cruelty had been proved. The State could now also act *in loco parentis*, taking children into its custody in the workhouse, or other Poor Law institution, if a parent was found to be unable or unwilling to care properly for a child.[26]

Except in cases of violent or sexual assault, court proceedings were seen as the least desirable form of intervention, and the NSPCC itself sought instead 'to improve the home life of parents and children where it is possible by moral suasion, warning and supervision. In the majority of cases a warning is a sufficient deterrent.'[27] London-wide, in its first four and a half years, the Society investigated over 1,100 cases, of which just 180 went to trial, while around three-quarters resulted in stern warnings to parents.[28] The Society claimed that recidivism after a visit from the Cruelty Man was rare – but we have only its word for this, which is compromised, since if the Society had admitted that its warnings were not wholly effective, much-needed funds and subscriptions might have been put in jeopardy. Well over half the initial complaints to the Society about cruelty or neglect were made by neighbours and around a quarter by police officers, Poor Law officials, teachers or School Board inspectors. The NSPCC surveys found that 10 per cent of the allegations were made anonymously, and that 83 per cent proved to be well founded, with false complaints being the result of mistaken impression rather than malice.[29]

The Cruelty Men appear to have met with little resistance in their work, and the existing NSPCC records suggest that assaults upon inspectors were very rare. The Society stressed that its staff must use courtesy and tact and avoid 'all appearances of fuss and meddlesomeness'.[30] The poor seem to have acquiesced and co-operated with cruelty and neglect inspections and investigations; it was their vigilance and concern that led to the majority of the alerts to the Society in the first place. The NSPCC was harnessing the self-policing and inquisitiveness about neighbours that other philanthropists had already noted as a feature of slum communities. But there were many increasingly vociferous groups who believed that the deeper structural causes of poverty needed more concerted action. In the late 1870s and 1880s the Nichol began to be invaded by people with a wide range of ideas and strategies for solving the Nichol 'problem'.

PART THREE

ANY ANSWERS?

Tickling the Elephant

Two Anarchists, Frank Kitz and Charles Mowbray, believed they knew how poverty was created and how it could be ended, and they moved into Boundary Street to spread the news. Frank Kitz (1849–1923), a textiles dyer, had been living in lodgings with his wife and six children in King's Cross, but became aware that police detectives had his premises under surveillance. Kitz had a small printing press in the family home, on which he produced leaflets and pamphlets for hand distribution to the working classes throughout London. Kitz's colleague in this enterprise was Charles Mowbray (1857–1910), by trade a tailor, and in 1885 they moved their print operations into number 36 Boundary Street, where Mowbray also set up home with his wife Mary, who worked at home as a textiles machinist, and their four children. They were just two doors along from Arthur Harding's family's lodgings.

Boundary Street had been chosen because it was cheap, and with its (false) reputation as a police no-go area it appeared to offer some kind of sanctuary for Kitz and Mowbray's miniaturised political publishing house. There was the added bonus of being sited next door to a room shared by two deaf-mute beggars, who could neither hear nor reveal the print shop operations.

Kitz and Mowbray took the view that if revolution were to happen, it was the very poorest citizens who needed to be politicised – the *lumpen* (if they really existed), who fell outside the reach of any trade union, working-men's club, Liberal–Radical association or lecture circuit. Kitz believed: 'We should preach to the thieves, the paupers and the prostitutes. The first act of the Revolution ought to be to open the prison doors.'[1] Where better than the Nichol, with its higher than average proportion of hawkers, costers, beggars, day-hired dock labourers, former prisoners, unemployed and sweated-labour home-workers?

According to Reverend Robert Allinson, pastor of the non-denominational London City Mission, which had been active in the Nichol since 1836, the penury of the Nichol's inhabitants made Socialism quite attractive to a sizeable minority of them. Allinson wrote: 'Under the pressure of want, men with keen, pinched faces and bright, glaring eyes have said to me, "We want a revolution, and we must have it" . . . They are so much ready-made material for dema-gogic orators to work upon.'[2] Allinson was sure that many times when he knocked on Nichol doors for an evangelical chat, even when revo-lutionary feeling was not expressed directly it was 'partly smothered, or concealed, but all the same, it is there . . . They are out of love with the Queen, the Royal Family, the Government, the bishops, the Church, and all ministers of religion. They are at variance with most of the institutions of the country, and would "overturn, overturn, overturn", till they had completely changed the aspect of our social fabric.' But Allinson believed 'this is not the characteristic of the people gener-ally. The majority of them bear the hardships of their lot with surprising fortitude, and display far less of the revolutionary spirit than their circumstances might lead us to expect.'

Street-corner preaching was one method that Kitz and Mowbray used to excite the undecided. Both men were excellent speakers, capable of grabbing the attention of the weariest passer-by and making theoretical concepts seem relevant to working-class lives. The second front of their attempts to enlighten and organise the very-poor was an energetic campaign of pamphleteering. Kitz and Mowbray could not afford sophisticated apparatus, and used an aged hand-press together with a paving slab lifted from the street as both ink slab and 'making-up stone'. The seating of their print shop comprised upturned orange boxes, and, unable to afford an oil or paraffin lamp, they worked at night by candlelight. Kitz recalled: 'We sallied out on nocturnal bill-sticking expeditions, and despite the destruction by the police of some of our handiwork, we managed to placard the East End with incendiary manifestos.'[3] Kitz and Mowbray considered their remit to be a broad one, and among the paving-slab appeals they published were 'Fight or Starve', calling on the casual dock labourers to organise themselves into a single body and take strike action; while

'An Appeal to the Army, Navy and Police' stated the case against militarism and urged the abolition of the standing army. There was also the pamphlet 'Are We Overpopulated?', which attacked both 'emigrationism' (the sending to the colonies of pauper infants) and the fashionable view that if working-class families would only practise birth control they wouldn't be poor at all. The only emigration that was desirable was that of the 'useless' aristocratic and capitalist classes, claimed Kitz and Mowbray.

From Boundary Street they also started a local anti-sweated-industries agitation, with particular reference to the clothing and shoe trade; and for their No-Rent campaign against landlords they allied themselves to the London-wide Local Rights Association for Rental and Sanitary Reform, and created their own offshoot branch, the Anti-Broker Brigade – formed specifically to counter forced evictions and the 'distraining' (seizure in lieu of rental arrears) of belongings by landlords' bailiffs and house agents. This anti-slum-landlord campaign was distinct from the *Daily Telegraph*/Lady Jeune efforts, and there seems to have been no acknowledgement by either that the other existed. One of the wonders of these years is that the various political agitators and politically motivated philanthropists who urged the working classes to unite and organise to combat social injustices often failed to co-operate with one another: single issues dominated, and charismatic individuals had a tendency to be wary of other charismatic individuals.

In a similar way, Kitz and Mowbray's attempts to get casual workers and home-workers to organise/unionise were not part of the (ultimately more successful) efforts in this direction of Annie Besant, Charles Bradlaugh and Cunninghame Graham (among many others), who, in July 1888, helped the Bryant & May match-girls of the East End – who earned 4s a week for a twelve-hour day and were disfigured by 'Phossy Jaw', caused by the phosphorous in the matches – to strike and win better wages and conditions from the management; by the end of the campaign, there were 1,300 unionised match-makers in London. One year after the strike, hoping to build on this success, May E. Abraham of the Women's Trades Union Provident League came into the Nichol to lecture to the home-based matchbox-making women on the advantages of joining a union. The match-women of the Nichol had a saying about how exhausting and physically debilitating their work was: 'We're driving life out to keep it in, at this 'ere sweat work.'[4]

Abraham was a young working-class Irish woman who had been employed as a secretary by Lady Emilia Dilke (wife of the Radical Liberal former MP for Chelsea, Sir Charles Dilke); she went on to marry into the wealthy Tennant family and became one of the first female factory inspectors employed by the Home Office. Abraham, along with Lady Dilke, toured the country in the mid- to late 1880s, explaining to poor women workers, mainly in the sweated trades, the benefits of unionisation. Around 57,800 women in Britain were members of unions, and the Dilke/Abraham campaign had initial success in increasing that number. Unionisation, in their view, far from fomenting militancy and class antagonism, would be a civilising force for the casual worker, eradicating the dispiriting individualism and competitiveness that were features of the non-organised labour market. In fact, Lady Dilke managed to make the unions sound like a super- ior form of Mothers' Meeting:

> Learning to act with others and for the good of others is in itself an education; self-respect is evoked by a sense of responsibility; the intel- ligence is aroused and cultivated by the effort which must be made more or less by every member of a Trades Union to understand the economics of the particular trade. Each woman gradually learns that the future of her children as wage earners is directly affected by her own conduct and her influence on the policy of her Trades Union.[5]

Lady Dilke, her biographer tells us, had a beautiful voice, but her speeches to union rallies almost always ended up in 'a high-flown peroration', which could not help but sound out of place in the poorest of districts.[6] London proved to be the most disappointing place on Dilke and Abraham's tour, and by 1899 just 2,000 of the nation's 120,000 female union members were Londoners.

As with charity, Socialism was a crowded field in the 1880s, and the political careers of Kitz and Mowbray throw an intriguing sidelight on its various furrows. Kitz had been born into great poverty. The illegitimate son of a Kentish Town housemaid and a German émigré, he had started work at a very early age – as an errand boy and porter

– and as a child had attended political rallies. (He decorated the walls around his bed with coloured pictures of the French Revolution.) Kitz was described by one contemporary as 'a rebel by temperament, rather than Anarchist by philosophy'.[7] In appearance, he had 'a fine burly figure, with a mass of light brown curly hair, blue eyes, rather heavy features, a pleasant jolly smile always hovering around his countenance, the very antithesis of the person with a grievance and grudge against society'.[8] He refused the offer of an apprenticeship with a textiles dyer, knowing that he had no taste for workshop routine and hierarchy, or for subordination to a foreman. For this reason, Kitz was only ever a journeyman dyer, and spent part of his late adolescence and early twenties 'on tramp' around Britain in search of work. He wanted professional independence but, as millions had learned, the cost of such freedom was often very high.

In the early 1870s there were many active Radical-hued trades associations and working-men's clubs and societies in London. They were a mixed bag, mainly pursuing single goals, such as enlarging the franchise; land nationalisation; temperance; or English Republicanism. There was usually, but not always, a strong secular, anti-clerical flavour to such bodies, and a tantalisingly brief glimpse of early, pre-Socialist revolutionary feeling in the Nichol comes from the memoirs of London City Missioner John Weylland, who, at number 11 Devonshire Place, discovered a gang of six 'translators' (cobblers who turned ancient, thrown-away shoes and boots into reusable footwear), led by an ardent, self-educated 'Positive Religionist'. Positivism (or Comtism) replaced theology with reason and logic: the new 'Great Being' was mankind, not God. The founder of Positivism, Auguste Comte (1798–1857), had devised his Religion of Humanity to try to discover the laws that governed human society, in order to improve it. This unnamed Devonshire Place cobbler, claimed Weylland, 'being of a reflective, philosophical order of mind, had worked out a system of opposition to Divine revelation. The infidels of the neighbourhood regarded him as their "coming man" and his fame was spreading, as he was clever in argument and powerful in debate.'

A Nichol man called Roly Poly who sold pudding and cake in the streets, and his wife, who sold sheep's trotters, were among the cobbler's acolytes, and Roly Poly told Weylland that having been lent a copy of Tom Paine's *The Age of Reason* (1793) he had now turned against the Bible: 'It's made up of lies by the parsons, what dusent produce nuffin, to keep us down and to get our money . . .' Roly Poly had in turn passed *The Age of Reason* on to the omnibus-washer who lived next door, and this man told Weylland, 'I'm the best scholar down here or in the [bus] yard either, and I've found out how we are kept down by the "haristocrats", and now I understands what are our rights, I'll have my share of the wealth which is the people's which produces it. And if fighting for it is to be done, I'll do my share.' The bus-washer's wife agreed, saying, 'The people are becoming enlightened and are not to be kept down by religion.'

A branch of the National Secular Society was founded in a coffee-shop in the Nichol, with a well-decorated meeting room featuring busts of Paine, Byron, Shelley and Voltaire; a bible was placed alongside a dictionary, and at meetings the latter was used to demystify the Good Book. The Nichol branch of the Society started with thirty members, but this figure quickly swelled to around 180. They described themselves to Weylland as 'freethinkers', whose aim was to 'revolutionise and destroy until we are able to build up a new moral system'. They published pamphlets to this effect and delivered them around the Nichol, but Weylland – horrified at the underbelly of atheistical revolt he had unearthed in the slum – visited immediately after the delivery, reclaimed the pamphlets and replaced them with his religious tracts.[9]

This sudden growth spurt of Republicanism and ultra-Radicalism among the poorest of workers was partly caused by the slashing of dockers' wages in the summer of 1871, which led to the formation of a Labour Protection League, with fifty-four branches in the metropolis. Also in 1871, picketing was criminalised, which led to a huge number of gaol sentences, whipping and fines for the new offence, causing nationwide resentment. The massacre of 20,000 (the conservative estimate) members and supporters of the Paris Commune by troops in May 1871, and Gladstone's refusal to recognise the Parisian workers' government, was a third factor behind this brief revitalisation of English Jacobinism among the poor.

As a fluent German-speaker and writer (his mysterious father appears to have stayed on the scene), Frank Kitz was to be a crucial bridge between these types of advanced Republican/Radical bodies and the Continental Communists, Socialists and Anarchists who fled

In the early 1870s, pastor John Weylland discovered a group of secularists and Radicals in the Nichol, who met regularly to demystify the Bible, discuss the works of Tom Paine and plan for the coming of an English Republic.

to London from suppression in their home countries in the 1870s and early 1880s. Kitz started his political club life by joining the Manhood Suffrage League, which met at a variety of pubs in Soho. In the late 1870s he co-founded the English Revolutionary Society with German Anarchist–Communist Johann Most, who had fled Bismarck's regime in 1878 when a crackdown on political dissent began to bite. Most appears to have been a powerfully persuasive force on Kitz, convincing him that government and State would always be the enemy of the working man and, no matter how it was composed or elected, would inevitably find some way to rob him of the fruits of his labour and deny him his freedoms. Every kind of authority would, by its very nature, degenerate into tyranny.

In 1881 Most was sentenced to sixteen months' hard labour following an Old Bailey trial for incitement to murder. In his Anarchist journal *Die Freiheit* (Freedom), Most had celebrated the recent assassination, by the Russian Nihilists, of Tsar Alexander II and called for the same fate for all European heads of state. Kitz operated Most's defence fund and published seven English-language issues of *Die Freiheit*. For the time being, though, Kitz seemed happy enough to merge his Anarchist sympathies with the broader aims of Socialism. While Most was in gaol, Kitz became a founding member of the Labour Emancipation League (LEL) – a movement that fused some of the older Radicals/Republicans with new Socialist, Communist and Anarchist theorists, many from the Continent or inspired by Continental revolutionaries. The LEL, which had around 5,000 members by 1883, sought universal adult suffrage, freedom of speech, the abolition of a standing army, and free secular education; but it also called for the public ownership of all means of production.

At around this time, Kitz met Charles Mowbray, who had joined the LEL. Born in Bishop Auckland, County Durham, Mowbray had served in the Durham Light Infantry before becoming a master tailor. Physically, Mowbray was impressive – tall, with an athletic build, a mop of black hair and blazing eyes. One contemporary described him as 'one of the greatest working-class orators who ever spoke in public';[10] but an American Anarchist, Emma Goldman, considered his intellect inferior to his eloquence and wondered how much reason and analysis underlay Mowbray's passion.

Hoping to improve his prospects, Mowbray came to London but found that his trade was being increasingly sweated, with the prices paid for piecework driven ever downwards as working conditions deteriorated. Recent waves of factory legislation had placed the regulation of workplaces under a large new centralised inspectorate, but the typical manufacturing environment of the Nichol – the family room – was far harder to 'police' and indeed Bethnal Green had no workshop inspector at all until 1893.

When he moved to the Nichol, Mowbray was desperately poor, and so unwittingly found himself on the visiting rota of the London City Mission. Reverend Robert Allinson, who had been the Nichol's missionary since 1882, dropped in on Mowbray for a pastoral visit, taking with him his 'pledge book' in which he tried to sign up locals to a promise to stop drinking. Allinson later recorded:

> I often visited him and he always treated me with the greatest respect. He was an intelligent, well-informed man, with reasonable views on religion, and we had many interesting conversations together. But his life

was one incessant struggle with poverty . . . Gradually he drifted into Socialism and began publicly to advocate it. From that time, his career became a chequered one . . . From Socialism, he drifted into Anarchy . . . From what I personally know, I unhesitatingly affirm that poverty – sheer, incessant, galling, grinding poverty – has made this man what he is.[11]

Mowbray joined in with efforts to organise tailoring workers in the East End to campaign collectively for better wages and conditions. Under the auspices of the International Tailors' and Tailoresses' Union he began to lecture at working-men's clubs and street corners, but later he would come to believe that union activity was merely a facet of the capitalist system – it was the system itself that needed to be destroyed and replaced. If workers' wages and conditions improved, what impetus would they have to bring about revolution?

Mowbray had by this time come under the influence of Josef Peukert, an Austrian Anarchist–Communist who had arrived in London in 1884 and was involved in the bitter *Bruderkrieg* (Brothers' War) raging in West End Anarchist circles – partly a doctrinal battle, but largely personality driven. Peukert had been expelled from Johann Most's International Club in Stephen's Mews, Rathbone Place, off Tottenham Court Road, and set up the rival, popular talking-shop cum social venue Club Autonomie, initially in Charlotte Street and subsequently just around the corner in Windmill Street. An eyewitness gives an atmospheric account of the physical fabric and the habitué(e)s of Club Autonomie in its Windmill Street incarnation:

It was a very dingy, badly furnished place. A few rough benches, chairs and tables were the only accommodations offered to regular frequenters or the casual visitor. Anyone could enter unquestioned, and take part in the discussions . . . If half the threats which made the rafters of the Club Autonomie resound . . . had been meant, few rulers or millionaires would have been left to end their days in peace . . . Most of the men affected sombrero hats and red neckties; the women usually cut their hair short, wore trilby hats, short shabby skirts, red rosettes in their mannish coats, businesslike boots.[12]

MURDER!

- WORKMEN, why allow yourselves, your wives, and children, to be daily murdered by the foulness of the dens in which you are forced to live?

The average age of the working classes is some 29 years, and the average age of the rich 55 years.

It is time the slow murder of the poor, who are poisoned by thousands in the foul, unhealthy slums, from which robber landlords exact monstrous rents, was stopped.

You have paid in rent the value over and over again of the rotten dens in which you are forced to dwell. Government has failed to help you. The time has come to help yourselves.

PAY NO RENT

to land-thieves and house-farmers, who flourish and grow fat on your misery, starvation, and degradation.

_____

A MASS MEETING

WILL BE HELD IN

VICTORIA PARK,

(NEAR THE BAND STAND)

On Sunday, July 26th, at 3 p.m.,

When the following Speakers will address the meeting in support of a No Rent Campaign :—
D. J. Nicoll, W. B. Parker, S. Mainwaring, C. W. Mowbray, J. Turner, R. Jane, and E. Hall.

_____

Hurrah! for the kettle, the club, and the poker,
Good medicine always, for landlord and broker;
Surely 'tis best to find yourselves clobber,
Before paying rent to a rascally robber.

One of Mowbray and Kitz's No-Rent campaign posters.

Doctrine was less important in the _Krieg_ than it should have been, but, for what it's worth, Peukert followed Anarchist–Communist Prince Peter Kropotkin in considering that the views of mid-century Collectivist–Anarchist Michael Bakunin (whose teaching Johann Most followed) were outmoded and potentially authoritarian; by allowing individuals unlimited ability to acquire and possess, Collectivist–Anarchism contained the seeds of future inequality and domination. Followers of Kropotkin favoured Mutualism – a system of co-operative production and exchange with community-shared ownership of means. Kropotkin, a geologist by training, claimed that the writings of Charles Darwin gave authority to Mutualism, and that _Origin of Species_ (1859) and _The Descent of Man_ (1871) offered a wholly different reading of evolution theory to that of the Survival of the Fittest/Struggle for Existence school of thought. Before fleeing persecution in his native Russia Kropotkin had accompanied zoologists on field trips to remote regions of Siberia. 'We vainly looked for the keen competition between animals of the same species which the reading of Darwin's work had prepared us to expect,' he wrote in 1890. Instead, they found co-operation and a range of altruistic behaviours. Kropotkin cited a passage in the second, 1863, edition of *Origin of Species*, in which Darwin stated: 'Those communities which included the greatest number of the most sympathetic members would flourish best, and rear the greatest number of offspring.'[13] Kropotkin noted that while political economists had appropriated Darwinism and the ideas of other evolution theorists to bolster their own cruel creed, eminent Russian natural scientists had developed the notion of Mutual Aid as the chief factor of human development, though their works had not been translated and so had received little attention outside Russia. Kropotkin's romantic history and character, and his idealism, were highly attractive to Kitz and Mowbray.

In this heady world, alliances were made and dissolved with alacrity and usually not a little drama. Kitz and Mowbray joined the Socialist League, and this was how they came to the attention of William Morris – artist, poet, craftsman, utopian Socialist, and *de facto* leader of the League. The League had been founded in 1884 as a splinter group from the Social Democratic Federation (SDF), which was committed to achieving parliamentary representation for the working man, which they believed would lead to State Socialism; Morris and the League, on the other hand, wanted revolution, not tinkering with the ballot-box system. For a while, the revolution that Morris wished for looked very like the one that Kitz and Mowbray were thinking of too. Morris was an anti-parliamentarian: he wished for a new world of human self-government, not State Socialism. Morris's revolution would be one of the spirit, with mankind moving from a benighted age of individualism and exploitation to fellowship and co-operation. The first task of Socialists, he wrote, was to define Socialism and explain it to the workers, 'educating people into desiring it [and] next, organizing them into claiming it'.[14] While Morris conceded that some degree of force might be inevitable as capitalism reaped the whirlwind, he had a hatred of the bloodier aspects of revolution. He wrote of his first meeting with Kitz, in February 1885: 'Like most of our East Enders, he is certainly somewhat tinged with anarchism, or perhaps one may say, destructivism; but I like him very much. I called on the poor chap at the place where he lived, and it fairly gave me the horrors to see how wretchedly off he was; so it isn't much to wonder at that he takes the line he does.'[15] Morris in the Nichol is a lovely notion: he dreamt of a world of craftsmen working cheerily in sylvan surroundings to earn honest pay for high-quality items that were useful as well as beautiful. The Nichol embodied the antithesis of this – its decayed, jerry-built physical fabric 'housing' workers enslaved by the mechanistic, profit-driven production of gimcracks for the bourgeoisie and 'slop' clothing and footwear for the mass market.

Morris tried to find Kitz work as a dyer at Morris & Co.'s Merton Abbey Works in Surrey, where Morris's fabrics, carpets, tapestries and leatherwork were produced, but in the event Kitz proved to be too busy with his political work. Kitz helped Morris to gain greater experience of public speaking, bringing him into contact with the most downtrodden of London's citizens. Morris by his own admission did not have a powerful platform presence and found it difficult to address the working man in his own terms, sensing acutely the cultural abyss between himself and an East End crowd. Kitz would use his own charisma and understanding of the local people to convene a crowd in slum streets for Morris to address. Later Kitz recalled that the listeners were slightly mystified by Morris but always gave him a fair hearing. The impression the listeners made on Morris was not so positive, and after two years he was confiding to his diary that 'the frightful ignorance and want of impressibility of the average English workman floors me at times'. And two months later, a lecture that he gave a quarter of a mile north of the Nichol brought Morris 'a fresh opportunity . . . of gauging the depths of ignorance and consequent incapacity of following an argument which possesses the uneducated averagely stupid person'.[16] This was the artisan class Morris was describing, whom he had hoped to convert from their trade union/parliamentary reform stances to his broader vision of Socialism. Morris never said what he thought of his unskilled, casual-labour listeners.

Frank Kitz did, though. He would eventually have serious doubts that preaching and pamphleteering were effective in stirring the most degraded and disenfranchised of workers into action. He came to suspect that the various Socialist and Anarchist efforts had had 'about as much effect upon the masses as trying to tickle an elephant with a straw.'[17]

This was a view shared by Kropotkin, who complained of London as a city of old-fashioned Radical/Republican pragmatists and isolationists: 'Better a French prison than this grave,' he said, when he realised what stony ground London would be in which to plant the seeds of Anarchist revolution and international fraternalism.[18]

For the time being, though, the tickling of the elephant continued to be carried on with great energy, despite an increase in police vigilance and attempts to interrupt legal demonstrations and open-air meetings. On 20 September 1885 William Morris and Charles Mowbray were speaking on the subject of free speech and free assembly at a site in Mile End, at the corner of Dod Street and Burdett Road – by custom, a large open space where public meetings had been held for decades. The Dod Street meeting had already ended when the police moved in, claiming that Mowbray and Morris were obstructing the highway. The crowd was dispersed with violence, banners were seized and destroyed and those carrying them taken into custody. This was Morris's – but not Mowbray's – first experience of malicious prosecution and police perjury, and it shocked him to the core. 'I may note here for the benefit of well-to-do West Enders that the police are incredibly rough and brutal to the poor people of the East End,' Morris would later write.[19] When the magistrate discovered that it was *the* William Morris standing before him, the charges were thrown out.

Then, for a short while in early 1886, it looked as though the revolution was finally getting under way. A depression in trade that had started in 1884 had, by 1886, led to London trade union unemployment of over 10 per cent, up from a 'norm' of 2–3 per cent at the start of the decade. This figure applied only to established skilled and semi-skilled trades, and indicated that a far worse condition existed in the casual, unskilled job market. In the coldest February for thirty years, building and dock work had been suspended. The afternoon of

Monday 8 February 1886 saw the first of a series of mass demonstrations of the London unemployed, terrifying and astonishing the West End. It was one thing to read accounts of privation and the appalling conditions in the London slums; it was quite another to see British labouring men (widely thought to be docile, inarticulate and apolitical) going so far as to organise themselves and march behind banners that appeared to question the social and economic foundation of British civilisation. In Trafalgar Square the crowd was addressed by two rival working-men's groups. The 'Fair Trade' faction wanted to see the imposition of trade tariffs against foreign imports in order to protect British manufacturing and agriculture. The SDF was there too, demanding that the State provide employment for able-bodied men whenever the free market failed to do so; the Metropolitan Board of Works had plenty of projects to get under way – why not use unemployed men to build them?

The Socialist League was also there in force. Supporters of the rival groups clashed with each other and with the outnumbered police. Sections of the 20,000-strong crowd broke away and stoned the windows of Clubland, looted shops in Piccadilly and went on to Hyde Park to rob carriage-riders before wrecking their vehicles. Socialist observers said that the police had waded in first, with unwarranted violence; and that club members shouted provocative obscenities at the crowd passing along Pall Mall in order to goad them. They claimed that their march had been infiltrated by the usual small set of violent, apolitical riff-raff that always infested working-men's meetings and marches – the *lumpen*, with no interest in anything other than riot and plunder. At the subsequent trial of the SDF leaders for seditious conspiracy, the jury agreed with the defendants' view that the rioters had had no connection with the Socialist factions, and – to the astonishment of the nation – acquitted them. In fact, of those arrested, at least one-third were skilled or semi-skilled tradesmen, many of whom had suffered seasonal downturns in their trades.

Throughout the capital, the fear of a brutalised labouring class rising up and seizing power with violence remained intense for weeks. But no disorder on this scale recurred in 1886. Demonstrations continued over the next eighteen months, but a huge body of police was now primed for action, and even a section of the army would be deployed. In the autumn of 1886 the SDF organised a march of the unemployed to accompany the Lord Mayor's Show through the streets, calling on workers to 'Leave your slums and follow the pageant along the thoroughfares in solemn and silent order'. This they did, but a year later, on 'Bloody Sunday' – 13 November 1887 – mass violence again erupted in central London. Unemployment had remained at a record high, and the policy of offering only the workhouse to the able-bodied poor remained in place. A meeting originally convened in Trafalgar Square to protest at the imprisonment of Irish Nationalist MP William O'Brien, as well as to challenge the prohibition of public assembly in the square that had been issued on 8 November by Metropolitan Police Commissioner Sir Charles Warren, turned into one of Britain's most infamous riots. At twenty to three in the afternoon the mounted police charged the huge crowd, and an hour and a half later the Foot Guards fixed bayonets in Whitehall and waded in. The *Daily Telegraph* reporter, stationed at nearby Charing Cross Hospital, watched as a stream of casualties was brought in, nine-tenths of them suffering bloody scalp and skull injuries from police truncheons, the rest having been bayonetted, most of them in the back. The reporter saw truncheons, boots and fists used on people who had already fallen.[20] One man died, and two sustained injuries that would eventually prove fatal, while Bethnal Green's police superintendent, James Keating, who sat all day on his horse in a soaking wet uniform, died sixteen months later, aged forty-six, his premature death brought on by the conditions of that day.

Charles Mowbray had taken no part in Bloody Sunday. In the late summer of 1886 he had travelled to East Anglia as part of the Socialist League's programme to reach out to the rest of the country. He organised a series of well-attended unemployment rallies in Norwich and wrote to William Morris that 'Socialism is going like wildfire'.[21] But on 14 January 1887 Mowbray and a fellow activist were arrested when the city's authorities alleged that the crowd they had rallied had damaged a savings bank and shops in Norwich's market place. The two were convicted of inciting a riot and disturbing the peace, and Mowbray was given a nine-month prison sentence – which William Morris described as 'ferocious', even had the charge been proved, which, Morris claimed, it hadn't. Morris had noted that whenever 'respectable' men, like himself, had been arrested for open-air lecturing, their cases were either dismissed by the magistrate or a light fine was imposed; working-class men, like Mowbray, Morris said, received a rough justice that reflected their social standing, not the offence committed. Morris organised a committee to care for Mary Mowbray and their children while Charles was in prison, and wrote a play satirising the judiciary at the Norwich trial of Mowbray, *The Tables Turned; or, Nupkins Awakened*, which was performed on 15 October at the Farringdon Road headquarters of the Socialist League.

Mowbray's imprisonment was one of a number of factors that would see the Anarchist–Communists within the Socialist League start their lurch towards incendiary rhetoric and increasing sympathy for 'Propaganda by Deed' – an extreme position advocating revolution by assassination that had been adopted by a minority of Anarchists in Continental Europe and America. Propaganda by Deed would ensure that the entire Anarchist movement would for ever be linked in the public mind with bombings and other atrocities – to the delight of Anarchism's enemies.

Even more extremists were created by the Haymarket Affair, or the Chicago Martyrs Case. On 11 November 1887 (just before Bloody Sunday in Trafalgar Square, and adding to the strong feelings among the marchers on that day) four American Anarchists were executed in Chicago. On 4 May, a bomb had been thrown into a cadre of policemen who were breaking up a meeting in Chicago's Haymarket district, convened to call for an eight-hour working day. Eight police officers died in the blast. No pretence was made by the prosecution that the men on trial for murder had thrown the bomb; simply that they were members of the organisation that convened the rally at which the fatal bomb had been thrown. They were executed for being Anarchists.

The creation of the Chicago Martyrs recruited many previously apathetic or apolitical workers throughout the industrialised world to the banner of Anarchy; and it encouraged many existing Anarchists to consider that Propaganda by Deed had now become legitimate. Within weeks of the Chicago Martyrs' deaths Charles Mowbray had emerged from gaol – gaunt, emaciated and embittered. His position on political activism had changed: pamphlets and street preaching were not enough any more. 'I feel confident,' Mowbray wrote, 'that

WHEN WILL HE GET THERE?

An Anarchist poster.

a few determined men – and when I say determined, I mean men who are prepared to do or die in the attempt – could paralyse the forces of our masters, providing that they were acquainted with the power which nineteenth-century civilisation has placed within our reach.' That power was dynamite. 'The people could carry it around in their pockets . . . and destroy whole cities and whole armies,' wrote Mowbray, who also urged the use of 'Gatlings, hand grenades, strychnine and lead . . . Everywhere there are signs of the bloody conflict which is about to take place between the workers and their masters.'[22]

Wild words, and William Morris would tolerate such outpourings no longer. The shift towards support for violence among several of the Anarchist–Communists within the Socialist League precipitated Morris's departure, at the end of 1890, from the body he had co-founded. Morris would, however, remain personally fond of Mowbray and Frank Kitz, and his loyalty to the former was proven in the events of April 1892, when Mowbray's life took another dramatic downward turn.

Anarchist groups in Britain and on the Continent had been fully infiltrated by spies, or *mouchards* (flies), as the Parisians called them, working for any number of foreign embassies keen to keep their eyes on their revolutionary countrymen; or working for the police as *agents provocateurs*. An American journalist in London reported being escorted to a masked fancy-dress ball at Club Autonomie by Scotland Yard's Inspector William Melville; all the club members recognised Melville beneath his mask and he was most cordially welcomed.[23] Melville would also pose as a sanitary inspector in the East End in order to gain entry to the cheap lodgings favoured by Anarchists. There were five Anarchist clubs in the East End in these years; the biggest, in Kingsland Road near the Nichol, was said to have over 1,000 members, but, according to one in the know, 'like all similar clubs, it is largely patronised by detectives'.[24]

One *agent provocateur*, working for Scotland Yard, was Auguste Coulon, who had for years kept up the façade of trusted comrade within Anarchist groups in London, the British provinces and Continental cities. With police pay, Coulon sent instructions, unrequested, to a six-man group of Anarchists in Walsall on how to put together an incendiary device that would help the Russian Nihilists to attack the Tsar. When the police swooped in Walsall, they found the men in possession of items that the police claimed were the components of a yet to be constructed bomb. Sentences of ten years were imposed on three of the men for possession of explosives; a charge of conspiracy to cause an explosion had been dropped early in the proceedings.

Charles Mowbray was by now printer and publisher of the former Socialist League newspaper *Commonweal*; his editor was the Anarchist David Nicoll and the paper had been relaunched with the subtitle 'A Revolutionary Journal of Anarchist Communism'. When Mowbray was absent from the office, nursing his wife Mary in her final stages of tuberculosis, Nicoll wrote an article for the *Commonweal* of 9 April 1892 about the Walsall case entitled 'Are These Men Fit to Live?' in which he made rude remarks about the judge at the Walsall trial, Henry ('Hangman') Hawkins ('a barbarous brute . . . a hyena'), the Home Secretary, and Inspector Melville. Both Nicoll and Mowbray were put on trial for incitement to murder, Mowbray being arrested at his home within four hours of Mary drawing her final breath. William Morris, while abhorring the article (and wondering at Nicoll's sanity), stumped up £500 in bail fees for Mowbray so that he could attend Mary's funeral.

Nicoll for his part claimed that the prosecution was wholly malicious and that he, Nicoll, was only being proceeded against because he had in his possession a great deal of written evidence proving that the Walsall affair had been a police set-up, with Auguste Coulon as a paid-up Scotland Yard spy instigating a non-existent plot, and that during Nicoll's arrest, papers proving this to be so were seized by police, never to be seen again. To some contemporary journalists, it seemed harsh that Mowbray was on the incitement charge, since he had not been in the *Commonweal* office at the time of the writing or printing of the offending article, because of his wife's illness – in fact, he hadn't been at the office for weeks. The jury acquitted him, but Nicoll was found guilty and given a sixteen-month sentence.

Mary Mowbray's funeral became an Anarchist rally and a valuable recruitment tool, with several thousand people following her hearse from its starting point at the Berner Street International Workers' Club in Whitechapel to Manor Park cemetery in the eastern suburbs.

There was a mysterious explosion of some tiny contraption on the front steps of the Tilney Street, Mayfair home of Judge Hawkins, in November 1893. The device had included a type of acid often used by French Anarchists, though as one reporter noted, 'Mr Justice Hawkins was disliked by many criminals other than Anarchists, and this affair was never satisfactorily tabulated.'[25]

The fiery invocations being published in the *Commonweal* were relegating Anarchy to the lunatic fringe of British politics – an exile from which it has yet to return. Once the concept of Propaganda by Deed had been given any legitimacy at all by members of the movement,

"COMMONWEAL" PRISONERS, COMMITTED TO THE OLD BAILEY ON THE CHARGE
OF INCITING TO MURDER IN THE SOCIALISTIC PAPER.

Mowbray in the dock at the Old Bailey.

it was simple for Scotland Yard to use its spies within Anarchist circles
to utilise bloodier and bloodier rhetoric, which would create the
impression that the entire theory and all its advocates were murderous
in intent. The penetration by spies also exacerbated the lack of trust
that existed within the movement; as comrade came to suspect
comrade, the centre began to fall apart. As much energy was being
put into feuding, intrigues, denunciations and paranoia as into
fomenting revolution. Mowbray himself was suspected of being a
police spy – why should anyone want to shout so loud about dynamite unless they were attempting to lure moderate Anarchists into
bloody deeds, an Old Bailey trial and a prison sentence? It was an
accusation that caused Mowbray pain and anger.

While Britain would see only one Anarchist bombing incident (in
which Martial Bourdin, a twenty-six-year-old tailor, managed to blow
himself up near the Greenwich Observatory in February 1894),[26] sick-

ening atrocities by bomb-tossing Continental Anarchists, from the spring of 1892 onwards, were resulting in the deaths of restaurant diners, opera-lovers and churchgoers in France and Spain. As it would turn out, the British Anarchists were violent in print only, but even this was quite enough to cause most leading Socialists to sever their connections with them. Many Socialists also came to doubt Anarchism's relevance, or practicality, in setting social wrongs right. Anarchy was an exotic plant that had had a brilliant but brief flowering in arid British soil. As Socialist League member Bruce Glasier recalled:

> There appeared to be something mysterious in its origin and mode of diffusion. It was hardly to be ascribed to any circumstance in the political or industrial situation of the time ... Nowhere did Anarchism spring up spontaneously in the country, as Socialism so often did. It grew and spread only within the Socialist Movement, parasitically in the branches ... Anarchism is not an innate predisposition in man; it is an acquired state of mind, and a very unstable one, usually. The Anarchist is either a Socialist who has got muddled with individualist ideas, or an individualist who has got muddled with Socialist ideas.[27]

Charles Mowbray continued to call himself an Anarchist, but in fact he now mingled with trade unions organisers and would appear on any platform erected to support the unemployed, workers' rights and the battle against the niggardliness of the Poor Law. In 1894 he left for America, and lectured throughout East Coast blue-collar communities, eventually settling down to work as a tailor in Boston with his second wife and the children he had brought over from London. He took to drink, and moved south to New York to open a saloon. During a crackdown on political immigrants following the assassination of President McKinley, Mowbray was deported as an undesirable. He spent the last years of his life in Chestnut Grove, Forest Gate, suburban East London, still active, still inflammatory, but now seeming to have abandoned Anarchism altogether. Affected by the jingoism of these years, Mowbray embraced 'Fair Trade', or 'Tariff Reform', as a way of protecting the English working-man's income and employment prospects. Tariff Reform was called Protectionism by its opponents – the supporters of Free Trade – and sought to limit, by the imposition of import duties, the manufactures and foodstuffs that were entering Britain from the increasingly successful producers around the world, the biggest 'threats' being the fast-growing and efficient economies of Germany and America.

Mowbray had come a long way from 'Workers of the World Unite'; the internationalism and fraternalism of his early political life had given way to fear of the foreigner and the romanticisation of the English labouring man. The speaking tours that he undertook in his final years were funded by Conservative Party enthusiasts for Tariff Reform. He died in a Bridlington hotel room on Friday 9 December 1910, the night before he was due to urge locals to vote for the anti-Socialist, anti-Irish Home Rule candidate at that week's general election. The sitting MP, Sir Luke White of the Liberal Party, was also the local coroner and oversaw Mowbray's autopsy.

For his part, Frank Kitz never gave up on Anarchism, but became bitter about those who had drifted back to the parliamentary democracy/trade unions version of Socialism. He believed that the Left had had its aims watered down and had suffered *embourgeoisement* by the Christian Socialists ('superstition-mongers', as he called them) who had flourished in influence in the 1890s and who advocated steady progress towards an egalitarian world, informed by the teachings of Christ. Kitz was also disdainful of the other main school of gradualists – the Fabians, who sought the common ownership of London's utilities and who wanted to diminish class inequalities by getting working men and women elected into local government and on to such bodies as the London School Board and the Guardians of the Poor. ('Gas and Water Socialists', Kitz called the Fabians.) Kitz never believed that the State or any of its institutions would ever do more than slightly soften the painful side-effects of capitalism.

With regard to the Nichol and its inhabitants, Kitz had come to the sniffy conclusion that revolution was too good for them. The man who had once seen the thief, the pauper and the prostitute as the first in line to be radicalised despaired of what he saw as the minuteness of their outlook, after having had close contact with them during his time in Boundary Street. Their territorialism, their lack of curiosity and inability to see beyond their own fears and desires depressed him beyond measure. Kitz wrote of Boundary Street, 'The denizens of the street looked askance at our intrusion into their region, regarding us as police "narks" ... Mowbray reassured them, and their suspicion changed into contempt for lunatics who could open a printery in "our street".'[28] Kitz showed scant sympathy or understanding that one of the worst aspects of extreme poverty – intense competition between individuals for jobs and dwellings – was its potential to shatter fellow-feeling and to keep minds fixed exclusively on the matter of earning enough to stay alive. That there was as much kindness and sense of community as there was in the Nichol utterly passed Kitz by.

A Voice of Their Own

Where Kitz and co's incendiary rhetoric and Continental theory failed, a little local Bethnal Green squabble brought unity and defiance amongst some of the very poorest workers: it was the parish vestry that pulled off the trick of galvanising the costers and hawkers of Bethnal Green into coming together to organise and protest, and in the process eliciting no small level of public and newspaper sympathy. In January 1888, the vestry decided to revive a disused by-law dating from the reign of George III to clamp down on stallholders and other street traders, mainly in the Bethnal Green Road but also along Sclater Street, just south of the Nichol, and at the Nichol end of Brick Lane. This sudden adherence to the letter of a very old law was widely seen in the parish as an attempt by the shopkeepers and tradesmen who dominated the vestry to oust the purveyors of cheaper wares and foodstuffs from their pitches, and thereby inhibit competition in trade at a time of economic slump. The vestry claimed that the costers' stalls and barrows caused obstruction and encouraged gamblers, prostitutes and other undesirables into the streets, particularly on Sunday mornings, and ruled that they must be cleared away by 11 a.m. This was the very time at which most casual workers' major purchases of the week were made – at prices and in small portions that suited the precarious finances of the poorest.

Although perennially hard-up, the vestry found the cash to create a salaried post of street inspector, appointing one John Angell, and formed a special Streets Regulation Committee. One of the first to be prosecuted, at Worship Street, was a very poor man, William Beard, who had six children to support from the takings from his crockery stall in Bethnal Green Road. He was fined 5s, but three of the Radicals on the vestry – furious that their colleagues were taking this heavy-

handed approach at a time of great hardship for the casual poor –
went along to court to pay Beard's fine for him, which caused a huge
brouhaha at Vestry Hall.

Next, the Streets Regulation Committee demanded the removal of
the parish's many coffee stalls by 7.30 a.m. each day – the very hour
at which the stallholders were most likely to be serving cheap hot
drinks and food to working men on their way to work. Again, the
justification by the vestry was that coffee stalls were a magnet for
'ignorance and vice', as they put it, attracting criminals and prostitutes to gather around them. Over 700 residents petitioned for the
hours to be extended to 8.30 a.m., but the vestry was not moved, and
immediately issued twenty-three summonses of coffee-stall keepers,
of whom twenty-one were fined between 10s and 20s each, plus costs.

The ancient bird and animal market of Club Row was also targeted,
with the policemen who tried to enforce the by-law being verbally
abused by the 200 or so 'rough boys' who regularly came from across
London to sell pigeons, dogs and white mice among the more established songbird-sellers.

In February 1888 the Bethnal Green Costermongers' and
Stallkeepers' Protection Society was formed, and its inaugural meeting
was held at Beasley's Coffee-House in Virginia Road. The Society
declared that its aim was to fight prosecutions at Worship Street with
the help of a solicitor to whom the Society paid a retainer. Discovering
that a similar crackdown had been put in operation in two nearby
parishes – St Luke's, and St George's in the East – the Society made
contact with other coster groups that had sprung up in defence of
their trade, and before long the agitation had spread citywide, with
the formation of the London United Costermongers' Protection
League. Some 500 East End members came together to demonstrate
in the Nichol end of Bethnal Green, despite a snowstorm that
continued throughout their march.

In the summer, the crackdown on the eighty or so stalls in Sclater
Street intensified. The vestry claimed that the food-purveyors left vast
quantities of leaves, stalks and meat and fish offcuts to be cleared away,
at the vestry's expense. On Sunday 19 August, twenty-three police officers and Street Inspector Angell turned up to ensure that all the stalls
were removed by 11 a.m., and hundreds of locals sympathetic to the
stallholders heckled and jostled the police, taking each stall as it was

A shop in the Club Row bird and animal market.

dismantled and re-erecting it further along Sclater Street. The more obstinate had their stalls impounded, notably the colourful pony and cart of a sarsaparilla seller, Mr Moss, who had all his produce poured down the drain by police officers and was fined 5s and 2s costs for obstructing the street with his vehicle. When Moss got his cart back, he returned to Sclater Street but now sold his drinks with his pony whip in his hand, ready to take off as soon as the police approached.

Montagu Williams, JP, always keen to see things with his own eyes,

Brick Lane on a summer Sunday morning in 1895, looking north towards the Nichol. Sclater Street is the first turning to the left.

strode along to Sclater Street on 9 March 1889, and concluded that the vestry had very little ground for complaint. From then on he charged each summonsed stallholder only the cost of his summons (2s). After that, the by-law fell back to sleep again, and the shop-keepers of the vestry seemed to lose interest in the fight they had started.

Four years later, the local unemployed, unaligned with Anarchist or Socialist organisations, began their campaign of direct action. A

A Brick Lane stallholder.

group of jobless labouring men started to march on vestry meetings in both Bethnal Green and Shoreditch, requesting that necessary parish tasks be given to them. These large deputations, led by boot-maker John Jewers, house-painter Charles Williams and car-man Lambert Heather, also picketed the Board of Guardians' meetings, occupying the public gallery and demanding that the notorious filth and dilapidation of the Bethnal Green Workhouse be put right by the direct employment of local labouring men, who wanted to clean, paint and refurbish the House for a regular wage. Jewers had fallen behind with his rent at the laughably named 3 Paradise Cottages, in Hoxton's 'Land of Promise' district (sardonically so nicknamed by residents because a local man had bequeathed some property in the area to the parish in his will, but his widow had refused to yield it up). Bailiffs attempted to remove Jewers's pitiful belongings, and around fifty of the unemployed barricaded themselves in the cottage to guard it against the seizure. A large crowd gathered outside in support, singing the 'Marseillaise' and 'The Starving Poor of Old England'.

Jewers and co wrung a small victory from the vestry. Following a

number of high-profile contractual scandals that had fleeced the
Bethnal Green ratepayers, the vestry, in 1893, agreed to experiment
with creating its own workforce of street-sweepers and rubbish collectors, to be paid the going rate for such work of 24s a week, with
reasonable hours, while more skilled men – such as masons and
paviours – were to earn 36s.

Additionally, an early form of labour exchange was reluctantly set
up at Vestry Hall to match jobless men to local vacancies. But only
five employers replied to the 1,500 letters sent out by the vestry asking
for details of vacancies on behalf of the 1,300 unemployed men who
had signed up, and the experiment was abandoned. The vestry soon
shut down its direct-labour section too, grumbling that it had cost
some £1,200, and that this was the sort of problem for which central
government should be finding solutions.

Two other issues particularly riled the Nichol poor: compulsory vaccination for infants, and compulsory school attendance. The 1853
Vaccination Act required the inoculation against smallpox of babies
under the age of three months, and follow-up Acts brought in stiff
penalties for those who refused to have their children under the age
of fourteen vaccinated. Opposition to this medical coercion existed
throughout the nation – most of it based on the grounds of the attack
on liberty, and much of it for its class bias – and the Anti-Vaccination
League was formed. One of the League's affiliates, the London Society
for the Abolition of Compulsory Vaccination, discovered that it had
an extremely strong cell in Bethnal Green, with hundreds of people
of every social class regularly meeting at street rallies and demonstrations against the Acts. The London Society summarised its objections
thus: 'While no scientific explanation of vaccination has been advanced
by our opponents, the government, which enforces the practice, has
never defined what vaccination is, the views of its advocates are mutu-
ally destructive, and the writers against the practice have proved that . . .
it is only another form of medical quackery, which will in due time
pass away and be forgotten.'[1] Many medical men could not understand this point of view, nor the level or nature of the opposition
among the poor to this State-supplied measure that had the potential
to save life – all provided free of charge to the user. (The old arguments about State-funded measures undermining the independence

of the poor seemed to melt away for the proponents of compulsory vaccination.)

Bethnal Green had been very hard hit by the smallpox visitation of 1870, which killed around 11,000 Londoners (and over 44,000 people nationally). The outbreak led to the passing of the 1871 Smallpox Act, imposing a huge fine of up to 25s on parents who refused to have a child inoculated. The fines were imposed each time a parent refused to comply with a vaccination order. A journalistic eyewitness of the 1870–71 outbreak in the Nichol end of Bethnal Green noted the fear and suspicion of locals at State medical intervention:

> The epidemic is raging and increasing in virulence in many of the districts we passed through, hingeing on one side to Hackney and on the other to Shoreditch, and we had great difficulty in obtaining information, from the reluctance of parties to allow any of their family to be sent to the hospital. In certain quarters we found the poor people entered into 'a solemn league and covenant' to render no information to visiting officers, if they suspected them as such. They choose to nurse the smallpox at home, and in many instances they doggedly refuse to let their children be vaccinated. It is curious to hear their reasons and the foolish notions they entertain. In some instances, they have a show of reason upon their side; for we find that some few medical men have not taken particular care with the cases they have attended . . . If the poor are not properly vaccinated the rich will assuredly, through one channel or another, eventually suffer.[2]

There is a sense here that the real reason for this expensive intrusion into working-class family life was far from selfless – that if the poor were allowed to go sick, the pox would continue to be free to infect the wealthy. Certainly, one of the factors that made vaccination so unpopular among the poor was that it was one of the tasks given to the Boards of Guardians; for many, this made the measure appear to be yet one more punitive Poor Law attack upon the poor – operating under the guise of care and concern. There was disquiet in some medical circles, too, that the guardians might be tempted to pare costs and show general parochial ineptitude in administering the vaccine. A coroner's case from April 1889 suggests a lack of unanimity among local doctors on the vaccination issue. Anna Mathews, the wife of an unemployed porter of Boundary Street, went to bed with her nineteen-day-old daughter Kate resting on her arm; the child had been vaccinated that day. In the morning Anna woke to find the baby dead beside her. At the coroner's inquest Anna said she had been entirely sober that night, and that since her husband had been unable to find employment for the previous year, she 'had not had the means to be otherwise'. A doctor told the court that he believed the vaccination might have precipitated the convulsions that he said had killed the baby.[3]

Despite all the penalties, the people of Bethnal Green and Shoreditch continued to refuse to comply with vaccination orders, and in 1898 over two-thirds of infants in the two parishes remained unvaccinated.

The mass education of the children of the poor was also seen by many as a temporary fad that might soon be abandoned when it was proved to be of no use, and which was an attack on the freedom of the individual – and expensive too. In London, before the passing of the 1870 Education Act, the city's 750,000 children could be schooled, if their parents so wished, for a small fee, in either 'National Schools' run by the Church of England – by far the largest operator in the field; in the 'British Schools', which were run by a variety of religious Nonconformists; the 'Ragged Schools' – philanthropic ventures set up for the poorest of street children, many of whom were too dirty, diseased, ill-shod and poorly clothed to mingle with other children; and the 'Dame Schools' – small private concerns more often than not set up by women in their own homes.

The Education Act created the nation's School Boards, but schooling remained varied for many years, with Church, charitable foundation, Ragged and Dame schools continuing to exist alongside the massive new Board Schools. The Board's inspectorate was able to compel attendance at whatever school the child was enrolled at, and to ensure that the parents of non-attendants signed up for a Board School place. This education was initially not free (the average cost in London was 2d a week), although the very poorest were almost certain to have their fees remitted to them. But this remittance took time and required the parent to give detailed data on earnings and outgoings to a stranger; some 80 to 100 families in the Boundary Street area were visited each week in the fee-remission exercises. Children between five and ten years old had to attend school full-time unless there was 'reasonable excuse' (such as chronic ill health, or there being no school within two miles of home). Those between the ages of ten and thirteen could be 'half-timers' if it could be proven that the child's employment was crucial to a family's well-being.

For the parents of persistent non-attenders, an 'A' notice was served – warning that if the child's school attendance were not improved, a 'B' notice would follow. The issue of a B notice required the parent to be present at a specially convened meeting of the B Committee, to hear the reasons for the absences. If a child still did not attend after a B meeting, a summons was issued and fines of up to 2s 6d could be imposed if the magistrate were in favour of compulsory educa- tion (many were not; Montagu Williams persistently refused to convict). One extremely poor Old Nichol Street flower-hawker faced fourteen separate summonses for his children's absenteeism; his defence was that he needed their help selling flowers at Dalston railway station.

In October 1889 Bethnal Green schoolboys decided to mount their own insurrection against compulsory attendance, and against the use of physical chastisement at schools and the imposition of homework. On Tuesday the 8th, between four and five hundred boys of around fifteen years of age marched through the parish streets calling out, 'No more cane!', 'We want shorter hours!' and 'No more home lessons!' Their leaders were two schoolboys wearing scarlet caps and carrying red flags, signifying the fight for liberty, they told newspaper reporters. The demonstrators marching behind them were pupils at a variety of schools – Board; church-based – and as they paraded past each local school they called upon children to leave their lessons and march with them. The next day, children from Hackney joined the protest and police now routed the crowd, giving chase and warning of prosecutions, and the children's protest quickly petered out.

Dissent was usually more intimate and fractured. John Reeves worked in the Nichol for sixteen years. His initial task, during 'sched- uling' – by which every house in the district with a rental value of £25 or less per annum had to be visited and the presence of school- age children established – was undertaken in plain clothes and with no identification. When Reeves knocked on the door of the vicarage of St Philip's church in Mount Street and asked how many children were in the ménage, the clergyman, Robert Loveridge, told him that

B Committees were convened by the London School Board to investigate why a child was persistently absent from school.

it was outrageous that home life should be interrupted with such impertinent questions. Poor families were legally obliged – middle-class families were not – to impart this kind of personal information to the schedulers, and many objected – some aggressively. In his memoirs, Reeves recalled being 'dreadfully abused and harangued', with neighbours joining in the harrying: 'All of this was very unpleasant,' wrote Reeves. 'One had simply to carry on quietly but firmly, until the anger burnt itself out. After some years they got to understand that we were not co-operating with the police, and that they had nothing to fear on that account.'[4]

These localised stand-offs had none of the inspirational rhetoric and personalities of such exciting, heroic labour disputes as the Great Dock Strike of 1889, or the match-girls' strike that forced the hand of Bryant & May, and which appeared to turn the tide, for a while at least, in favour of the worker and captured the imagination of many in the West End. But the Bethnal Green street-trading rumpus, the calls for a parish employment programme and the non-compliance with vaccin-ation and schooling edicts did at least show that the very poorest could organise themselves to protest. They were not the inert rabble that both Socialists and supporters of *laissez-faire* took them to be. Ben Tillett, hero of the Dock Strike, said at the end of the century that 'many of those who lived in the black spots of misery had been so demoralized by want that they no longer had any desire for anything better . . . It was from these quagmires of degeneration that the hyenas of the revolution emerged. A Socialist government would therefore have to think of ways and means to get rid of this scum.'[5] But in fact, by the Edwardian era, London's costermonger unions had a membership of over 1,000, with the majority of London's estimated 7,500 costers having at least some kind of link with a local trade-defence organisation. These bodies had no clear political allegiances, and at general election time costers' barrows were as likely to be fluttering with the blue flags of the Conservative candidate as with the orange and yellow of the Liberal. The parliamentary seat of Bethnal Green South West was held by Radical Liberal Edward Pickersgill from 1885 to 1911, with a six-year interruption by Conservative & Unionist anti-immigrationist Samuel Forde Ridley, between 1900 and 1906, who had been backed by the local coster union, possibly, but not definitely, because of his anti-alien campaigns in parliament. The costers returned to Pickersgill in 1906, but in 1911 were backing the Socialist candidate.

The poor of London were as complex and contradictory as any other social class in their political allegiances, and close investigation fails to substantiate claims made then and now that they were naturally Tory, or inherently indifferent to politics.

According to Arthur Harding, political talk was silenced in the local pubs, where every publican was a Tory and displayed Conservative politicians' pictures. No one was ever allowed to criticise the Tories in a Bethnal Green pub, Arthur claimed. An anecdote from the early summer of 1889 appears to corroborate the notion that politics plus East End pubs equalled a punch-up. In Joseph Jacobs's Nichol pub, the Victory, a celebration was under way to mark the re-election of Jacobs as a vestryman, in the Conservative interest. A small group of drinkers who had supported a rival Radical Liberal candidate loudly heckled Jacobs's supporters and a brawl erupted at around midnight. A supporter of Jacobs called James Mayes, aged thirty – known locally as Mace – suffered a blow to the face during the fracas. Mace had only recently been discharged from the Mildmay Mission Hospital in Turville Street and had a weak heart and just one lung; he had been advised to avoid commotion and excitement. Mace wandered down to the Mildmay, checked himself back in and died three days later. The rumour that did the rounds in the Nichol was that the fatal fight had taken place inside the Victory, after closing time, and not outside on the pavement, as Jacobs claimed at the subsequent coroner's hearing. It was also said that the coroner, Dr Roderick Macdonald, had decided not to pursue this line of inquiry further in order to avoid embarrassing or compromising a powerful local man such as Jacobs.[6] Despite this incident, Jacobs always maintained, proudly, that his clientele had no interest in politics, and that 'snarling Socialism',[7] as he called it, held no appeal for the inhabitants of the Nichol, who were 'genuine working men, not a Socialist or sacker of shops among them'.

But a significant number of working men had voted with their feet, and if politics was not to be discussed in pubs, they took their drinking money to the East End's burgeoning clubland. Clubs and their membership boomed in the late 1880s, and Charles Booth, in his *Life and Labour* survey, found thirty-two political clubs in East London (as distinct from church/philanthropic clubs, and purely social clubs); twenty-two of these were Liberal and Radical; six were Conservative; three Socialist and one supported Irish Home Rule. The overall tone he detected was 'not so much Liberal or even Radical, as Republican, outside of the lines, authorized or unauthorized, of English party politics, and thus very uncertain at the ballot box. There is also a good deal of vague unorganized Socialism.' Although such clubs tended to attract the skilled or semi-skilled worker, Booth believed 'keen dialectic to be the especial passion of the population at large',[8] and visitors to common lodging-houses, home to the most impoverished strata of London men, similarly noted a strong taste for political and theological debate. When 'missionaries' came to preach in the lodging-houses, heated discussions often began, to the surprise of the visitors, who believed the submerged to have no interest in, or intellectual capacity for, such abstractions.[9]

The bizarre thing was that the Nichol had an extraordinarily high level of enfranchisement for parliamentary elections, considering that more than 80 per cent of its population were estimated to be living in chronic poverty. Some 46 per cent of Nichol males over the age of twenty-one were on the Bethnal Green South West parliamentary electoral roll in the late 1880s and early 1890s, against a national figure of 60 per cent; in Old Nichol Street itself, enfranchisement levels hit 85 per cent in 1887. Between the years 1891 and 1901, Bethnal Green South West and impoverished Poplar had the joint highest levels of enfranchisement in the whole of the East End.[10] And it was the Nichol's unfortunate architectural history that led to the strange anomaly whereby the most socially and economically excluded men found themselves with disproportionate access to the ballot box.

The 1869 Poor Rate Assessment and Collection Act had accidentally enfranchised many sections of the working class who paid 'compounded' rates through their landlord, as a proportion of their weekly rental money. Landlords were now legally obliged to supply to the electoral authorities the names of all their tenants; what this tended to mean in practice was that the 'principal', 'chief' or 'responsible' tenant was named as 'householder' or 'occupier' and so was automatically placed on the register, while the further down the subletting chain a tenant was, the less likely he was to make it on to the register. Later on in the process, 'revision barristers' would comb the lists attempting to pick off paupers (receipt of poor relief, except a medical order, automatically disenfranchised the recipient), as well as those who had moved home in the past year, and non-naturalised citizens from abroad. In 1891 the Conservatives did a sweep of the parliamentary electoral rolls of Bethnal Green and successfully challenged and removed a quarter of the parish's electorate on these three grounds. The barrister criticised the Bethnal Green Vestry for its lack of scrutiny of the names that had been supplied by landlords. Nevertheless, some 636 Nichol adult men – of a total of 1,574 counted in the 1891 census – retained their right to vote, and more than half of the slum's hawkers, over one-third of its labourers, and 29 per cent of the textiles and footwear workers remained on the parliamentary voter list for 1892.[11]

As one historian of the franchise has pointed out: 'A man of voting age was most likely to get on to the register and stay there if there were no other adult men living under the same roof', because he was more likely to be considered the 'principal tenant' and the rates element of his rent would entitle him to the household vote. 'Franchise law and registration practice were least problematic in cases where one household occupied one separate dwelling . . . Neither a humble occupation nor a humble dwelling was in itself a disqualification for the franchise.'[12] By contrast, only around 37 per cent of adult males on the census in such wealthy districts as Belgravia, Mayfair and Kensington were found on the electoral roll. The mansions and town houses here made it more likely that family homes, with resident domestic staff, would award the paterfamilias the sole occupier/household vote, disenfranchising his sons, brothers, or any other adult males under the same roof who could not be said to contribute to the rates.

The most thrilling data – whether the Nichol men bothered to vote; and for whom they voted, and why – can never be known. It is tempting to extrapolate from the notable, pervasive Radical Liberalism of Bethnal Green South West (and of the equally poor and equally highly enfranchised Poplar) that where impoverished working men did have the vote, they tended towards the left.[13] Did the elderly and failing artisan men of the Nichol fulfil their traditional political profile and back Radical Liberalism? Were the more casually employed and unskilled workers more likely to abstain, to vote for Home Rule, for anti-vaccination, the Empire, Free Trade, Tariff Reform, better poor relief or any other kind of social progress? These are tantalising and unanswerable questions: the secret ballot has been one of civilisation's greatest leaps forward but has done the historian no favours at all.

The Scientific Slum

During the street traders' disputes, London took the side of the little people, with 10,000 Londoners signing petitions supporting the costers, and large meetings attended by the public; the local and national press, too, berated the shopkeeper class for the clampdowns. Support for the threatened markets surrounding the Nichol came from another unlikely source. Charles Booth, forty-six-year-old shipping magnate and gentleman amateur statistician, had, in the spring of 1886, set about organising a project that would emerge as his highly influential seventeen-volume *Life and Labour of the People in London*, published from 1889 to 1903 in three series, 'Poverty', 'Industry' and 'Religious Influences'. The sights and sounds of the Sclater Street, Club Row and northern Brick Lane markets thrilled Booth when he visited them as part of his fieldwork for his first volume, 'East London'. Of Sclater Street on a Sunday morning he reported: 'The streets are blocked with those coming to buy, or sell, pigeons, canaries, rabbits, fowls, parrots, or guinea pigs ... Through this crowd the seller of shellfish pushes his barrow; on the outskirts of it are moveable shooting galleries, and patent Aunt Sallies, while some man standing up in a dog-cart will dispose of racing tips in sealed envelopes.' Around the corner, 'Brick Lane should itself be seen on Saturday night, though it is in almost all its length a gay and crowded scene every evening of the week, unless persistent rain drives both buyers and sellers to seek shelter ... [with] the flaring lights, the piles of cheap comestibles, and the urgent cries of the sellers.'[1]

Booth had commenced a sort of double life, forsaking his marital home in South Kensington (and later, just to the north of Marble Arch) and taking lodgings in the East End, moving frequently once he felt he had assessed the spirit of a locality. He was not the first gentleman of wealth and leisure to savour the joys of slumming – it was a pastime as established in the 1880s as bicycling, bridge or angling; he was simply one of many with the privileged gaze, perambulating strange streets and partaking of the sights, sounds and smells of this other world. (Some even dressed up to do so: 'After a good dinner a crowd of men and women in evening dress would be personally conducted through the worst slums known, prying into people's homes and behaving in an intolerable manner,' recalled one young university settlement worker in Whitechapel in the late 1880s.)[2] The diary that Booth kept of his time in London lodgings is lost, but fragments that his wife Mary typed up for her memoir of Charles reveal the enjoyable time he spent at three London addresses, one of which was in Shoreditch. Mary noted, 'He is really enjoying his East End life . . . He likes . . . the people and the evening roaming and the food! which he says agrees with him in kind and time of taking better than that of our class . . . the oatmeal porridge and thick bread and butter of his East End landladies.'[3] But his sensual enjoyment of poor London had a very serious purpose: his restless mind was determined to fathom the true extent and causes of poverty in London. In the social and economic crisis of the mid-1880s, many alarming statistics were being thrown around, and Booth rejected the trade union / Socialist notion, widely disseminated and cautiously accepted as fact, that 20 per cent of Londoners were existing in dire poverty and extreme want.

The first volume of Booth's survey, published in April 1889 as the earliest in the 'Poverty' series, had entailed the visitation of 3,400 East London streets by Booth or one of his hand-picked team of six 'secretaries' after they had examined written and oral testimony from a variety of people who had made house-to-house visits on Booth's behalf: clergymen, philanthropists, rent collectors, Charity Organisation Society members, and the police. The most important source of information was the London School Board inspectorate, which had an extraordinary level of access to the home life of the poor. Booth stressed that information for his survey was to be extracted from the poor with tact and discretion, that the 'delicate machinery' of the School Board's scheduling work should be subject to no 'unwarrantable impertinence' on the part of the inquiry team; and in the printed volumes of *Life and Labour* false names were given to residents and the streets they lived in. So, for instance, Half Nichol Street was given the (possibly ironic) pseudonym 'Summer Gardens'; Boundary Street was 'Cutter's Row'; Old Nichol Street was 'Baxter Street'; Mount Street was 'Fount Street'.

Booth saw himself as a disinterested investigator, using scientific methods of inquiry to state more clearly the nature and extent of the actual problem; after this, it was for others to decide what was to be the solution. Common sense, facts and figures and the true meanings behind the numbers that were being bandied about were desperately needed, he felt, and Booth intended to supply these where others had produced lurid and harrowing anecdotal and impressionistic accounts of the sufferings of the very-poor. Journalistic slumming had given rise to a successful literary sub-genre, with such titles as Andrew Mearns's *Bitter Cry of Outcast London* becoming an instant bestseller, despite being written as an earnest exposé by a concerned churchman. Other titles about slum conditions that sold well and made a splash in the newspaper and periodical press included James Greenwood's *Low-Life Deeps, An Account of the Strange Fish to be Found There* and *The Seven Curses of London*, and George Sims's *How the Poor Live* and *Horrible London*.

Booth's closest friends, even his wife, had little idea where he was coming from, politically and philosophically. His own son-in-law considered him 'an unique personality, as baffling in his inner thoughts as in his personal appearance'.[4] (He was tall and thin, and dressed shabbily.) One of the journals reviewing the first volume of *Life and Labour* referred to Booth's 'severe impartiality'.[5] But Booth did have a political motivation for his survey: he wished to overcome the 'help-lessness' that he believed was temporarily paralysing a thoroughly commendable capitalist system. In the introductory paragraphs of his first volume he wrote,

> With regard to the disadvantages under which the poor labour, and the evils of poverty, there is a great sense of helplessness: the wage earners are helpless to regulate their work and cannot obtain a fair equivalent for the labour they are willing to give; the manufacturer or dealer can only work within the limits of competition; the rich are helpless to relieve want without stimulating its sources. To relieve this helplessness a better stating of the problems is the first step.[6]

Booth believed that the poverty problem had been wildly overestimated. What he was expecting to find was widespread fecklessness, laziness, drunkenness and physical or mental debility as the explanation for any chronic poverty that might exist. However, he admitted at the outset that he was more than willing to be persuaded otherwise on any of his views, should the data be convincing. This was just as well: Booth had not believed the figure of 20 per cent living in chronic poverty – by 1889 his researches had revealed that the proportion in the East End of London was 35 per cent, and in the Nichol, 83 per cent.

Although it had been Booth's stated intention that he would not suggest remedies for any social problems he and his researchers might encounter, he would soon prove hugely influential in promoting the controversial idea of old age pensions. This form of 'limited Socialism' (his words) would allow to the most vulnerable and worthy of the poor (as Booth saw them) the dignity of independence. State support of this limited kind, allowed only to the 'respectable' and provident elderly poor, could assist – rather than undermine – self-help. Aligned to no political party and in need of no social or financial support from any individual or cabal, Booth could laconically toss out such suggestions as a State pension – an idea that horrified many who knew him well. On the night in December 1891 on which Booth gave a speech in London putting forward his pension idea, a dense fog had come off the Thames and entered the Jermyn Street lecture hall in which he was giving his address. From the barely visible crowd came a series of objections to his proposal; not one supportive voice was heard from the mist. 'Very hostile meeting,' Mary Booth noted in her journal.[7] Others of Booth's circle, most notably his cousin by marriage, Beatrice Webb (who was one of his six researchers on the 'Poverty' series of Life and Labour), began to distance themselves from Booth for the opposite reason, having come to believe that one or other form of Socialism – in Webb's case, Fabianism – was the only answer to the social crisis, and despairing of Booth's attachment to market forces.

Booth was born into a Liverpool family that had made a fortune in corn trading. By religion the Booths were Unitarian – a Dissenting sect less interested in dogma and more concerned with the human than with the divine, believing that mankind was essentially good, and that there had been no Fall. Later, like many in his family and

Charles Booth as a young man.

circle of associates, Charles came under the influence of Positivism, whose founder, Auguste Comte, came up with the word 'Sociology' for a new discipline that would use empirical methodology to deduce the laws by which societies behaved. The 'Positive Religion' formed a useful bridge for many in Europe who had lost their faith but not their earnestness.

When his schooling finished, Charles Booth went straight into business, and made his own quite separate wealth with the Booth Shipping Line before a mental and physical breakdown led him to add new, non-work-related, interests into his life. Booth found statistics fascinating, and the results of the 1881 census, and the meanings that were extrapolated from the figures, were particularly stimulating to him. Was the data being interpreted sensibly? Were there new questions that could be devised for the next census, in 1891? Booth joined the Royal Statistical Society and in 1885 undertook one of its surveys, which had the aim of exploring how best to spend the huge sums that were being given in charity for the aid of the unemployed of London. With Socialism on the rise, and London charities squandering (in Booth's view) cash according to misunderstood data, *Life and Labour* developed from Booth's hunger to delve ever further into the strange society he had come across during his Statistical Society work on poverty and need.

Twentieth-century critics – particularly in the field of social science, to whose very creation Booth contributed so much – have denounced Booth for the lack of a consistent theoretical basis for his inquiry; but it is because he was a maverick that his own written contributions to the *Life and Labour* volumes are so sprightly a read. One of the many joys of *Life and Labour* for the modern reader is watching the struggle on the page between Booth's insistence on 'pure' data, and the moralistic judgmentalism from which he believed himself to be quite free – the wrestling match between the dry statistician and the amused anecdotalist who keeps cropping up between the charts and tables. Quite apart from anything else it does, *Life and Labour* reads as a fascinating index of late-Victorian middle-class anxieties about the modes of living of the very-poor: wives who work, lack of fiscal or social ambition, nomadism, casual marital relations, promiscuous social lives, lack of thrift, lack of interest in home and hearth, insufficient attachment to material possessions or the accumulation of wealth.[8] The work is by turns knowing and wry, shrilly contemptuous, world-weary and baffled by the unmanageability of the task of surveying London. A tension arises from the constantly thwarted ambition to be comprehensive, tabular, empirical; throughout the seventeen volumes, the authoritative tone is undercut by admissions that some things cannot be known, or can be accessed only by imagination or hearsay or sweeping generalisation. 'I should have been glad,' wrote Booth, of the very poorest – the 'blackest' – streets,

> if I could have given as full an account of some black streets elsewhere in London, but such localities do not lend themselves satisfactorily to parochial visitation, and the material is scarce. There is moreover much uniformity. Certain types cover all the black streets . . . None will be all bad together. Everywhere mixed in with the rest are to be found the victims of drink or folly or misfortune, and the description of some mixed streets in which poverty rather than vice prevails may serve, with a slight allowance, as illustrations of worse places.[9]

Every so often, Booth throws in the towel.

Booth had to open his 'Poverty' series with a caveat. Because of his heavy reliance on the School Board inspectors, he knew that perhaps only between one half and two-thirds of the population of the East End had been reached in the survey, and that he had had to do a great deal of extrapolation when assessing non-family-based Londoners. Despite separate essays on 'Women's Work' and the various trades in which female labour predominated, *Life and Labour* is handicapped by the inherent bias that arises when the family unit, with a male head of household, is the basis of inquiry, with all other types of labour considered to be to some extent ancillary. Aware of this, Booth stated that he suspected that the condition of the families he and his team had been able to survey was likely to have been better than average, and he confessed to erring on the side of pessimism in his written reports to try to balance this out. However, his overall summary of the state of London, with regard to revolution, was immensely comforting for his readership. He concluded that, 'The hordes of barbarians of whom we have heard, who, issuing from their slums, will one day overwhelm modern civilisation, do not exist. There are barbarians, but they are a handful, a small and decreasing percentage: a disgrace but not a danger.' [10]

He aimed to disentangle the various strands that comprised the working classes, separating off, as best he could, the 'residuum', who culturally were alien to the majority of the aspirational 'true working classes, whose desire for a larger share of wealth is of a different character'.[11]

Booth found that a family of husband, wife and three children required between 18s and 21s a week in order to be able to maintain 'decent, independent life'. This was his famous 'Poverty Line'. The 'poor' were those who barely managed to do this and who struggled constantly, while the 'very poor' were those who could not raise 18s a week to cover the rent and food for themselves and their dependants and who lived in a state of 'chronic want'.

From the forty-six notebooks that his East London researchers compiled for him, Booth devised his famous colour-coded social stratification. London's 909,000 East Enders fell into eight Booth categories:

Casuals waiting to be picked for a day's work at the gates of the London Docks.

Class A: The lowest grade/occasional labourers, loafers and semi-criminals. 1¼% of East Londoners (11,000 people)

Class B: Very poor/casual earnings. 11¼% (100,000)

Class C: Ordinary poverty/intermittent earnings. 8% (75,000)

Class D: Mixed with poverty/small regular earnings. 14½% (129,000)

Class E: Working-class comfort/standard regular earnings/above the Poverty Line. 42% (377,000)

Class F: Well to do/higher class labour. 13½% (121,000)

Class G: Wealthy/lower middle class. 4% (34,000)

Class H: Upper middle class. 5% (45,000)

Booth also created a categorisation of income and regularity of work, to be cross-referenced with the colour-coded social classes A to H.

These types of labour were: 1. Occasional work; 2. Casual employment; 3. Intermittent earnings; 4. Regular work, but with low pay; 5. Regular work, with standard pay; 6. Highly paid work. Booth stressed that the six types of labour were not discrete: 'These sections not only melt into each other by insensible degrees, but the only divisions which can be made are rather divisions of sentiment than of positive fact.' Even artisans and clerks will flock to the dock gates, Booth admitted, if times and trade became bad enough. For this reason, Booth considered the London Docks to act as a 'sort of "distress meter"'[12] of the London labour market as a whole.

The smallest of the East End classes, according to Booth, was Class A, which he admitted to be 'no more than a very rough estimate, as these people are beyond enumeration . . . My tables are obtained by adding in an estimated number from the inmates of common lodging houses, and from the lowest class of the streets. With these ought to be counted the homeless outcasts who on any given night take shelter where they can, and so may be supposed to be in part outside of any census.'[13] This was far less than scientific; and the language Booth used to describe Classes A and B was also far from neutral. Of Class A he believed, 'Their life is the life of savages, with vicissitudes of extreme hardship and occasional excess. Their food is of the coarsest description, and their only luxury is drink.' The Class A description gathered a momentum of its own, and Booth even thundered at such qualities of Class A as sharing, generosity and the will to work hard:

> It is not easy to say how they live; the living is picked up, and what is got is frequently shared; when they cannot find 3d for their night's lodging . . . they are turned out at night into the street, to return to the common kitchen in the morning. From these come the battered figures who slouch through the streets, and play the beggar or the bully, or help to foul the record of the unemployed . . . They render no useful service, they create no wealth: more often they destroy it. They degrade whatever they touch, and as individuals are perhaps incapable of improvement.

Booth described a large number of Class B as 'shiftless, helpless, idle or drunkards', making an exception of the single women, either deserted wives or widows. He thought the average Class B man worked as much as three days a week, in wretchedly paid casual work, and that wives and children were crucial to the family economy for this reason: 'The ideal of such persons is to work when they like and play when they like . . . They cannot stand the regularity and dullness of civilized existence, and find the excitement they need in the life of the streets.'[14] He noted that many former soldiers were A and B males and claimed that Class B 'is not one in which men are born and live and die, so much as a deposit of those who from mental, moral, and physical reasons are incapable of better work'.

It was Class C, he thought, who felt hardest the seasonality of certain jobs (dock and labouring work, for instance); they wanted to work hard, and many were reasonably skilled, but when trade was bad they found themselves in competition with Class B for the worst kinds of casual labour. When times were good, Class C men could be in Division 5 of labour (Regular, with standard pay) but their own personal failing, thought Booth (namely, lack of thrift, and a taste for drink when wages were good), made them ever vulnerable to falling back down into Class B. Cs were, in Booth's words, 'hard-working, struggling people, not worse morally than any other class, though shiftless and improvident . . . They are thus a somewhat helpless class, not belonging usually to any trade society, and for the most part without natural leaders or organization.'

The Ds faced competition for jobs and occasionally suffered from the seasonality of trades, but at a wage level high enough to be regarded as a regular income. The men of Class D tended to be gasworkers, or the more skilled dock labourers, car-men, and porters. 'They are as a body, decent, steady men, paying their way and bringing up their children respectably. The work they do demands little skill or intelligence . . . A good wife, and a thrifty one, is what helps this class keep up appearances.'

The largest single class was Class E, small-shopkeepers and the most skilled home-working artisan – the majority earning between 22s and 30s a week, with wives who therefore did not need to work. Class E female children tended to go into service, while the boys would learn their father's trade. Class E would never accept charity, Booth said, and, together with Class D, comprised the nearest the East End had to a middle class.

Class F earned 30s to 50s a week, typically as foremen, ware-housemen and in the skilled river and dock trades; their sons became clerks and their daughters worked in the better-class shops.

The Gs of the East End were mainly clerks, the bigger tradesmen and 'subordinate professional men'; while the servant-keeping Hs congregated mainly in the salubrious district of Hackney.

What made the poorest poor? Booth was satisfied that there were three major causes: Questions of Employment, which included lack of work, and low-paid jobs. Questions of Habit: drink, lack of thrift. And Questions of Circumstance: illness, injury, old age, and having a large family. For Classes A and B, he found that 4 per cent were 'loafers' and therefore entirely responsible for their own poverty; 55 per cent came under the Question of Employment heading; 14 per cent had bad habits; while 27 per cent were impoverished by their circumstances. In Classes C and D, none loafed; 68 per cent had employment problems; 13 per cent bad habits; and 19 per cent unfortunate circumstances.

Booth found a remarkable way of illustrating his model of the socio-economic make-up of the metropolis: his Map Descriptive of Poverty coloured each street of London according to his eight class designations and is one of the nineteenth century's most arresting, not to say beautiful, icons. Black streets indicated the dense presence of 'the lowest grade (corresponding to Class A), inhabited principally by occasional labourers, loafers and semi-criminals – the elements of disorder'. Dark blue represented the very-poor (corresponding to Class B), 'inhabited principally by casual labourers and others living from hand to mouth'. Dark blue edged with black was where Booth and his team could not make up their minds about where criminality and bad habits stopped and 'honest' chronic poverty began. Light blue meant standard poverty (Cs and Ds). Purple, meanwhile, was an almost incoherent blending of poverty and small businesses, being home to everyone from B to F. Pink was 'working-class comfort' – Classes E, F and G, keeping no servant. Red was 'well to do', with one or two servants. Yellow indicated the wealthy, with three or more servants and houses rated at £100 or more.

The Poverty Map manages to be two contradictory things: it is a testament to a daunting energy and determination to name and order an unruly city – an obvious labour of love, the product of painstaking work and keen, if not deep, thought; but it is also clearly the work of a madman, or, at least, the product of a crazy and cross-eyed society. It looked like empiricism, but wasn't. Who in all seriousness could look at the map and believe that it tells us anything about actual, lived

human experience? The simplification required for a graphic representation of wealth distribution undercuts the extraordinarily complex
findings and ambivalent conclusions of Booth's written work.

Booth recognised the limits of his cartographic rendering of the
contents of *Life and Labour*, particularly with regard to trying to depict
'character' as a facet of socio-economic failure or success:

> At best, the graphic expression of an almost infinite complication and
> endless variety of circumstances cannot but be very imperfect, and a
> rainbow of colour could not accomplish it completely . . . Here and
> there an attempt has been made to give a little more elasticity to the
> system by combining the colours. Dark-blue in especial will frequently
> be found with a black line upon it, to indicate that great poverty is
> mixed with something worse . . . It must be borne in mind that every
> street is more or less mixed in character, that the black streets taken
> together contain some of every class from A to F, or even G.[15]

That's why the colour purple was such a catch-all: 'We find in these
streets a very wide range of character . . . In some, the mixture of
poverty is to be found almost in every house . . . In others, it goes by
houses and then is more easily distinguished . . . Finally we have streets
that are poor only at one end . . . becoming first purple and finally pink
before the eastern end of it is reached.'[16] Booth then feebly suggested
that one distinction for purple streets was that they contained large
houses that were no longer inhabited by the class they were built for.

The map is an elaborately concocted fantasy of a city that never
existed. The insistence on linking 'moral' failure (or character flaws)
to economic destiny means that, for instance, a yellow street with
black edging would be required to reflect the high figures, for these
years, of both white-collar crime and alcoholism within the
'respectable' family. And what colour could represent a street where
a slumlord dwelt? Pink, red or yellow edged with black, surely; but
no such designations existed. Booth wrote: 'Class A must not be
confounded with the criminal classes. Every social grade has its criminals, if not by conviction, at least by character.' But despite his protestations, morality, to Booth and his team, only really mattered when it
caused, or somehow interacted with, poverty; if bad habits went hand
in hand with riches – what then?

Among the five biggest splodges of black and dark blue on the Poverty Map are the streets of the Nichol. Mount Street and Old Nichol Street are pure black, 'representing the very rough vicious class'[17] – the ink spillages of shame. The rest are dark blue, though Boundary Street itself was designated purple, reflecting its high level of business and shopkeeping activity, which helped to override its black and blue inhabitants. (Charlie Burdett, the felonious fried-fish-shop keeper at number 18, jailed for firing a gun during a burglary, combined proactive criminality with sound business skills, and so should, by rights, have had his empire reproduced as black tinged with purple, which didn't exist in Booth's schema.) When local vicar Reverend Robert Loveridge of St Philip's, Mount Street, came across the Poverty Map he was indignant that Mount Street and Old Nichol Street had been painted black, saying that this was 'a malignant lie . . . that the dwellers in the Boundary Street area though desperately poor were rather virtuous than otherwise'.[18] Booth's Nichol data was supplied to him by rival cleric Arthur Osborne Jay and his curate Rupert St Leger, whose boast it was that he visited every home in the parish three times a year. 'What do you want to come poking about in poor people's houses for?' St Leger was sometimes asked when he knocked at Nichol doors, though when it was established that he was not acting in concert with the police he was more often than not welcomed in, and his questions answered. Once, after knocking several times at a door, St Leger entered and found the female occupant asleep on her bed. He left, but the next day was assailed in the street by the woman. 'They told me you came in my room yesterday. How dare you come into a lady's room when she's drunk? You're no gentleman.' St Leger found this highly amusing.[19] He took it as read that the poor were surveyable and to be subject to the privileged gaze. It was for their own good, after all.

St Leger's handwritten notes in the Booth Archive are a catalogue of misery – miniature tales of struggle and endeavour by many; of the slide into drink and hopelessness by others. What fascinated St Leger most were the stories of those who had come down in the world. The dollmaker, Mr Read, at 18 Half Nichol Street, 'a dirty disreputable-looking fellow' in his sixties, told the curate that he 'should be busy when the Germans were all dead', since imports of German toys were wrecking his trade. Read's father had been a successful toymaker employing eighteen craftsmen, and Read had inherited this business but failed. He was now supported by his wife's work as a charwoman.

Mrs Gavigan in the ground-floor back room of number 4 had once been fairly well to do – the wife of an optician. But her husband had been confined to Hanwell Lunatic Asylum suffering from suicidal melancholia. She was supporting herself, her surviving children and two grandchildren by washing and charring. One of these infants could not attend school because he had no boots 'and only came out from behind the table when told that "it was not the School Board man"', noted St Leger.

In the ground-floor room at number 7 were 'two miserable-looking widows'. Mrs Flaherty had been born in Hatton Garden and her father had been a master tailor, employing sixty men. He disinherited her when she married against his wishes. She had been in the Nichol two years and was 7s 6d in rental arrears. She did washing and charring occasionally, and all her decent clothes were pledged in a pawnshop. Her room-mate, Mrs Jackson, had been born in Snow Hill, near Holborn, and sold fruit and flowers in Paternoster Row, behind St Paul's Cathedral. On the day St Leger called to investigate her, she had had no takings and her feet had got very wet – her boots were an odd pair because she had had to buy them one at a time, and they were of too poor quality to keep out the rainwater. She had just pawned two aprons and her pocket handkerchief to pay the week's rent.

Upstairs at number 20, Huguenot-descended satin-weaver Mr Coquard, in his eighties and twice a widower, had once had six looms. He had lived in the Nichol, weaving, for over forty years, and was now deaf and had breathing difficulties. This was the same room in which his first wife had hanged herself.

At number 40 Half Nichol Street, St Leger was charmed by Mrs May, the orphan of a Brighton businessman. St Leger found her 'respectful', 'civil' and 'evidently of superior origin'. She had come to London to find work and had become destitute. She was currently taking care of another woman's children, one of them 'semi-idiotic, unable to utter any but incoherent sounds'. Mrs May was trying to help out their mother, Mrs Richardson, of Boundary Street, whose husband was tantalisingly noted to be a 'medical man of loose character'. Mrs May was paying 4s 6d a week to her landlord for a supposedly 'furnished' room, whose

By 1895, when this picture was taken, a few silk-weavers were still eking out a living in a trade that had once employed tens of thousands in the East End.

bareness and dilapidation she described to Leger with 'graphic contempt'.[20]

Door after door opened on to scenes of illness: measles, respiratory problems and, most commonly, rheumatic disorders rendered Nichol inhabitants bedbound, or floorbound, if there were no bed. 'Mrs Noble, a widow, in bed on the floor with rheumatic gout, does needlework when she can, 1 son disabled through accident, another at a sawmills, 1 grandchild with them, been here 9 years, very poor.' 'Spall, carman, in bed with rheumatism, wife and 8 children, only 1 at work, 1 very ill, not expected to live.' 'Davis and rheumatic wife, with five children. Wretched home – windows broken, floor rotten, walls crumbling, eaten alive with bugs, chimney smokes fearfully . . . Rent 3/9. Are in arrears and pay off 3d weekly back rent. Mrs Thompson owns house and is very strict regarding rent. Puts their goods in back yard.' 'At Bates's, child came to door and said "Not today" . . . Grandmother lying down, and a sign by the name – a black cross with dots in each of the four quarters. On a second visit, very poor indeed . . . upholsterer, wife and five children, two with measles, wife weakly.'

'Parsons, a hatter, whose wife, 67, has been laid up for three years with rheumatic gout, a very talkative, cheerful woman although suffering with great pain. Says [famous Baptist minister] Spurgeon has same symptoms as herself and so had Lord Palmerston.'[21]

After Booth had read St Leger's notes he headed for the Nichol himself, on a raw February day in 1891. He stood and observed while two groups, one made up of women, the other of children, waited for a local church mission house to start its daily dispensation of soup. He wondered how they could stand the cold.

> I passed several times and still the same women, and I think, the same children stood waiting in the freezing air. The children looked well enough, more common than wretched. The women looked exceedingly cold, and no wonder, for they seemed to have run over from their houses without throwing on either bonnet or shawl, in their working aprons, bare-armed as well as bare-headed, dangling their jugs and gossiping till their turn might come. At the corner as I passed along, two boys met.
>   ''Ad dinner?' said one.
>   'Yes.'
>   'What did you 'ave?'
>   'Soup.'
>   'Was it good?' I put in, and the answer came promptly.
>   'No.'

Booth walked on past gutters filled with frozen dirt, past costers' baked-potato vans and barrows laden with oranges ready to be wheeled to Liverpool Street for vending, the fruit papers littering the pavements and roadway. 'In one street is the body of a dead dog and nearby two dead cats, which lie as though they had slain one another. All three have been crushed flat by the traffic which has gone over them, and they, like everything else, are frozen and harmless.'[22] This was, wrote Booth, 'a district of almost solid poverty, in which the houses were as broken down and deplorable as their unfortunate inhabitants'.[23]

   Booth had devised a plan for dealing with Classes A and B, who typified Nichol-dwellers – a modest proposal that policy-makers might want to consider. 'The disease from which society suffers is the

'The Cockney is working out his sad destiny': Charles Booth's Life and Labour survey pondered the 'extinction' of certain types of worker, in the light of evolutionary theory.

unrestricted competition in industry of the needy and the helpless,' was his diagnosis of the ailment afflicting late-Victorian capitalism.[24] Classes C and D, Booth believed, faced the biggest threat to their livelihood and ability to make social and financial headway, not from an economic system that exploited, not from rack-renting landlords, cheap imports, mass immigration from the provinces and the Continent, or hard-hearted relieving officers and COS workers, but from Class B. 'To the rich the very poor are a sentimental interest: to the poor they are a crushing load.'[25]

Class A, meanwhile – 'this savage semi-criminal class' – was beyond all assistance, and in this view Booth was broadly in line with Marx and Engels and their fixed idea of the wholly separate *lumpen*. However, in Booth's eyes, the As – being such a tiny proportion of the working classes – did not pose too much of a problem.

Booth believed that they took over whole streets, turned them 'black' and made them 'ripe for destruction'. The answer was to tear

down the black streets, so that As could find no sanctuary: 'Persistent dispersion is the policy to be pursued by the State in its contest with them, for to scatter them is necessarily to place them under better influences.'[26] Booth believed that although people could, through great misfortune or character flaw, drop down into Class A, 'A-ness' was a condition largely transmitted through the generations. Evolution theory had, by the late 1880s, shifted towards the proposal that moral, as well as physical, attributes had some hereditary basis, and concepts of human fitness/unfitness in both body and mind were being used to bolster *laissez-faire* as well as Socialist State intervention and Anarchist–Mutualist arguments. Booth stated that the character of Class A was a biological 'taint'. 'There appears to be no doubt that it is now hereditary to a very considerable extent,' he wrote. The boys 'naturally' took to loafing in adolescence; the girls 'naturally' to prostitution. However, he conceded, 'Those who are able to wash the mud may find some gems in it. There are, at any rate, many very piteous cases.' With Class A, the State should step up its pincer movement on family life by removing the children from the influence of their parents. He cited the good work being done in this respect by the Board Schools, Dr Barnardo and the industrial and reformatory school movement.

Class B posed far more of a problem for the future of Britain. It was a 'quagmire' upon which the whole of the structure of labour was built. Like Marx, but for wholly other reasons, Booth recognised that some 'margin' of unemployment was necessary to the capitalist system, allowing some degree of flexibility of movement for the employee, but more importantly for the employer. (The radical newspaper the *Star*, reviewing Booth's work in its 7 May 1889 issue, pointed out that he had unconsciously quoted Marx, and the newspaper editorialised that 'the "unemployed" are, in fact, as much a necessity of the capitalists' profit as is the gold reserve at the Bank of England'.) But having a large, 'inefficient' superfluous working population acted to degrade a country's economic health, Booth believed, and employers did not benefit from having such people in the labour pool; the effect of Class B was to speed the deterioration of Classes C to E.

Class B was both more numerous and more complex than Class A. 'B-ness' was not hereditary, though some inheritable physical or mental debility or criminal tendencies may have caused an individual to become a B. 'On the whole,' suggested Booth, 'I regard the individuals of Class B as suffering severely from loss of position and of the comforts to which they have been accustomed.'

In pondering what should be done with Bs, Booth considered and dismissed protectionism, State-aided emigration, the exclusion of pauper immigrants, the State regulation, or even total suppression, of home industries. Each of these seemed to him to be worse than the original problem. What the State needed to do was to regulate the very existence of Class B. He recommended labour colonies in which whole B families would be well housed, well fed, kept warm and educated and trained all day, every day in self-sufficiency. They would build their own homes, farm their own food and manufacture their own goods. 'They would become servants of the State.' Those who turned out to be 'ambitious' after all could then be rehabilitated into mainstream society and a life of independence and self-respect.

Booth's industrial colony suggestion was little advance on the 'Less

Eligibility' concept behind workhouse incarceration for the able-bodied, as drafted in the 1834 Poor Law. Booth saw the New Poor Law as a 'Socialistic' intervention that allowed the 'Individualist nation' to continue to flourish. Socialistic also, in his view, were Board Schools, hospitals and charitable institutions. If this type of Socialism could help out business, then he was in favour of it:

> Our Individualism fails because our Socialism is incomplete. In taking charge of the lives of the incapable, State Socialism finds its proper work, and by doing it completely, would relieve us of a serious danger . . . Thorough interference on the part of the State with the lives of a small fraction of the population would tend to make it possible, ultimately, to dispense with any Socialistic interference in the lives of all the rest.[27]

He suggested they pilot the industrial-camp scheme in Stepney. This would never happen.

Booth's only worry was that individual liberty would be compromised, and he crucially failed to address how – other than by compulsion – Bs would take up their place in these encampments. He merely hoped that circumstances would arise in which As and Bs would be increasingly unable to find a 'fresh opening in an ever-hardening world', and that they would probably die out, like a failed sub-species.

Powerful stuff, and particularly chilling for the modern reader, because we know – as Booth could not – just where this sort of talk could lead. Indeed, reviewers of *Life and Labour* took up the encampment concept and ran with it, taking it to a more extreme position than Booth's. The *Saturday Review* heartily endorsed the eradication of Class A: 'Nothing can be done for it except kill it out,' said the *Review*, adding that Booth should additionally have demanded the withholding of all charity, since 'more good would be done in the long run by a general hard-hearted determination to drive the weak into the workhouse and leave the idle to starve'. The article ends, 'Among the very poor there are many who have been crippled in the battle of life, to whom help and pity are due. But there are many more who are malingerers and skulkers, who have run from the discipline and the bullets. With these last, what is to be done?' The *Spectator* was rather too eager, too, referring to 'the criminal scum' who should be 'harried out of existence' by the police.[28] Perhaps they had been

reading Nietzsche: 'The great majority of men have no right to existence, but are a misfortune to higher men.' Certainly they will have
read the various evolutionary scientists. One of Booth's own
researchers, Ernest Aves, was clear that a large section of the East End
working class was already facing extinction: 'It is a fairly safe general
conclusion that in those districts in which a greatly disorganised and
excessively specialised industry prevails, combined with a considerable
amount of allied or supplementary home and female employment,
that there, the Cockney is working out his sad destiny.'[29]

There is a highly unsatisfactory mismatch between Booth's plans
for As and Bs, and his ongoing uncertainty about what exactly caused
or contributed most to unemployment and to irregular or casual
employment. The aged, the infirm and young children were not the
issue: it was the adult able-bodied males and, to a much less known
extent, females that puzzled him. What role did ill luck, or weak character, or working in a doomed industry play in their 'unfitness' for
work? To what extent was character destiny – or did destiny adversely
affect character? While he vividly noted vile housing and atrocious
slum conditions, Booth never put forward an environmental argument: that bad surroundings could swiftly undermine such notions as
self-respect, let alone health, and send the average working man or
woman into freefall, financially, socially or ethically. 'The imagination
must be drawn upon to complete the picture of Class B,' he wrote.[30]
But that's not good enough: if they were to be subject to draconian
State intervention, more than mere supposition was needed. The anecdotal evidence gathered for *Life and Labour*, such as Rupert St Leger's
notes on the Nichol, showed that a significant number of people living
there had enjoyed better fortune in the past – that some had drifted
to the district because of its cheap rents and prospects of earning any
money at all in such degraded trades as matchbox-making, shoemaking, tailoring and hawking. Others had been born and remained
there for years, practising dying professions such as silk-weaving, or
engaged in the cut-throat speculative furniture-manufacturing trade.
There was a higher than average number of female-headed households in the Nichol, and these lone mothers were over-represented in
the figures for pauperism. St Leger and Booth noted with sympathy
those Nichol women who were widowed, deserted, had been subjected
to marital violence, or who had large numbers of children to care for;

but they gave no indication of whether such females were to be considered as 'superfluous' and 'inefficient' labour, or were simply trying to hold things together for themselves and their dependants by working at the only trades open to them. Like most commentators of the day (many leading male trade unionists included), Booth and his team saw labour as an adult male's prerogative, and believed that when women or children entered the workplace, undercutting wages and adapting themselves readily to all forms of slop and debased work, the family, as well as the economic mechanism of the nation, was undermined. On the one hand economically self-sufficient women were to be praised for their tenacity and independence; on the other they were viewed as part of the disease afflicting working-class London. So were these women part of the residuum? If conditions were right, could they ever again be reabsorbed by the true working classes, with all their aspiration and respectability? Or had they condemned themselves to 'A-ness' or 'B-ness' for ever? Was any form of salvation possible?

Our Father

Two months after reporting to Charles Booth, Rupert St Leger moved on. Having served for two years at Holy Trinity, Shoreditch, he was offered and accepted the position of vicar of Ridgewell, a hamlet in Essex. It is possible that he was having difficulty adapting to the singular ways of his extraordinary boss at Holy Trinity. Arthur Osborne Jay, boxing enthusiast, (very) High Church Anglican, favourite of many a West End society lady (and not a few gentlemen), liked to claim that he had been handpicked to be the incumbent of this most challenging of East End parishes by the Bishop of London himself. It was a false claim – one of many that would litter his colourful career.

Six feet tall, and built like a prize-fighter, he strode the streets of the Nichol in a long black coat and a top hat and insisted on calling himself, and being called, *Father* Jay. One of Booth's investigators noted 'his pugnacity, his want of tact, his coarseness, even his brutality [and] a certain touch of vulgarity' and claimed that he was very much a man's man: 'I have always got on better with men than women,' Father Jay admitted.[1] Many lady philanthropists would have been devastated to hear it.

Father Jay, twenty-eight years old at the time of his appointment, had been the Bishop of London's third choice for Holy Trinity – a parish that had been carved out of the larger parish of St Leonard's, Shoreditch, in 1867 but which was failing to justify its separate existence. There was even talk, at Lambeth Palace, of joining it back with St Leonard's. So neglected was Holy Trinity, it did not even have a church building. Its home for several years had been the first floor of number 56 Church Street, above a stable, rented on a weekly basis. (The landlord of number 56 was a local hero, boxer Bill Richardson, who had made a great deal of money from prize-fighting and had

invested most of it by becoming a slumlord.) The smell of manure
was a permanent feature of Holy Trinity, and there was the occasional
whinny or snort from a horse below. The room was 40ft long and had
a small annexe that did duty as a miniaturised chancel. The previous
vicar, the Reverend Henry Henderson (a former tutor in the Gladstone
household), had done his very best, installing a harmonium, pictures
and flowers in an attempt to make the church a more welcoming
retreat for his poor parishioners. He himself lived on-site, sleeping on
a camp bed, and in April 1886 was found collapsed at his desk, pencil
in hand; he died three days later at the age of fifty-five. To hear Arthur
Osborne Jay tell it, the parish work of Holy Trinity had been utterly
moribund. In fact, Henderson had given seventeen years of unosten-
tatious kindnesses and had probably knowingly shortened his life by
living among his parishioners (many East End Church of England
vicars did not do so); he had been spotted during outbreaks of contagious diseases carrying sick children out of their houses and on to the
horse-drawn ambulance come to fetch them.

Father Jay's first service at Holy Trinity, on the eve of the new year
of 1887, brought just fourteen people through his door, from the
huddled thousands surrounding. To Jay's horror, Henderson had been
handing out to every member of the congregation in attendance a 4d
ticket for food or coals; it had been a misuse of church 'doles' in
Father Jay's eyes, and this largesse was stopped immediately.
Henderson's services had lasted two hours, and his sermons had been
sprinkled with Ancient Greek; Father Jay slashed the length of the
services and arranged them so 'that ignorant persons can easily join
in. I do not find <u>one</u> person here who can find their place in the Prayer
Book.'[2] (One elderly lady thought that she had to follow all of Father
Jay's motions as he conducted worship, and she would mirror his
movements throughout the service.) With the Bishop of London's
permission, Father Jay devised a severely truncated Sunday evening
service comprising one psalm, one lesson, one hymn, and with 'Sit',
'Kneel', 'Stand' instructions printed in capitals in the appropriate spaces.

Very little of Father Jay's pastoral work would be focused on women
or children. He had a kind Irish housekeeper, whom Arthur Harding
recalls handing out roly-poly pudding to children on an indiscriminate
basis, which went against Jay's insistence on precisely targeted assistance that was given only after rigorous investigation. Jay delegated

most of his parochial care of women and children to two female ministries who knew the area well – the Kilburn Sisters, a High Anglican sisterhood; and the Mildmay Deaconesses, who were lower-church and had been helping out in the Nichol since the late 1860s, doing what they could for women in need of medical assistance, for mothers-to-be and nursing mothers, but with a view to proselytising as they cared, which made many shun their help. Father Jay would have no unseemly playfulness among his helpers and sacked as 'unsuitable' one of Henderson's mission women when he caught her skipping with a rope with other women in the street outside. Father Jay had been horrified to discover how Henderson's Mothers' Meetings had been run, walking in on 'one of the most noisy and remarkable assemblages I have ever entered'.[3] Three hefty middle-aged women were playfully rolling each other about on the floor, shrieking with laughter and swearing. None of the women knew how to sew, Jay complained, and all they wanted to do was 'gossip'. Seemingly disgusted at all female levity, he reformed the Mothers' Meetings to include a Litany, two hymns and no laughing.

Father Jay had been warned not to be too optimistic in his dealings with the Nichol: 'In such a neighbourhood you can do nothing. Do not attempt the impossible,' one bishop told him; another said, 'Nothing will ever rouse the people of that part, save the last Trump, and then they will respond too late.'[4] Their Lordships also pointed out that the small congregations of Father Jay's close neighbours, St Philip's in Mount Street and St Leonard's in Shoreditch High Street, suggested that there was, indeed, no need at all of this third Anglican church in or abutting the Nichol. What they hadn't foreseen was Father Jay's astonishing ability to conjure up money. Within eighteen months he had raised £5,000 of the £6,000 he had set out to collect in order to build a proper church, and had secured the interest and backing of such illustrious figures as Princess Christian (Queen Victoria's fifth child), the Marquis of Lorne (a son-in-law of Victoria's) and the Duchess of Albany (a daughter-in-law of the same). The immensely wealthy Miss Betsy Dash had stumped up £1,000 towards the construction costs of new Holy Trinity, while philanthropist Lady Edith Heather-Bigg and heiress Evelyn Shuster offered Father Jay cash, contacts and hands-on help in the Nichol. Lord Salisbury's wife, and the president of Magdalen College, Oxford, laid the foundation stone

Father Jay in 1895.

of the new Holy Trinity when Princess Christian was indisposed. The appearance of the great and the good in the slum on visits to Father Jay caused good-natured amusement among the locals. ''Arf your luck! After you with the ice-cream coat! I suppose you did a click [burglary] yesterday,' a lad called out to one of Father Jay's female visitors when she emerged from a carriage wearing a white fur. Father Jay inaugurated his birthday suppers, inviting to dinner a selected 300 men from among his parishioners, with guests of honour such as Maharajah Duleep Singh (Jay's father had been Singh's personal chaplain) and the Duke of Bedford. The Duke began to send two deer a week to the Nichol from his deer park, and the local mission house made stew with them for the free children's dinners – the Nichol children greatly enjoying venison in comparison to their usual meat fare of sheep's head, faggots and tripe.

Father Jay had secured as the site for his new church the several-times-condemned Orange Court – a favourite spot in the Nichol for cock-. and dog-fighting, bare-knuckle boxing, Pitch & Toss, and for stashing stolen booty when on the run from the police. Orange Court was entered from Old Nichol Street via a narrow, tunnelled entrance

HOLY TRINITY CHURCH
AND LODGING HOUSE
SHOREDITCH

Holy Trinity in Old Nichol Street, consecrated in 1889, was described by Lord Leighton as having the most beautiful church interior in England. Ultra-Protestants deplored it for what they perceived as Roman Catholic echoes.

and one Sunday morning when two policemen made their way along the passageway, the first to emerge into the court was floored by a fire-grate hurled down from a first-floor window, which, surprisingly, failed to hurt the constable very badly. This backwater of backwaters was not difficult for locals to escape from, though, since those in the know could leap over its brick wall and into the open doors of the houses backing on to the court, from where they could scatter in all directions. Orange Court was described by one visitor as 'The inner hell of this awful place',[5] and in fact its local nickname was Little Hell. In February 1887 sanitary investigations revealed illegal, jerry-built drain pipework beneath the houses surrounding the court and a brick septic tank that was full and leaking; when Father Jay's building work began one year later these defects had not been remedied, and Jay's architect, Richard Lovell, sketched the elaborately cobbled together tangle of pipes and antiquated cesspool. So appallingly dilapidated were the houses in Orange Court that the coroner at the July 1887 inquest into the death of Mary Pope claimed that she had hanged

herself from a nail in a wall of her room with a piece of string, knowing that the house wouldn't have withstood the use of a rope and a lintel or beam. Mary took in washing for neighbours and, with the rent overdue, pawned one of these bundles of clothing for two shillings so that her flower-hawker husband could buy some stock at the wholesale market to sell in the streets. But he was unable to sell what he had bought, and on the day that Mary was to return the laundry, she hanged herself in despair.

The building of the new church required the eviction of 500 people from the court and from two adjoining properties on Old Nichol Street, with no compensation for the weekly tenants. The labourers who demolished the court complained that they were riddled with vermin as soon as they set foot within the buildings. 'Yes, they do bite in this weather,' a passer-by said, as they scratched and itched.

The birth of new Holy Trinity involved Father Jay in a serious row with Lambeth Palace, since the Bishop of London had caught Jay out in breaching the conditions of his church building grant of £1,600, and had heard tales of Father Jay's rudeness to the Bishop's staff and of furtiveness bordering on deception. Lambeth Palace believed that the Holy Trinity plans were for a simple mission hall; Lovell's design, though, was for a full-scale, consecrated church with Carrara marble, mosaic work from Rome and the finest-quality stained glass imported from Germany – so fine was the finished building, in fact, that Lord Leighton, artist, sculptor and president of the Royal Academy, declared it the most beautiful interior of any church in England (according to Father Jay). A bit more than a mission hall, then, and the Bishop of London couldn't quite work out how all this had come about. He went into a sulk, refusing to attend the consecration in April 1889, until Father Jay had apologised to his staff.

Father Jay believed that the very-poor felt alienated from religion by the traditional cold, cavernous Anglican churches of the East End – St Leonard's, Shoreditch, being a fine example of unwelcoming neo-classicism – and he intended to offer them a homely, well-decorated place in which they would not feel unworthy of God's love. Father Jay and his curate had established for themselves a universal truth of the East End: that the poor never felt quite so poor as when they were unable to clothe themselves adequately for church. Jay also claimed that far from having no aesthetic sense, people of the Nichol were highly adept at telling quality from dross, 'having a tendency to despise anything which is not costly'.[6]

The completed Holy Trinity was almost unique in England in being one of very few churches on a first floor. The ground floor and base-ment of the building were taken up by Father Jay's *pièce de résistance* – his Men's Club and gymnasium. It was an article of faith for him that religion should not be forced upon the poor; that a working man could be led to the Light only by slow degrees, when his trust had been won and a bridge had been made between his world, his culture, and that of a priest, who chose to live among the poor rather than scuttle home to the suburbs. The club cost 1d a week and was open to any Nichol man over the age of eighteen. For his penny, the club member could play dominoes, cards, chess and billiards and read all the current news-papers and journals of the day; a small bar served lemonade, tea and coffee. Most impressive of all, there was a boxing ring, gloves, dumb-bells, punch-ball, a pommel horse, parallel bars, rings and a trapeze. By supplying all the equipment of the noble art, Father Jay had cannily broken the link between boxing and the illegal street prize-fight, and between boxing and drink; the Nichol's two long-standing boxing halls were extensions of pubs, but at Father Jay's club, no alcohol was allowed. It was a brilliant move, and many a famous East End boxer would find his start in this ring, overlooked by a plaster saint and with a whole church above his head – all this on the spot where men used to prize-fight without gloves, sometimes to the point of near death. The walls were filled with pictures: half of them depicted Christ on the Cross, and half were photographs of London's top pugilists stripped to the waist, and as the years rolled past, the collection on the wall would feature the graduates of the Holy Trinity Club. Many entertainers had their start at Holy Trinity, too, using its small stage or its gym equipment, including music-hall comedian Harry Rich and future stars of the trapeze Nero and Neroni, Levano and the Unrivalled Tricolini.

Father Jay had been an intelligent, critical observer of the several university settlements and missions that had started up in East London in the mid-1880s, and he intended to learn from their mistakes. The settlement movement was born of a strand of thought dominant at Oxford University, chiefly at Balliol, that saw good citizenship as the working out of Divine Will – a 'restless altruism',[7] as one commentator has put it, in which faith was expressed through action rather than introspection and concern for one's own soul. A fractured society could be healed as part of the expression of the Almighty's love for Man as shown to us in the Incarnation. This Idealism differed from traditional Evangelical good deeds and right living in that it accepted that God had become immanent since the Incarnation: the Almighty was not a separate entity, to be placated through personal atonement via Christ, but was 'alive in it all'.[8] In 1884, two of the most influential university settlements began life in the East End. Toynbee Hall, under Canon Barnett and his wife Henrietta, was a set of collegiate-style buildings inserted into the very middle of one of the poorest and most overcrowded parts of Whitechapel, and housed a Guild & School of Handicraft and an art gallery (today's Whitechapel Gallery), with evening classes galore. In the same year, Oxford House was set up twenty-five minutes' walk away in central Bethnal Green, offering a range of clubs, societies and classes to 'rough lads' and working men, but with a more obviously religiose, High Church atmosphere than the seemingly secular Toynbee Hall.

The young men from the universities were supposed to form a bridge across the chasm between the classes, to offer their skills to those who needed them and to learn about the lives of the poor at close hand. The gentry had long since abandoned the East End, leaving its (mis)management to the shopocracies that comprised the vestries. What was needed, it was felt at the universities and public schools, were new squires, wisely governing, carrying their idea of 'civilisation' into the slums and acting as models upon which the working man could refashion himself. But there would be gains, too, for the settler, who could finish off his education by experiencing a very different world. Many of the men who passed through Oxford House, for instance, were headed for careers in the Church, and chose to substitute this new form of postgraduate study for the traditional spell at theological college. Some from Oxford House and Toynbee Hall would become teachers, or would decide to work in the emergent field of social science, devoting themselves to the serious study of class relations and economics. Others simply stayed in East London to carry on the classes and clubs they had started. (One such man was Clement Attlee, who became a Socialist during his time spent running the Stepney Boys' Club at the outreach settlement of Haileybury public school; William Beveridge, meanwhile, had been a Toynbee Hall settler.)

There were other less pure motives intermingled with the altruism; some we can guess at more easily than others. That some of the settlements were, among other things, a method of proselytising was stated quite openly in an 1895 essay, 'Working Men's Clubs', by Arthur Foley Winnington-Ingram, head of Oxford House from 1888 and later Bishop of London. In this article, Winnington-Ingram additionally let slip another aim – by keeping working-class men and boys busy in their leisure hours, the mission would interrupt courtship and so help prevent the pre-marital hastiness that gave Bethnal Green its notably low marriage age and, correspondingly, one of London's highest birth rates. The settlement's activities could help to make more 'refined' fathers, with fewer children – a tame form of neutering, achieved by keeping the sexes apart in their most fertile years.[9] The first women's university settlement opened in 1887, and many more would follow (aimed at improving poor girls' leisure time and helping out wives and mothers); and the gender segregation of the settlements was striking in comparison to the free-and-easy sociability between unmarried men and women, girls and boys, in the slums. The settlers inhabited entirely separate spheres; but how close homosociality was to homosexuality for some of the settlers remains to a large extent cloaked in the fog of nineteenth-century euphemism. In his memoirs, one homosexual Toynbee Hall settler wrote of another, 'He believed, in a way that is characteristic of the Romantic phase of Socialism in the 1880s, that homosexuality could be a vital part of the new ideal for which they were working . . . that homosexuality could become a positive spiritual and social force, breaking down the barriers of class and convention, and binding men together in comradeship.'[10]

More typical in its vagueness, and open to the prurient musing of later generations, are the thoughts of Henry Scott Holland (1847–1918), Canon of St Paul's and involved in the founding of Oxford House. Of his first exposure to the slums, during a trip to a temporary mission hut, Scott Holland wrote:

> I did enjoy my glimpse of rough London thoroughly – that thrilling sight of the black and brutal streets reeling with drunkards, and ringing with foul words, and filthy with degradation – and the little sudden blaze of light and colour and warmth in the crowded shed, with its music and its flowers, and its intense, earnest faces – and its sense of sturdy, stirring work, quick and eager, and unceasing – God alive in it all. It is most wonderful to me – the contrast with our rich solemn days, our comfortable Common Rooms, and steady ease . . . It certainly does one good to get touched up by a rough strong bit of reality like that.[11]

Scott Holland later picked up on the fact that this very enjoyment and excitement – this gorging on the sensation of poor London – was one of the things that was wrong with Oxford House, and indeed of the whole settlement idea. He worried that the settlements served to educate and entertain the settler, acting as a tonic for the over-refined and spiritually jaded; but that, despite many minor triumphs, the movement had failed to give the East End whatever it was that it needed. He came to see the settlements as primarily acting as 'a home for the rich unemployed . . . submerged gentlemen'. Oxford House and Toynbee Hall brought 'these unfortunates under the healthy influence of contact with the working man. They gain the hope and vigour that comes from real usefulness.'[12] What wasn't happening, Scott Holland felt, was the encouragement of the working classes to fight and win their own battles. He was not alone in this worry. George Paddock Bate saw Oxford House as a failure because its settlers only really reached out to the upper echelons of the Bethnal Green poor and were unable to find any route across the abyss to the most outcast: '[they] get hold of a better class altogether. They are afraid to touch the real thing.'[13] And the patronising nature of the cultural outreach work was spotted by journalist and author William à Beckett, who pointed out: 'I am not sure that we would feel greatly complimented were the costers of Shoreditch and Hackney to organise a society to provide the upper classes with amusements suitable to their station.'[14]

This was also Arthur Osborne Jay's point of view. He was scathing about the failure of outsiders to understand, accept and even value the culture of the slums, and saw all that energy, good will and money being squandered on a quest that could only prove futile. He had already had first-hand experience of the right way to reach 'outcast' men but had also seen the hostility that this could arouse in the more traditionally minded. Jay had been in the East End since his ordination in 1882, and from 1884 had been part of the controversial St Martin's Mission at Burdett Road, Mile End, which had been largely funded by Magdalen College, Oxford, as part of that college's own settlement outreach. The Reverend Robert Dolling who set up St Martin's had initially wanted to supply local postmen with a place where they could read and relax, away from slum conditions, family, the pub and bad associates. This burgeoned into a mission house with a chapel on the top floor, and Dolling encouraged many Magdalen men to come and help out in running various men's clubs, boys' clubs and Sunday schools. A Socialist and a High Churchman who did not curry favour with his superiors, Dolling's unusual set-up at Burdett Road was frowned upon, and Church support for the mission was withdrawn (he had worked there unsalaried for two years). A local campaign was started to save Dolling's mission, but the Bishop of London was having none of it. It was the Magdalen connection that got Father Jay the job at Holy Trinity, Lambeth Palace not being slow to spot the potential for funds from such a wealthy college if Jay could maintain the connection with it.

Dolling's St Martin's Mission had given Jay the germ of his own experiment. There were few rules at the Holy Trinity clubhouse, for

Jay appreciated that it was the tiniest permissions that tended to be the most appreciated. No drink, gambling or swearing were tolerated, and the card game 'Banker' was banned since it involved chance only, and not skill; but apart from this, Father Jay only insisted that each man on entering shake his hand and say 'Good Evening', with the same on departure – Jay standing at the threshold in full college cap and gown. Father Jay would never initiate a conversation about religion, but would answer any questions that a club member might put to him. On Sundays, at a quarter to three in the afternoon, the 300 or so men who spent their Sabbath afternoons at the club were only too happy to stay on for a short religious service – entirely separate from the one upstairs a little later. Hats could stay on throughout, pipes could be smoked, and the jolliest, most rousing hymns were chosen, accompanied by the harmonium, with the more confident of the men singing a solo or reciting verse. Afterwards, tea and bread-and-butter were served up, occasionally to the accompaniment of one of Father Jay's West End ladies who had come along to sing and play. Guest speakers at the club included the bishops of Stepney, Worcester, Zululand and Japan. The Bishop of London preached for fifty minutes on the benefits of renunciation, to a congregation who had very little to renounce, but instead of lynching him, they listened earnestly.

Some of Father Jay's flock were naturally courteous and forbearing; others had to be coaxed into good behaviour; and a few had to be banned. Father Jay had targeted his work at the very poorest men and boys of the Nichol, many of whom were ex-convicts, while most were either unemployed or casually employed. Some of those who were in full employment earned just 8–10s a week. Many were young and married, turning up with unwashed hands and faces and wearing tattered corduroys, with closely cropped hair to lessen the appeal to vermin. 'For a long time it [the club work] was carried on in the teeth of a kind of sullen, silent contempt . . . "Shake hands with you?" sneered one of the members to me on entering, "I don't come here for that, I come here to enjoy myself . . .",' Jay recalled.[15] Like so many visitors before him, Father Jay had to work hard to reassure his parishioners that he was in no way connected to the police. The problem as Father Jay saw it was that the 'moral atmosphere' of the Nichol had made belief in disinterested altruism impossible; the environment had brutalised its inhabitants, destroying all notions of virtue, he

Holy Trinity Men's Club at Night.

believed, and he found extremely tiresome the Nichol's insistent search for ulterior motives.

Almost all the men gave false names on first joining the club, hoping to pass themselves off as any number of Thomas McCarthys or Michael O'Donovans. Others were known only by their nicknames – Jack the Bender, Lord Dunfunkus, Facey, Old Squash, Scrapper, Donkey. A small number of hard-men had made the very existence of the club perilous. 'Tommy Irishman' was one, repeatedly stealing all the games and the billiard balls; another, unnamed, floored a young helper-out at the club with a heavy bound volume of the *Illustrated London News*; another club member was Mount Street costermonger Robert Rattray, jailed for eighteen months for the violent robbery of a man in Little York Street; a lad called Boko was temporarily banned for openly boasting of his thieving expeditions and he took it in good spirit, singing on the doorstep, 'Oh Father Jay's a very good man/He does you all the harm he can'.

Father Jay was surprised at the level of humour in the Nichol, with its blending of grim sarcasm with perky observation. 'There can be no hell hereafter,' one aged Nichol man told him, when they were discussing the afterlife. 'We live in it already.' 'Oh yes,' said another, 'the Lord is very good – if he does not come Himself, He often sends two policemen for you.' Jay used his own withering wit to savage effect if he felt like it, and one observer said that he had seen locals wince when Jay wanted to have fun at their expense.

At ten o'clock, the gas lamps of the club were turned down and the room became a night refuge, with built-in wooden berths accessed by a shelf-ladder; on particularly cold nights the additional men who came in for shelter slept on the club's benches or the floor, using their boots for pillows. Sulphur was burned and the next morning the men had to wash themselves and their berths with disinfectant to try to keep the place free from vermin. Jay himself slept on a wooden platform suspended over the room at one end, so that he could ensure that order was maintained throughout the night. But he also wanted to study them, by listening and watching. By 'careful and ceaseless supervision' Jay intended to ensure that 'the vicious and degraded' did not 'herd' together.[16] It is possible that Jay was here politely indicating to his more worldly readers that 'abominations' (as the late-Victorians called it) took place between vagrant men in shelters.[17]

Jay briefly interviewed each man before admitting him for the night, and developed a no-tramp rule, intending only to help out the temporarily 'submerged', as he put it – the working men who were in search of a job rather than those who knew no other life but loafing. He was interested to see that drink had undone so many, recalling a doctor, a lawyer and a butler from a West End mansion among the fallen who had slept at Holy Trinity. He was excited to find a genuine Romany in for the night, and amazed at the very high number of former soldiers who were homeless. The room at night did not smell good, and after three years of living like this, Father Jay became seriously ill; he blamed 'breathing the noisome atmosphere' for his six weeks of influenza, from which he was not expected to recover. Around fifty parishioners came to visit him with gifts that he dismissed as 'of a more or less unsuitable character'. As he lay prostrate, in through the window came the noises of the Nichol, including conversations about his likely demise and the remark that he was too fat to shake off the flu, while some children played a new game called 'Father Jay' in which they lay down and pretended to be dead.

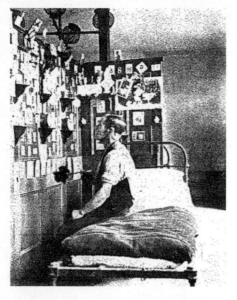

Father Jay's Trinity Chambers
lodging house offered beds and
cubicles from 2s a week.

On his recovery he was instructed by doctors not to resume his
habit of sleeping above the homeless, breathing in their exhalations
and those of the gas mantle and sulphur burner. So he went and raised
thousands more pounds to be able to build a proper lodging-house,
with staff, which he called Trinity Chambers (in true university settlement style), abutting the church. Here, he had space for ninety-two
men, who paid 2s 6d a week for a cubicle (or 2s for a bed in a common
dormitory), with hot baths, a kitchen and a common room; and
another small refuge for shipwrecked mariners. Like the boxing
saloons, the privately run common lodging-houses of the Nichol were
being undercut by Jay.

He also asked many of his men to consider either a life in the army
('that's a dog's life,' many of them told him) or being emigrated to
Canada or Australia – like a benign, *fin de siècle* form of transportation.
The walls of the gym featured photographs of his successful exports
to these New Worlds. But Father Jay lagged far behind Miss Annie
MacPherson, whose evangelical School of Industry (teaching trades and
giving basic schooling to destitute boys) on the edge of the Nichol, on
the corner of Club Row and Bethnal Green Road, had, over twenty-
five years, exported 6,000 poor boys and girls – whom she saw as 'surplus'
labour – to the colonies; by the time of her death she had sent out
12,000 of them. There was little mutual regard between MacPherson

and Jay; she attracted around 530 worshippers to her gospel meetings within the Home of Industry, a success that may have piqued him.[18]

Father Jay found further money to extend the church westwards, claiming that the capacity for 300 was regularly exceeded and that at one harvest festival a woman had her arm broken in the throng in the nave, and on another occasion a celebrant attempting to kneel in a tightly packed service had fractured her kneecap. Jay's fundraising success was partly the result of his facile penmanship. He produced three full-length books in his first ten years at Holy Trinity and several pamphlets, and secured the interest and rapturous approbation of a number of influential journalists. James Greenwood spent an evening at the club and reported it highly favourably in the *Daily Telegraph*; *Home Magazine* featured Jay in its series 'Men Who Are Moving the World'; while the *Temple* magazine dubbed him 'the saviour of Shoreditch'. He did nothing to disabuse his interviewers of their notion that he may have represented the Second Coming.

Jay's views on the nature of his parishioners, the causes of their condition and the best solutions to it were highly slippery. Across the range of his publications he veered from admiration of their fortitude to fury at their shortcomings; on the one hand they were 'the victims of the unjust incidence of mistaken laws, the very martyrs of the modern world . . . [and] some of the poorest and best people in the world', but on the other they exhibited 'dense, impenetrable ignorance; utter, entire lack of moral perception; deep, unfathomable degradation'. He blamed low wages, slum landlords and an irrelevant, lazy Anglicanism – that had done too little, too late – for creating an 'environment [that] renders virtue or decency impossible'; but he also believed that many of his flock suffered 'inherited defects and taints of blood'. Only a return to a parochial system, with resident clergy, could tackle the social problem, he stated at one point; yet elsewhere he urged full State interference, with pensions, sick benefits and subsidised housing for the deserving. Intellectually, he was a feather for each wind that blew. Hyperbole made for great, impassioned prose – crucial to a fundraising literary endeavour – and this need to strike attitudes underlies the massive inconsistencies in Jay's writing.

In the Nichol, Father Jay had created his own little world, and he saw that it was good. But he had made enemies.

Tainted Blood

Monday night, 25 February 1889, eight lads, none over nine and a half stones, were fighting in Father Jay's gymnasium for a large marble clock, goaded by an excited crowd of over 600 that included the Mother Superior of a priory in Hackney. The event was Jay's biggest boxing tournament to date, and it aroused the ire of the Reverend Robert Loveridge of St Philip's, Mount Street, who asked sympathisers to post the *Sporting Life*'s match report of Jay's contest to the Bishop of London and to various Bethnal Green and Shoreditch bigwigs. Jay was breaking local mothers' hearts, Loveridge said, by inveigling their sons away from home life to become professional or semi-professional pugilists. What's more, it was well known that Jay harboured known thieves and knife-men at his Men's Club, refusing to assist the police in pursuit of named individuals, and failing to use his pastoral care to reform moral character. When the Bishop of London wrote to Father Jay to find out what exactly was going on in darkest Shoreditch, Jay replied that instead of complaints, he should be receiving praise for the fact that he had gathered that number of labouring-class males together with no swearing, no rowdiness and no drink served – that this was precisely the sort of activity a Christian should be involved in. The Bishop wearily replied that he would pursue the complaint no further but that Jay must try to avoid 'giving offence to good people'.[1] Father Jay went on to preach a sermon at Holy Trinity entitled 'May a Christian Box?' to which he invited his critics, who came and sat among his club members. He declared that boxing was 'rational exercise and healthy recreation'; it improved health, and taught discipline and sportsmanship. The first hymn was the thoroughly manly 'Hold the Fort',[2] roared out by the Shoreditch pugilists to the surprise of the visitors.

Loveridge had been the incumbent of St Philip's since 1871, and was previously its curate. The blizzard of publicity that Jay had generated about himself and Holy Trinity had had the effect of whiting out of the picture all the other church activity in the Nichol. This was particularly galling for Loveridge, who had advised against keeping Holy Trinity as a separate parish, arguing to the Bishop of London that it was of no use having yet another church in a secluded slum. Drawing up a sketch map of the locality, Loveridge declared to the Bishop that the Nonconformist/Dissenting churches – the Baptists, Wesleyan Methodists and Congregationalists – dominated the main byways of that part of Bethnal Green and Shoreditch. 'We want no more back-street churches in Bethnal Green without some in commanding position to cope with Dissent, which leaves the back and is taking to the front all round,' he wrote.[3] The latest survey of church attendance had shown that of a parish population in Bethnal Green of 126,591 (the 1881 census figure), some 9,885 people went to morning and evening Sunday services at Nonconformist churches (which had seating for 11,000), while 7,339 attended Church of England worship, in churches that could seat 14,000. An audit of local worship for Sunday 24 October 1886 showed that St Philip's attracted 121 to its morning service, and 285 in the evening; in the hayloft that was Holy Trinity (just before Father Jay was installed) forty-one people and fifty were in attendance morning and evening respectively; Jay's new building after its enlargement would seat 400, and he claimed to attract this number on a regular basis, but a private researcher saw just sixty in the congregation on an unannounced visit one Sunday night in March 1898.

Other local Anglican churches were also at half-capacity, but the Nonconformists were doing somewhat better, and overshadowing all of them was the Shoreditch Baptist Tabernacle, in its large new building on the northern fringe of the Nichol; here, the Reverend William Cuff preached to 1,033 people in the mornings and 1,486 in the evenings.[4] Cuff's huge congregation did not include many people from the Nichol, attracting mainly the aspirational upper-working/lower-middle classes, many of whom travelled across London to hear his practical, home-spun message of hope that appeared to have more in common with the Self-Help movement than with spiritual enlightenment. This was the best-dressed congregation for miles around, and their arrival and

The Holy Trinity boxing ring, gymnasium and night-shelter was on the ground floor, beneath the church.

departure regularly caused a traffic hold-up in the Hackney Road, underlining the Baptists' ostentatious success in unpromising surroundings. Small wonder that Loveridge was concerned at Nonconformist success.

Loveridge was in his seventies, toothless, very hard of hearing and blind in one eye. A local Baptist rival, Edward Smith, minister of the Gibraltar Walk Chapel two streets east of St Philip's, described him as 'a dear old gentleman, but with more heart than head, whom cadgers of all kinds marked out as their prey'. Another commentator agreed that charitable giving was 'Mr L's strong or weak point', according to whether you agreed with indiscriminate alms-giving: 'Mr L is a regular old woman in appearance, manner and in the conduct of his parish,' continued this rather unkind verdict.[5] Although Loveridge's congregations were small, his real work lay in his pastoral provision for Nichol children, including his massive 'National School' – a remnant of the Church of England-based schooling system that was in the controversial process of being superseded by the Board Schools. For those children who had to work, there were also evening classes and Sunday Schools at St Philip's, and Loveridge claimed to have over 2,000 enrolled in these. His 'Little Dots' classes were for the very youngest children. The buildings of St Philip's were fifty years old, and the church itself was peculiarly gloomy; Loveridge spent so much on charitable giving that he had neglected its fabric. Visitors noted the seemingly permanent scatterings of confetti and rice which were never swept away after weddings.

He gave 1,000 free dinners to his schoolchildren in winter, and held Christmas feasts for 600 parishioners each year. But his most spectacular act of largesse was the annual day outing to the Essex countryside. Each August, 1,500 very-poor Nichol children and around 500 aged and/or infirm adults were conveyed north-eastwards by carts, with tea urns, trestle tables and supplies of bread and butter. The encampment would be set up in a meadow near Epping Forest, and Loveridge and fifty assistants would spend the day brewing tea and buttering rolls as the children romped. Then the vast party would pack up and roll back home again to the Nichol.

None of this work gets the slightest mention in any of Father Jay's books; nor do the huge efforts of the Congregationalists and the non-denominational London City Mission, which together ran the Nichol Street Ragged School and mission house in Old Nichol Street. Nor do the thousands thronging to see Reverend Cuff at the Tabernacle a few hundred yards away. The way Father Jay told it, the Nichol had been 'for long, left without any Church at all'.[6] The opposite was true: religion surrounded the Nichol on its outer perimeter and had also penetrated deep into the maze; the trick for most Nichol adults was to avoid getting inveigled into any of these houses of God unless there were some material benefit to obtain. (One Nichol shopkeeper told Father Jay that if she was ever seen in church, it would be assumed by her customers and rivals that her business was failing and that she was after a handout.)[7]

Spiritual life in the Nichol often ran along more folk and Romany channels, while Catholic worship not infrequently took place in customised 'chapels' in domestic spaces. At 11 Devonshire Place a tiny Roman Catholic place of worship had been created in an Irishwoman's back parlour and it was used by as many of her countrymen as could fit in. It contained a small cheap table dressed as an altar in fine silk and with a finely wrought cross, and to the side a little font-like vessel for holy water and a picture of the Virgin with some artificial flowers at her feet.

An old, deaf whelk-cooker in the Nichol told the London City

Missioner that 'I ain't got no larning, mister', but, as he understood it, to avoid dying suddenly in the night he must place his mattress in a certain configuration in relation to the floorboards, in accordance with the Crucifixion, 'as we never knows what may be, and they says as it's hard to die the Cross-way of boards'. Worship Street magistrates' court often heard cases against local fortune tellers, brought under the Vagrancy Act. Emma Machim, aged thirty-seven, of Gibraltar Gardens, just east of the Nichol, was jailed for fourteen days with hard labour for telling fortunes for money. Machim had told Esther Pickles that she would soon come into property but would first have trouble with a dark lady (Pickles had picked up the ace of diamonds). Meanwhile the ''Strology Woman' rented a room in a Nichol court and read the zodiac and the tarot for her mainly young and female clients. Wearing an Egyptian-style head-dress and a large coral necklace with many charms hanging from it, she also dispensed Fate Powders (3d; made of brick dust) to summon up visions of the future, Compression of the Damask Rose to make the face irresistibly beautiful (6d; comprising rouge and lard in a small pillbox) and the Spirit of Love (10d; cheap scent). 'Them silly girls like to be befooled and none of 'em 'ardly believes the cards when I cuts 'em and what I says about their stars and nativities. But it amuses 'em and does 'em no 'arm,' she said.

Old Joe Lee and his wife were called the 'Gypsy King and Queen of Shoreditch' and were descended from the original Romany settlers of Mount Street. Joe was a celebrated horse and donkey 'witch', and costermongers and others who relied on the well-being of their livestock brought him their animals to be cured or made harder-working.[8]

Hostility to conventional forms of Christianity in the Nichol was not violent but it was persistent. The nurse who was attached to St Matthew's, Bethnal Green, admitted that she concealed her link to the church until her third or fourth visit to a household, until she had 'got a hold of their feelings', and only then would she attempt to evangelise; she said that if it were known she was employed by St Matthew's, many locals would not have allowed her into the house, in spite of sickness.[9] As the Anarchists, Communists and Socialists had found during their efforts to convert the locals, preachers were for the main part politely ignored, or tolerated for a short while in puzzlement.

*   *   *

Boxing and egotism aside, there was a further source of rancour against Holy Trinity, resulting in numerous poison-pen letters to Father Jay and denunciations to the Bishop of London. Jay was among a number of charismatic 'Ritualist' – or High Church – Anglican priests who had set up in the slums of London and whose services appeared to many to flirt a little too intensely with Roman Catholic practice. An impartial observer lurking at the back of Holy Trinity during Sunday evening service noted that the place was 'like the chapel of some great Catholic house . . . highly ornamented with pictures and figures – "Images" they might be called. The altar is railed off with a high ornamented iron railing, and as Mr Jay stood at the altar and raised his hand to bless the people there was nothing that looked other than Catholic, except that his dress was a little different from that of the RC priest. The people mostly were on their knees.'[10] But who exactly were they worshipping? Father, Son and Holy Ghost? Or the Saviour of Shoreditch?

The schism in Anglicanism in the 1840s had seen the Oxford Movement, or Tractarians, propose a return to the earliest model of church hierarchy – the 'apostolic succession' that considered bishops a continuation of the apostles. The Reformation, they believed, and the subsequent drift of the English Church had severed Christianity from its origins. The Tractarians wished to see a return to catholicism: not to *Roman* Catholicism, but to the universality of the Christian Church. Reaching back across centuries of history, the English Church could reconnect with the earliest doctrine and authentic practice. As importantly, the Tractarians wanted the State to have no role whatsoever in Church matters – the spirituality of the nation should be the preserve of the bishops alone, their authority intact.

By the 1880s, the original split had changed in nature. While many in the early Oxford Movement did in fact go over to Rome, others stayed within the Church of England, considering themselves 'Anglo-Catholic', or 'High Church', and less concerned with such matters as apostolic succession and State intrusion than with the meaning of ritual and ceremonial, and with the role of the Church in assisting the poor and healing social rifts. Many of them would embrace Socialism of one flavour or another. They were criticised by Broad Churchmen and Low Churchmen for obscurantism – for their retreat into the mysteries of Christianity, miracles, signs, Holy Ghostliness.

Henry Scott Holland, who had co-founded Oxford House in Bethnal Green and taken an interest in the sanitary problems of the parish, wrote of the clash of philosophies between High and Low Church,

> However much you may shift the emphasis from off miracles, the pres-
> entation made of Christ is one that holds in it inherently and inevitably
> this supra-normal element, and we have got to take [accept] this
> element. If we try to form a judgement on Jesus Christ as recorded
> for us in the one story we know of Him, omitting this supra-normal
> factor, I think the whole record falls to pieces, and there is really nothing
> left that has stability enough to count. This affects the whole life, and
> culminates of course in the Resurrection.

Broad and Low Churchmen, Scott Holland claimed, attempted to argue away the miraculousness of the Gospels, and to claim that the deeds described in them were simply to be understood as metaphors; they had linked social progressiveness to this humanist, non-mystical interpretation of the New Testament. But Scott Holland wanted to prove that High Churchmen, who took the Gospels literally, were every bit as committed to ending suffering and injustice – to forcing the pace of social progress: 'The *more* you believe in the Incarnation, the *more* you care about drains . . . The Incarnation is above all things not an idea but an act, not an illuminating thought but a deed of the Divine Will. Historically we [the Ritualists] have steadily voted against the tradition that to be a social reformer you must be shadowy in your creed.'[11] In co-founding the socialist Christian Social Union in 1889, Scott Holland believed he was carrying out the natural progres-sion of the Incarnation, in which God became immanent in mankind in order to redeem the world He had created. Democracy and Socialism were to be the fulfilment of the Divine Purpose, as expressed in the Incarnation.

Anglo-Catholics emphasised the role of the sacraments in worship. In Anglicanism, there were just two: baptism and the Eucharist (the Lord's Supper). The sacraments conferred grace upon the recipient, but Low and High Church differed on whether the material phenomena of the sacraments (bread and wine in the Eucharist) were merely symbolic, commemorating events in the Gospels; or whether they were supernatural, containing Christ's real presence. The

Reformation had sought to demystify Christian worship, returning it to its authentic simplicity and insisting that priests indulge in no occult practices that conferred special powers upon themselves. Priestcraft was reined in by an Act of 1547: the gorgeous vestments of the clergy were banned, although clothing marking 'the superior dignity' of the Eucharist were permitted. Images, altar candles, incense, devotional pictures, the raising of the chalice above the head by the clergyman during consecration, turning eastwards to the altar during Holy Communion, rood screens and altar rails (which created a barrier between clergy and congregation), and making the sign of the Cross at benediction and absolution were now no longer permitted.

By the mid-1850s, because of the Oxford Movement furore, the militant Protestant body the Church Association had begun to spy on High Churchmen to see if their services contained any of these practices and could therefore lead to a prosecution under the Church Discipline Act of 1840. In 1874, the Conservative government passed the more stringent Public Worship Regulation Act, 'to suppress the Mass, in masquerade', as Disraeli put it. Between 1877 and 1882 five vicars were imprisoned for 'objectionable practices', but these prosecutions succeeded in arousing sympathy across the nation (even among the religiously indifferent) for persecuted Ritualist clergymen, and created instant martyrs. The Church of England had picked on a number of excellent parsons – living among their parishioners and wholly committed to their pastoral care – and now appeared to many to be despotic. A major trial of a Ritualist collapsed in 1889, and thereafter the Act was rarely invoked. By the 1890s, only the Church Association and other hardliners, such as the Protestant Defence League, would continue to urge prosecutions.

Which was just as well, because by the end of the nineteenth century just under a quarter of parishes in England were said to be High Church; just over a third were so in the East End of London, and Shoreditch, Hoxton and nearby Haggerstone were home to several high-profile Anglo-Catholic churches with resident clergy who were devoted to their small but ardent flocks. The beauty of the ceremonial was highly attractive to many who lived in appallingly ugly conditions. Women in particular seemed to find consolation in High Church services, and critics of Ritualism often noted with derision the large proportion of women and young people worshipping at such poverty-surrounded High churches as St Chad's and St Augustine's, both off

Hackney Road; St Michael's, Shoreditch; St Mary's, Haggerstone; and St Columba's in Kingsland Road.

Holy Trinity, Shoreditch, was one more addition to the Ritualist portfolio, and Father Jay was vulnerable, like many High slum vicars, to attack by Low or Broad Church rivals. Those who disliked him, such as Loveridge and the Nichol's London City Missioner Robert Allinson, pointed out Jay's various Romish posturings to anyone who cared to listen. Baptist Reverend Cuff, meanwhile, was implacably opposed to Anglo-Catholicism, and furious that it had taken root in Shoreditch. He wrote of

> the assumptions of priestcraft . . . made palatable to the vulgar taste by the tinsel of the playhouse . . . We are surrounded by Anglican Romanists, who accept the leading doctrines of the Papacy . . . To the hard-working pastor in a populous district, the system is a source of constant perplexity. At the best, it is a compromise between the truth of Christ and the rags of paganism.[12]

Jay had created his own body of pseudo-monks, the Brotherhood of St Paul, young men who took up residence together in the Nichol and helped out with Jay's Sunday School and Club, and sang in the Holy Trinity choir. They wore black habits, headgear described as 'quaint' and large crucifixes, but passed unmolested and unmocked through the Nichol. Jay's outreach work for females was delegated to two organisations with strong Nichol links: the Mildmay Deaconesses – a Broad Church Anglican sisterhood – worked with Jay under protest, disapproving of his High Churchness though approving of his total dedication to his flock; while the controversial Kilburn Sisters, an Anglo-Catholic sisterhood, ran their Orphanage of Mercy Mission Rooms at 34 and 35 New Nichol Street. The Kilburn Sisters were subject to persecution in print by fanatical Protestants. The Protestant Association issued a pamphlet on the 'Ritualistic Kilburn Sisters', filled with Gothic images of Romish cruelty which they claimed was to be found in the Sisters' orphan 'convents' – 'hair shirts, steel whips, knotted scourges, and crosses with sharp points that wound the wearer'.[13] In response to an outbreak of mutual masturbation amongst some of the older girls in the orphanages, the Sisters introduced individual wire-mesh cubicles, secured each night with a padlock *and* a bolt, and with brass spikes along the upper edges of each wire wall; an electrical device would alert the Sister on night duty to any attempts at escape from a cubicle. The Protestant extremist press enjoyed revealing the existence of these 'iron cages', while the more main-stream *Truth* magazine pointed out the lack of common sense and worldly knowledge that the Sisters showed in their over-reaction to this all too common adolescent misbehaviour. The Sisters' founder, Emily Ayckbowm, was so unworldly that she could not speak directly of her battles against 'an Evil of a peculiarly revolting type . . . it is not the kind of Evil which can be talked about'.[14] (*Truth* also pointed out the obvious risks of death in the event of a fire. The 1880s and 1890s witnessed a number of conflagrations leading to mass fatalities, and scandalous headlines, at Poor Law and charitable residential schools.)

The Charity Organisation Society, meanwhile, objected that 'in our opinion, no body entirely composed of and governed by women, to the absolute exclusion of all members of the opposite sex, could be wholly successful in matters of policy, of finance, and business'.[15] It was alleged that the Sisters accepted illegitimate children at £40 a time, with no questions asked of the parent, full confidentiality guaranteed, on the understanding that these children would remain with the Sisters until adulthood; this, claimed the COS, was an inducement for promis-cuous women to leave their bastard offspring to be cared for by public charity.

The Sisters rejected the Bishop of London's suggestion that a male should be elected on to their committee, and then they sacked his Lordship as patron. The Bishop subsequently received many letters from former inmates of the Sisters' orphanages, half of these stating how kindly they had been treated, and half alleging harshness. Father Jay stood by the Sisters.

Father Jay was thus a strange blend – a muscular Christian who never-theless had a love of the frocks, flowers, paintings, incense, candles and theatrics of Anglo-Catholic ritual. By 1893, Jay had added another facet to his already richly contradictory persona. Having pondered the objects of his pastoral care in various theoretical lights, he embraced the eugenics mania that had captured the imagination of so many armchair scientists by the close of the century. Jay wrote: 'Unhappily there are many who are not born, but damned into the world. It may not be the best theology, but is the soundest sense, to admit that some, by inherited defects and taints of blood . . . have no fair chance of being anything but bad.'[16] Three years later, in an interview he gave to the *London* magazine entitled 'To Check the Survival of the Unfit', he said,

> We are met by the incontrovertible fact that the major portion of the submerged and semi-criminal class are in their present position through physical, moral, and mental peculiarities. They have no nerve nutrition, no energy or staying power . . . Their natural gifts are small. Cunning, not wisdom; sharpness, not intelligence, are stamped even on their faces.[17]

The concept of selective breeding to improve (or at least to halt a perceived decline of) the British 'race' had been mooted since the early 1860s, and in 1883 Francis Galton – Charles Darwin's cousin – coined the term 'eugenics', and wrote of the human 'refuse' that was resulting from the overbreeding of the least 'fit'. In the 1880s, commentary and opinions on the social crisis in Britain frequently used the language and hypotheses of evolution theory. Many now believed that scientific progress was revealing that it was natural for circumstance or the environment to kill off the weaker members of society; others went further, stating that if sentiment could only be kept at bay, it would be highly beneficial to the human species if, by some process, this dying out could be artificially accelerated, starting with the prevention of breeding by those who were mentally or physically defective.

Some level of authority for this latter point of view came from Charles Darwin's *Descent of Man* (1871). Concurring with the findings of Galton and fellow evolutionary theorists Herbert Spencer (who coined the term 'Survival of the fittest'), T.H. Huxley, Alfred Russel Wallace and W.R. Greg, Darwin stated that caring for the feeble, and allowing them to breed, would lead to the degeneration of humanity: only Man allows his 'worst animals' to breed, and if this continues to be so, 'the nation will retrograde' – that is, begin to lose its 'higher' faculties.[18] But Darwin stated in the same chapter of *Descent* that 'the most noble attribute of man' is that our intellect and morality are so developed that we are the only species in which the capacity for disinterested love of all living creatures – other races, other animals, 'idiots' and other retrograde specimens of mankind – has emerged.

How could Darwin square the withholding of altruism towards our unfit with practising our most noble acquirement: sympathy? If we were to lose our altruism through habitual under-use, we would begin to regress. All he could suggest was that we continued to minister to the unfit – with our asylums, special hospitals, vaccination campaigns, provision of Poor Law relief, etc. – while trying, he knew not how, to ensure that the unfit would breed later and later in life, if at all, and therefore produce fewer progeny.

Without our knowledge of DNA and its behaviour, or sophisticated mathematical models with which to explore probabilities, Darwin and co were understandably fumbling when they tried to comprehend which characteristics were transmissible across the generations, and which were more likely to be the result of environment; and whether the latter could cause adaptations in individuals that became hereditary. A voluble body of opinion claimed that the appalling conditions endured by the very-poor were reversing the Ape-to-Angel direction of evolution. Evolution theory provided one of the tropes regularly used in descriptions of slum-dwellers in these years: Beatrice Webb wrote of 'the aborigines of the East End', while T.H. Huxley compared poor East Enders unfavourably with the 'Polynesian savage in his most primitive condition'; and General William Booth, co-founder of the Salvation Army, saw poor Londoners as analogous to the 'pygmies' whom explorer Henry Stanley had recently come across on his African travels. (The poor, however, also made use of tribal name-calling, revealing that the late-Victorian social gulf appeared to be as wide as that separating the earth's different races: playwright and journalist George Sims recalled how 'Hottentots!' was often shouted playfully when wealthy-looking strangers were spotted in the streets of poor districts.)

The criminality that was felt to be a common feature of slum life was posited as evidence of the reversion from the higher human moral and intellectual faculties of sociability and altruism. Darwin had discovered that oceanic islands – where creatures were cut off from their kind on the mainland – witnessed retrograde evolution; adaptations that were no longer needed began to disappear – the flightless bird, the sightless cave-dwelling mammal. Was Britain experiencing something similar within the physically secluded, socially isolated populations of its urban backstreets?

Shocking data seemed to bear out the fancy that the most numerous class of British children – the offspring of the poor – were showing an irreversible decline in physical and mental ability. Nationally, half a million schoolchildren would fail a whisper test for defective hearing, in 1902. Extreme hunger, leading to inability to concentrate, was said to affect one in eight schoolchildren in London in 1889; perhaps that slowness of mind would become hereditary. Meanwhile, data from the three schools in the Nichol in the 1880s and 1890s show the battle the London School Board teachers faced in combating poor physical health to provide even the most basic elementary education. Quite apart from the regular waves of infectious disease that saw school attendance plummet (and teachers themselves signed off for weeks), there were heartbreaking tolls of physical damage – weakness of sight and hearing, epilepsy and enfeebled intellect – to be contended with.[19]

The degeneration strand of thought would reach a peak in 1902 following the revelation of the vast numbers of working-class males deemed to be in too poor a physical condition to be accepted for service by army recruitment officers during the second Boer War. The shock findings that there might not have been enough reserve male strength to maintain the Empire would lead to the National Efficiency movement and a new impetus for the State to intervene to improve the British 'race', since *laissez-faire* had wreaked such damage.

It is important to point out that the racial degeneration theory – though it was widely publicised, being a pet subject for journalists and the popularisers of science – did not gain acceptance from serious investigators at this time. The medical men convened to consider the matter in the 1904 Interdepartmental Committee on Physical Deterioration (which was a direct result of the Boer War fiasco) firmly refuted 'progressive degeneration' and the notion that environmental damage reached any further than the immediate generation affected.[20] In a similar way, Francis Galton's books – including *Hereditary Genius* (1869), *Hereditary Improvement* (1873) and *Natural Inheritance* (1889) – had garnered many thoughtful, sceptical reviews. *The Times*, for example, on 7 January 1870, argued, in its analysis of *Hereditary Genius*, that improved national education would be a far better way to raise the quality of the British race than Galton's proposal for 'viriculture', by which men of genius and the more intelligent among womankind should marry and breed superlative offspring. These 'typically'

Victorian and Edwardian eugenicist/racialist theoreticians were, in fact, largely *out* of step with mainstream medical thinking.

Father Jay was swayed by them, though. He had read Darwin; he had pondered Booth's labour colonies; and he had more recently fallen upon Havelock Ellis's *The Criminal*, published in 1890 (as part of the Contemporary Science Series, making the latest thinking accessible to the nation's armchair eugenicists) as a digest for the British reader of the past fifteen years' worth of European work in the new field of criminal anthropology. The Italian Cesare Lombroso, whose 1876 book *L'uomo delinquente* (Criminal Man) created a sensation on the Continent, categorised criminal 'types', examining them as anatomical and physiological anomalies. Ellis suggested in *The Criminal* that a more promising field would be 'criminal sociology' rather than 'criminal anatomy' – examining how environment might show its mysterious hand in the production of criminality. But he went on to state that the science was still too young to be able to disentangle criminality's two aspects: innate disposition and environmental contagion. So while *The Criminal* begins as a promisingly sophisticated take on the subject, it descends into a series of descriptions and illustrations of the 'physical characteristics' of criminal man. Ellis selected statistics to back up a position he had already settled on, rather than collecting and analysing data out of which a theory might emerge. He also fell back on the extended anecdote and a set of highly entertaining illustrations – a sort of birdwatcher's chart against which to measure your fellow man. For all its scientific posturing, *The Criminal*, like the work of many early criminologists and their popularisers, is little more than the ancient art of physiognomy dressed in new robes.

Father Jay was most impressed, however, and, reading Ellis's findings, certain aspects of his parishioners began to make sense to him. While talking to Jay in a Nichol street one day, one of his club members said to the vicar, 'I should like to turn honest.' Jay laughed and took the boy's cap off his head, saying, 'Let me look.' The boy thought this was some kind of joke, but Jay stared at the skull and the facial features and deduced that 'anyone can tell what that sad, sloping forehead, those shifty eyes, those heavy jaws mean'. Father Jay told the boy that he did not believe he was capable of change – that 'the power of God can always work a miracle [but] nothing else in such circumstances could avail'.[21] He now threw his not inconsiderable weight behind the inheritance/degeneration movement, plumping in print for 'hereditary taint' as the single most powerful predictor in the creation of criminality among the poor, overriding such factors as hunger, squalor, hatred of misused authority and undeserved privilege, the example set by parents, clan or neighbours. It was society's duty to recognise that all men were *not* equal, said Jay, that special care was needed to deal with the large number of people who cost the nation so much and who propagated so much misery. It had already been mooted during discussions on the 1890 Lunacy Act that the insane and 'drivelling imbeciles' should be kept from breeding (the measure was rejected, but would become law in 1913 with the passing of the Mental Deficiency Act);[22] now the same treatment ought to be adopted in the case of the hereditary criminal, wrote Jay: to do otherwise would be 'monstrous and unfair'.

Jay had devised a solution. It was not unlike Charles Booth's idea for the As and Bs of this world, but it had been refined and perfected in the light of the scientific experts Jay had been reading. The existing workhouse system did not prevent the damned from 'continually adding to the sum total of human misery by bringing into the world children whose only inheritance can be defective wills, weak bodies, and uncertain intellects'.[23] What was needed was forcible encampment – a series of huge penal settlements, preferably on the South Coast, or perhaps on some breezy moorland. (Despite his biologism, Father Jay could not shake off his traditional Victorian belief in the benefits of Fresh Air.) Here, the 'moral maniac' would be contained for life, his (or her) mania established by the highest thinkers in the land, men of science who had studied criminal anthropology and so could be relied on to make no mistakes. Conditions would be comfortable, work would be plentiful and remunerated at market rate (wood-chopping and mat-making would be appropriate employments, for example), and there would be much enjoyable rational recreation in leisure hours. There would be beautiful gardens, a gymnasium, baths, reading rooms, a chapel, a theatre and a concert room. 'To the submerged temperament, such a place will be the best home they have ever known.' There would be no parole or any form of release, since these people were not capable of change. That's why they were there. The settlements would be single-sex, so there would be no opportunity for them to breed, and gradually a whole section of British society would become extinct. Officers at the camps would be selected for their ability to blend human sympathy with tough love, and penalties for bad behaviour by the detainees could include solitary confinement, a bread-and-water diet, and corporal punishment – the use of 'Father Stick', as Jay put it.

Yes, yes, he knew what the objections would be. Sentiment in England always swung behind the notion of individual liberty; and we hold it dear that a man should not be imprisoned without having committed a crime. That's why forcible detention would be very carefully decided by the criminal anthropologists' panel whenever anyone was convicted for a second or third offence of stealing. A parliamentary Select Committee acting on facts gathered under a Royal Commission could sort out the precise factors to be considered by the experts. The whole programme would thus be highly democratic in nature.

The major obstacle, Father Jay felt, was the party political nature of British government, where legislation (or the shelving of it) was decided by those keen to keep their seats; and the popular press was always able to raise a hue and cry about dramatic new measures. A strong 'Socialistic' state would not be hampered by such panics and sentimentalism, and would thus always be free to act to protect the interest of the most 'useful' in society, who formed the vast majority. His 'New Scheme' did sound harsh, but these were challenging times, and, as he put it, 'a virulent fever cannot be cured by doses of treacle'.

Jay's penal settlements never appeared in Britain, and until his retirement to Malvern in Worcestershire in 1926, Father Jay continued to live among his flock – single, overworked, devoting his life to their care through boxing as well as slightly more conventional pastoral measures. Jay never made any attempt to reconcile his State-interventionist proposals with his belief in the salvation offered through Christ; and it is tempting to dismiss his penal-settlement notion as one more attention-seeking gambit. Certainly, his New Scheme triggered another round of interviews, profiles and press cuttings. But he was by now performing on an even larger stage – inspiring three novels in the 1890s, each of the authors captivated by the magnetic physicality of the man and his curious blend of vehemence and painstaking self-sacrifice.

Telling Tales

To take the last first, T.H. Hall Caine's novel *The Christian* appeared in 1898, a piece of piffle that combines an attack on Broad Church laziness with a love story, in which the Reverend John Storm (Jay) and beautiful young orphan Glory Quayle find their path to happiness littered with troublesome relatives, who wish Storm to stick to the safety of ministering to the wealthy at the (fictional) All Saints, Belgravia. Caine persistently underlines that, while gentle, Storm is the manliest of men – an example of fine breeding, too, plus a dash of something more exotic, with 'a forehead like an arched wall . . . a well-formed nose, a powerful chin, and full lips, all very strong . . . His complexion was dark, almost swarthy, and there was a certain look of the gipsy in his big golden brown eyes with their long black lashes. He was clean shaven, and the lower part of his face seemed heavy under the splendid fire of the eyes above it.' Heathcliff in a cassock, Storm is 'a man of powerful moods', and Glory quite blushes whenever she feels she may not come up to his soaring intellectual and moral standards. Just to round him out, and lest he seem too coarse for *fin de siècle* tastes, Storm likes yachting and canoeing, and cries at beautiful sunsets and cruelty to animals.

Forsaking SW1, Storm signs up to the High Church Ritualist brotherhood the Society of the Holy Gethsemane (also known as the Bishopsgate Fathers) – a nice enough set of lads, if highly strung, but Storm realises that a life of monkish introspection is not for him, so off he trudges to a slum incumbency, is attacked by a rough, falls fatally ill as a result and has a deathbed wedding to Glory.

Twelve years later Caine was still in thrall to Jay, and contributed to a short biographical sketch of Jay and Jay's father, strangely entitled *Father and Son: A Study in Heredity*, in which he described Jay's blend of gentility and earthiness: '[He is] a gentleman, a scholar, a man of refinement, living down there in the lowest slums of the cruel city, year in, year out, without any real intellectual companionship . . . sharing little of the life which is natural to him, and cultivating none of the tastes to which he was born.'

Jay had also beguiled author Mrs L.T. Meade, a prolific bestselling writer of children's fables, detective yarns, historical novels and romantic fiction who created the new genre of girls'-school stories. A self-educated, self-made woman, Meade had been among the earliest to spot the potential for blending social realism and topicality with the traditional romance, and in 1875 published *Lettie's Last Home*, the tale of a poor East End girl whose mother is a baby-farmer; and in 1876 her *Scamp & I: A Story of City Byways* was the immensely popular, much-reprinted adventures of street waif Flo and her pet dog.[1] Meade's street arab stories focus on the nobility of the poor and their struggles as they overcome, or at least resign themselves to, their sufferings. (Meade warns that they must not be assisted by indiscriminate charity.) She produced some six books a year, and among her outpourings for 1895 was *A Princess of the Gutter* – the gutter in question being in the Old Nichol – featuring the brooding presence of 'Father Ranald Moore', the thinly disguised Jay.

Beautiful Cambridge-educated orphan and heiress Joan Prinsep is bored by her life with her relatives in their Bayswater mansion. Fortunately, her Uncle Ralph dies, leaving her everything, but a codicil to his will states that she can only inherit if she spends some time living among the poor. Joan is horrified to learn that among Uncle Ralph's bequests is an insanitary court in Saffron Hill, Clerkenwell, and when Joan investigates she learns that since Uncle Ralph has leased on the property to a third party, she can neither obtain full possession, lower the rents nor make any improvements to the buildings.[2] However, Uncle Ralph's ghastly property portfolio also includes some hovels over in Shoreditch, and the leases on these are shortly to expire. Joan ventures east to 'Frank Street', is introduced to Father Moore in his boxing club cum church but almost vomits at the appalling smell (it is like nothing she has ever ingested) and she notes 'the uniform ugliness of all the faces'. Not Father Moore's, though. Meade casts him in Mr Rochester mode: he has a large build, is abrupt and outspoken, full of energy, and his dark eyes 'seemed to glow with a sort of inward fire'. And that marvellous physiognomy again – the keen, firm lips, short dark hair and a fine intellectual brow (whatever that was). He walked with a 'quick, ungainly, but decidedly masculine stride'. A bundle of restless energy, Moore spends a great deal of his time while talking to Joan striding about before flinging himself across a sofa. 'I have seen many an East End worker since then,' Joan notes later in her diary, 'but I have never, never come across anyone so absolutely selfless as Mr Moore.'

Moore becomes Joan's mentor in her quest to spend her inheritance on improving the condition of the local poor. Joan moves into an attic (which somehow contrives to have eight rooms) in Frank Street, with views south to St Paul's Cathedral. She has it fumigated, plastered, painted china blue, with white muslin curtains, and Father Moore is rapt by her simple but tasteful choice in furnishings. It is a haven of cleanliness in a region of filth, and she buys herself an easy-wash skirt and blouse, knowing how soiled she is to become. She had hoped to be seeing more of Father Moore but she knows that 'the life of this good man was one long race against time and evil'.

Joan sets up her own women and girls' club, on university settlement lines, and Meade lovingly details for the reader the fixtures and fabrics Joan selects for the club on a shopping trip to Peter Robinson. Next, Joan has Joan Mansions built for the deserving poor. It's the least she can do, she feels, as she tells her snooty cousin Anne: 'We see life without any sham at all down here . . . In some way or other it seems to be all our fault. We grind the life out of them; we take everything and leave them nothing.'

None of this would have been possible without the help of Martha Mace – the 'princess' of the title – a self-described 'rough gel', buxom, dirty-faced, sporting the eyebrow-skimming fringe that every adolescent East End girl either had or aspired to, and magnificent in her crimson flannel blouse and going-at-the-seams black skirt. Martha initially suspects Joan of 'doin' the religious dodge', but then decides to be her protector in this rough company. One of the many lessons Joan learns in Frank Street is the phenomenon of the 'mate': the intense, one-on-one, non-sexual relationship between one rough gel and another. It comes as a revelation to Joan, who is told:

It's much more'n a friend – we're mates, that's wot we calls each other. It's as good as bein' married in some ways, an' with none o' the troubles; we sticks to each other through thick an' thin, an' fights for each other, and shares each other's bite and sup. There ain't a gel in our factory wot 'aven't 'er mate.

It took Mrs Meade's rather glutinous tale of slum life to make that aspect of the Nichol public; no other commentator had noted this fundamental part of its social structure.

Joan is told she will be safe enough so long as she avoids two or three of the more secluded, dark courts at night-time; so she wanders into the darkest, most malodorous one close to midnight and would have been robbed and assaulted by three evil-looking women had not the night air been pierced by the screams of a domestic assault, which distracts the robbers.

Because of the civilised example Joan has set, Martha begins to wash her face and hands, gives up her seven days a week, twelve hours a day job as barmaid at the Red Dragon, decides not to follow her mother into the watercress-selling lark (out in all weathers, all day, from 5 a.m.) and is taken on by the respectable haberdashers in Shoreditch High Street, earning £16 a year for an eight-hour day.

Like *The Christian*, *A Princess of the Gutter* appears to the twenty-first-century reader to contain a repressed eroticism in its descriptions of Jay. In Meade, there is also a powerful sense of the physicality of Martha Mace and her friends, an animal magnetism that is absent in the descriptions of beautiful but refined Joan. *A Princess* is a fascinating fantasy, supplying its female readership with not just an armchair tour of the slum (along with shopping and fashion insights) but a new kind of role model in fiction for women – the philanthropist creator of subsidised housing, dispensing aid wisely, loved by all, teaching manners but also learning from the mores of the poor, just like the real-life Baroness Angela Burdett-Coutts and Octavia Hill, the most famous of philanthropic lady-landladies to the poor. The novel is a rescue fantasy, on two levels: Joan rescues Martha and her kind, but Father Moore rescues Joan from a life of unfulfilling privilege in the West End.

The third fictional Father Jay appeared in the best-known and most controversial book of the trio, *A Child of the Jago* by Arthur Morrison.

Morrison was a freelance journalist and writer of short stories for the burgeoning weekly magazine market when, in 1894, at the age of thirty-one, he had a major success with *Tales of Mean Streets*, a compilation of fourteen stories of East London life, which was widely praised and caused a small furore for its graphic depiction of rough gels' and boys' courting rituals in the tale 'Lizerunt'; though in fact, 'Lizerunt' was atypical of *Mean Streets*, since what Morrison had been aiming to capture in the collection was the 'hopeless monotony' and dreariness, as he saw it, of the lives and culture of the 'respectable' poor (Booth's classes D to F) of East London.

Father Jay had greatly enjoyed (or so he said) *Mean Streets*, and wrote to ask Morrison if he would care to visit him so that Jay could show him a wholly different side of East End life that he might find stimulating for his fiction. Morrison visited, the two men bonded instantly, and yet another Jay mouthpiece came into being. Morrison was a willing slave – genuinely believing that Jay's approach to pastoral care was the best he had ever seen and approving of both the boxing and the penal settlement proposal. For eighteen months Morrison visited the Nichol daily, even staying for spells with Jay, and entering into all aspects of Nichol life: drinking in its pubs, helping out at Jay's club and trying his hand at matchbox-making. He invited several Nichol residents to his house in rural Loughton, Essex (including the man who had dropped the fire-grate on to a policeman in Orange Court) in order to note down their sayings and mannerisms. In November 1896 he published *A Child of the Jago*, which took the sub-genre of slum fiction into wholly new territory and started a war of words in the literary columns of newspapers and magazines that was still being fought two years later.

Morrison wanted to tell the tale of a small boy who, but for his dreadful surroundings, would have grown up to be a good citizen. He wanted to show how contamination by one's environment is effected. Morrison made little attempt to disguise the Nichol. He called it the Jago (it has been suggested that the inspiration for the name came from combining 'Jay' and 'go' – it's where Jay goes), and so persuasive was Morrison's nightmare vision of the place, so great the notoriety of his depiction, that from 1896 onwards, even within the East End, 'Nichol' and 'Jago' became interchangeable names.

Dicky Perrott is eight years old at the opening of the novel, the son of Josh, an habitual criminal who has been in and out of jail, and

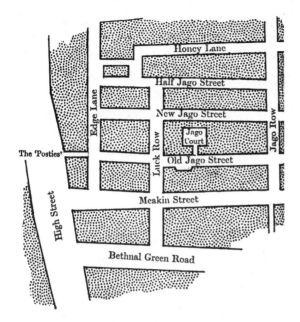

Arthur Morrison's map of his fictional Jago – a very thinly disguised Old Nichol. Edge Lane is Boundary Street; Honey Lane is Mead Street; Luck Row is Chance Street and so on.

Hannah, an honest, quiet and sober woman who has come down in the world, her move into the Jago from elsewhere in East London indicating her fall from grace. Dicky is told by one of the Jago's oldest residents that, as a Jagoite, the best the boy can hope for is to make it into the 'Igh Mob, since 'it's the best the world has for you, for the Jago's got you, and that's the only way out, except gaol and the gallows'. The plot of the book is the gradual entrapment of a basically decent boy into criminality. Between the ages of eight and seventeen, Dicky experiences the closing down of all other opportunities but crime, just as surely as the labyrinthine streets of the Jago inhibit his physical movements through the slum.

Always hungry, especially for cake, Dicky is lured in by coffee-shop owner Aaron Weech, 'a prosperous, white-aproned, whiskered, half-bald smirking tradesman', who hums hymns. Weech is also one of the Jago's biggest fences, and most of his 'clients' are youngsters. Fatally, Dicky accepts 'free' cake, buns and tea, but Weech runs up a tab that he demands Dicky pay off by stealing for him. In one of the book's many echoes of *Oliver Twist*, Weech, like Fagin, tries to block the child's every move towards 'respectability', even succeeding in having Dicky sacked from the one honest job he is able to obtain.[3]

Weech also snitches to the authorities about Josh Perrott's latest theft, and when Josh is imprisoned, the family becomes reliant on thirteen-year-old Dicky's ability to find cash and food.

Various sub-plots tell tales of Jago iniquity. The novel is punctuated by outbursts of faction fighting, on the one hand between the two biggest families of the Jago (the Ranns and the Learys); and on the other between the Jago and the Dove Lane (Columbia Road) gang. A family called the Ropers have their 'exasperating respectability knocked off' by various mean acts of their neighbours, until Father Henry Sturt [Jay] assists them to move out of the Jago, where everyone is 'as thick as glue and as wide as Broad Street'.

Contradicting his own assertion throughout the book that the polluting effects of the Jago/Nichol cannot be escaped by any of its natives, Morrison has two characters gradually redeem themselves – the squalid yet generous-hearted daft prostitute Pigeony Poll; and former semi-criminal costermonger Kiddo Cook, who is rewarded at the end of the book with a small business of his own and marriage to Poll, all arranged by Father Sturt.

Jay/Sturt is described by Morrison as 'tall and soundly built, with a certain square muscularity of face'. Sturt inspires 'a general, uneasy awe', and we see him putting down Cockney larkiness with withering High Table banter that sends its victims scuttling off in shame and astonishment at the cutting humour of this toff. 'No Jago could disobey Father Sturt,' Morrison assures us; but the reader is supplied with no scene or dialogue that shows how or why this might have been so – we are required to take it on trust. There is inconsistency in the portrait of Sturt. Repeatedly we are told that he does not give alms – but in set pieces that show how noble he is, he does indeed dish out some cash, coals or clothing. Similarly self-contradictory is the scene in which Kiddo Cook and Josh Perrott attend Sturt's boxing club and are surprised and delighted with its cleanliness, the flowers and the music played there, indicating that they are capable of an appreciation of beauty and the sublime. On the one hand Jago men are irredeemable; on the other, Sturt redeems them.

All of Father Jay's fads and fantasies are given full voice by Morrison, and even poor old Reverend Henry Henderson, Jay's predecessor, dead ten years, is attacked once again – with words put into the mouth of Father Sturt – for his simple-minded charitable giving and unmuscular brand of Christianity. Oxford House and Toynbee Hall are savaged in the guise of 'The East End Elevation Mission and Pansophical Institute'. Incidents of generosity and kindness in Morrison's Jago can be counted on one hand (they mostly fall to poor old Pigeony Poll). Women's sympathy for each other is, in Morrison's eyes, merely an excuse to go to the pub together.

The Jago is 'a howling sea of human wreckage', and Morrison was not the only one to use watery metaphors in describing the poor of Bethnal Green. That the poor were 'the submerged' was a common figure of speech in these years. Father Jay himself wrote of the 'ship-wrecks of humanity' and the 'helpless shoals' among his parishioners, while the master of the Bethnal Green workhouse described the 'able-bodied loafer' who passed through his wards as 'possessing all the attributes of the soft-shelled crab'.[4] Thinking of the poorest as crea-tures of the ocean not only dehumanised them but broke the link between their state and the wider economic world – they were just an unfortunate phenomenon, like barnacles, or flotsam and jetsam.

The foetid whiff of eugenics blows through *A Child of the Jago*, with such lines as 'Still the Jago rats bred and bred their kind unhin-dered, multiplying apace and infecting the world.' And when Dicky's mother gives birth to her third child, the young surgeon who attends her at home tells Father Sturt, 'Is there a child in all this place that wouldn't be better dead – still better unborn? But does a day pass without bringing you just such a parishioner? Here lies the Jago, a nest of rats, breeding, breeding, as only rats can; and we say it is well. On high moral grounds we uphold the right of rats to multiply in their thousands. Sometimes we catch a rat. And we keep it a little while, nourish it carefully, and put it back into the nest to propagate its kind.' Sturt agrees and says, 'But who will listen – if you shout it from the rooftops?'

The obnoxious moralising of the novel, and the sneering, arch tone, with the overuse of mock-heroic to ridicule the Jagoites, is partly redeemed by splendid passages, most notably those depicting scenes of Jago violence. The faction-fighting episodes, such as the following, aroused incredulity and distaste in some reviewers. Morrison claimed he had been reticent in his descriptions, and had not attempted to convey to the reader even a sense of the typical curses screamed and shouted during such bouts:

Parties of Learys were making for other houses in the street, when
there came a volley of yells from Jago Row, heralding a scudding mob
of Ranns. The defeated sortie-party from Jago Court, driven back, had
gained New Jago Street by way of the house-passages behind the Court,
and set to gathering the scattered faction. Now the Ranns came, drunk,
semi-drunk, and otherwise, and the Learys rushed to meet them. There
was a great shock, hats flew, sticks and heads made a wooden rattle,
and instantly the two mobs were broken into an uproarious confusion
of tangled groups, howling and grappling. Here a man crawled into a
passage to nurse a broken head; there a knot gathered to kick a sprawling
foe. So the fight thinned out and spread, resolving into many independent combats, with concerted rushes of less and less frequency, till
once again all through the Jago each fought for his own hand.

Morrison skilfully uses the twists and turns of the Jago/Nichol street
plan to add movement and drama to the prose. People and vehicles
suddenly appear around corners; fleeing Dicky has to pace himself –
dashing along a street, slowing as he enters a court, taking off again,
making sudden turns, then coming to a halt when he reaches his secret
hideout, a shed where he tells his only confidant, an aged donkey
belonging to a local coster (a beast so hungry it has started to gnaw
the wooden palings) what has been going on in his life, while hot
tears stream down his face.

Dicky is a triumph too – simultaneously villain and hero, pathetic
and vicious by turns; old beyond his years but with a child's reactions
to the injustices meted out to him by the Jago. This portrait of a boy
slowly succumbing to the dominant influences around him is the
novel's sole attempt to explore motivation, emotion and conscious-
ness. Only Dicky and the slum come to life on the page; all the other
characters are pieces to be moved around the squalid chessboard of
the Jago for maximum dramatic or pathetic effect. Even the portrait
of Jay fails to capture the spark that others saw in the Saviour of
Shoreditch. Partly strangled by its archness and wearisome sense of
superiority, A Child of the Jago suffers because of the author's unwillingness to consider Jago-dwellers as fully human. To Morrison, the
Jagoites are poor because they are born morally weak; the depreda-
tions of fences such as Weech feed on this weakness and create full-
blown criminals, while sentimental philanthropists finish off the job

Arthur Morrison (1863–1945) photographed in 1902 in his Essex home. Here, he entertained Nichol residents so that he could research their speech and mannerisms. His extraordinary literary success allowed him to indulge his love of paintings; he would abandon his writing career after fifteen years to become a dealer and expert in Japanese prints.

of ruining character with their injudiciously applied sympathy and charity. The same harshness of vision and one-sidedness is to be found in Father Jay's own three books about the Nichol, and the critic who reviewed the novel for the *St James's Gazette* claimed that Morrison had done little more than dramatise Jay's *Life in Darkest London, The Social Problem* and *A Story of Shoreditch*. Both Jay and Morrison angrily denied in the periodical press that *A Child of the Jago* had been written at Jay's behest by an enterprising journalist eager for a *succès de scandale*, still less that Morrison had committed mass plagiarism of his idol.

The most intelligent assault on Morrison came from literary critic H.D. Traill, who attacked him for being part of the New Realism movement yet producing a fantasy. Morrison had, in fact, never claimed allegiance to any literary school (he did not know that his work was to be considered alongside that of George Gissing, Rudyard Kipling and Stephen Crane) and wrote to refute Traill, stating that he had had to read up on Realism, Naturalism, (Emile) Zola-ism, and plenty of other artistic-isms, of which he had never previously been aware. His aim, he said, had been to record accurately what he had seen and heard for himself over months of careful scrutiny, since 'observation is my trade'. Nothing had been added or subtracted in his account of life in the Nichol. He hadn't made art out of the Nichol – this *was* the Nichol.

Traill found much to admire in Morrison's writing but felt sure that 'as described by Mr Morrison . . . the Jago never did exist'. Traill believed that by selecting some of the very worst aspects of East London life, Morrison had done exactly what an artist should do – he had created a dense, undiluted composite that bore little relation to its factual inspiration: 'the total effect of the story is unreal and phantas-magoric,' wrote Traill, and the reader feels like 'one who has just awakened from the dream of a prolonged sojourn in some fairyland of horror'. Morrison's skilful craftsmanship had produced this effect, and Traill thought that far from having a flavour of documentary, or reportage, *A Child of the Jago* was every bit as idealised, in its way, as the Venus de Milo.[5]

Morrison was apoplectic; oddly so, since his artistry was being so extravagantly praised by so eminent a critic. He stated that he had intended to present his comfortably off, leisured readership with a brutally honest look at a real social problem existing close to the heart of the imperial capital, in the hope that it would shake them out of their complacency: 'This book of mine disturbed those who had done nothing, and preferred to do nothing, by way of discharging their responsibility toward the Jago and the people in it . . . Personal comfort is the god of their kind. They firmly believe it to be the sole function of art to minister to their personal comfort – as upholstery does.'[6] Sounding identical to Father Jay in the latter's literary purple passages,

Morrison continued that the wealthy expected a novel to supply them with a 'debauch of self-delusion' but that he was not the man 'to coat truth with treacle'. In fact, no such feeling of socio-political purpose is discernible in the novel and, despite himself, Morrison actually paints a portrait of total hopelessness with regard to 'solving' the Jago. The ending of the book is wholly pessimistic, and Sturt comes across as achieving little more than offering palliatives to a tiny minority of reclaimable Jago souls.

Morrison challenged Traill to 'trot out his experts' – to find individuals who knew the Nichol well and who would go on the record to deny that *A Child of the Jago* was anything other than an exact transcript of life in that quarter. Perhaps to Morrison's surprise, Traill did exactly that, going to the Nichol and taking testimony, which he later published. One Mr Woodland Erleback, a manager of the Nichol Street Board School for thirty years, told Traill that

the district, though bad enough, was not even thirty years ago so hopelessly bad and vile as the book paints it. The characters portrayed may have had their originals but they were the exception and not the rule. Many poor, but honest and hard-working people have lived in these mean streets, and I can introduce you to several respectable men holding responsible positions whose early days were passed there, and who found their way out of the Jago that is represented as impossible to the hero (or rather victim) of the book.[7]

Henry Spicer, a fellow school manager and a former MP for South Islington, told Traill the same, and so did J.T. Henderson of the Nichol Street Ragged School. William Anderson, a Poor Law officer for Shoreditch, had lived in the Nichol for twenty years; while the Misses Matthewman and Newman had worked there for thirty years, running various Mothers' Meetings. All denied that *A Child of the Jago* was an accurate portrayal of the slum. Traill also pointed out that Vavasseur, Carter & Coleman was a large silk manufactory occupying numbers 15 to 18 New Nichol Street, and its owners had told him that they were happy to store their expensive stock there and had never had a break-in. (Traill might also have drawn attention to a huge theatrical scenery store between Mount Street and Turville Buildings, which had gone similarly unmolested.) Most angry was Robert Allinson of the London City Mission, who declared that the Nichol was no worse than several other poor districts of East London, and that Morrison had painted it much too dark, all on the word of one man (Jay).[8]

Jay and Morrison, in turn, trotted out Arthur Winnington-Ingram of the Oxford House settlement (but by now, the Bishop of Stepney) and Harold Boulton – businessman, philanthropist, magistrate in West Ham and Captain of the Queen's Own Cameron Highlanders. Boulton wrote that Morrison had, if anything, understated the notorious faction fights, but had otherwise captured in all its truth the Nichol's 'reeking filth and horror, its absolute lawlessness, its frequent murders, its untainted heathendom'. Boulton viewed the Nichol as 'an ideal Socialistic state . . . [where] there was no code, social, political or moral, and the Queen's writ did not run'.[9]

H.G. Wells weighed in, admiring Morrison's fiction but pointing out the fallacious heritability argument. Morrison (and Jay) had confused environmental factors and heritable characteristics and, as Wells wrote, 'neither ignorance, wrong moral suggestions, nor parasites are inherited . . . The Jago people are racially indistinguishable from the people who send their children to Oxford, and the rate of increase in the Jago population is entirely irrelevant to the problem. The Jago is not a "black inheritance", it is a black contagion, which alters the whole problem.'[10] Morrison hit back in a newspaper interview two weeks later:

> I don't say they are all hopelessly bad, but the majority of Jago people are semi-criminal . . . Heredity and environment are their greatest enemies . . . Look at these long lists of families going back to the third or fourth generation, and all criminals and lunatics . . . You never see a tall man amongst them, all the criminal classes are stunted. They have a certain strength, they can fight for a short time, but they have no staying power. Take them on a five-mile walk and you'll soon find that out . . . For my own part, I believe, as Father Jay does, in penal settlements; it would be far cheaper than our present prison system. Why not confine them as lunatics are confined? Let the weed die out, and then proceed to raise the raisable.[11]

Morrison's fictional Jago-dwellers never picked up a book or newspaper – probably weren't capable of reading. But according to Father

Jay, his parishioners in the Nichol took a lively interest in international, national and local affairs. Jay said that although most of the males preferred sporting papers, the general daily newspapers were read, too; indeed, he stocked them at his club. Those who were illiterate had the news passed to them by word of mouth, and in pubs and other meeting places a literate person could often be seen reading to small groups of the unlettered. Jay claimed that 'they are very severe on those who describe them as "roughs", or "thieves", or "English barbarians".'[12] They had read the reviews of all Jay's own books, and as Jay was walking through the streets one day he met a man he knew, whose dog he stooped to pat. 'Nice little dog that, Jim,' he said. 'Yus, 'e is a nice little dawg, and 'e don't go and write shillin' books about 'is friends . . . .'[13]

They knew all about the Morrison furore, and were deeply upset at how they had been depicted in his novel. Never mind, said Jay: as with the publication of his own books, funds for the Holy Trinity project had risen steeply after *A Child of the Jago* appeared, and the club's work won national fame. In 1901, the Prince of Wales – about to become Edward VII – had been able to state that 'all of us are familiar with the labours of that most excellent philanthropist, Mr Jay, in this neighbourhood'.[14] No one else had a look-in.

PART FOUR

STRIPELAND

The Dreamers of Dreams

In parliamentary elections, London had voted Liberal for most of the nineteenth century. Then, in the 1885 general election, London turned Tory, and Conservative delight at this electoral bonanza was reinforced at the general election of the following year, when the Conservatives won 45 of 59 London seats. Although he was the leader of a coalition government, and was dependent upon Liberal Unionist Cabinet colleagues for his government's survival, Conservative Prime Minister Lord Salisbury now felt secure enough that the metropolis was Tory at heart to delay no further the modernisation of London's administration, as part of the overhaul of the whole nation's system of local government – a policy urged upon him by the Liberal Unionists shoring up his minority government. Another reason for moving quickly on this matter was the publication of the report of the Royal Commission on the Metropolitan Board of Works, which brought fresh, unwelcome publicity (and 'Board of Perks' jibes) about the surplus-land-dealing and general jobbery and graft of certain members of the Board – an indirectly elected, unaccountable body that was looking increasingly outmoded after the latest Reform Act, of 1884. Salisbury could see the sense of acting now: of taking advantage of his healthy London parliamentary backing to impose the form of administration most congenial to his traditional supporters. If increasing democracy meant that one day the working man might get the upper hand, why not create a system of local government that would avoid the sort of massive centralisation that might help a huge caucus of the unwashed to wreak havoc on the traditional social order?

Salisbury gave the task of drafting such a bill to his Local Government Board minister, C. T. Ritchie, who saw a way of answering the call for London local government reform that would nevertheless

IN MEMORIAM
METROPOLITAN
BOARD of WORKS

PEACE
TO ITS
HASHES
Obiit, March 21, 1889.

TO THE MELANCHOLY MEMORY OF
THE METROPOLITAN BOARD OF WORKS.
IT WAS AN UNFORTUNATE INSTITUTION.
FLUSHED, IN THE EARLIER YEARS OF ITS
EXISTENCE, WITH A LAUDABLE AMBITION
TO COMMAND THE RESPECT AND ADMIRATION
OF THE RATEPAYERS
IT GAVE AN EMBANKMENT TO THE THAMES,
DRAINED LONDON
AND SUDDENLY SHOWED THE WORLD
HOW JOBBERY COULD BE ELEVATED TO THE
LEVEL OF THE FINE ARTS;
THEN, FIGHTING TO THE END, IT WAS MORE
ANXIOUS TO LEAVE AN INHERITANCE OF SPITE
TO ITS SUCCESSOR THAN TO RETIRE FROM
THE SCENE OF ITS LATE LABOURS WITH
DIGNITY TO ITSELF.
UNWEPT, UNREPENTANT, YET UNHUNG,
IT HAS PASSED FOR GOOD AND AYE TO THAT
OBLIVION FROM WHICH IT IS POSSIBLE THE
MORE THOUGHTFUL AND PHILOSOPHICAL
RATEPAYER MAY THINK IT WOULD HAVE
BEEN AS WELL, FOR THE INTERESTS OF
MUNICIPAL HONESTY, THAT IT HAD
NEVER EMERGED.

Punch   *March, 1889*

leave London's vestries as fully empowered bodies, locally elected. With the passing of Ritchie's Local Government (England and Wales) Act of 1888, the 'County' of London was created. Fifty-three years after Britain's other major cities had been municipalised, Home Rule for London had been achieved.

The London County Council (LCC) was to be directly elected, and its constituencies were the same as for parliamentary elections. Two councillors per seat were returned for a three-year term. The LCC took over directly from the Metropolitan Board of Works responsibility for the housing of the working classes, although, disastrously, sanitation and 'nuisance' remained with the vestries, while Poor Law administration remained with the guardians.[1]

Unlike most of his predecessors at Downing Street, Salisbury felt that he had little to fear by creating a new debating chamber just ten minutes' walk from the House of Commons: the LCC was to be housed in the old Metropolitan Board of Works' home at Spring Gardens, at the Trafalgar Square end of Whitehall. But Salisbury had – quite understandably – misjudged the strange cross-currents of Londoners' political leanings. On 17 January 1889 the first LCC elections delivered a whopping majority, of 73 to 45, to the reform-minded candidates, soon to name themselves 'The Progressives', over 'The Moderates' (as the Conservatives rebranded themselves for the LCC). For heaven's sake, there was even an avowed Socialist elected (John Burns, for Battersea).

Not one former Metropolitan Board of Works member was voted on to the Council, and in the press, the Board's passing was celebrated. In Bethnal Green South West, Radical Liberals Charles Harrison and James Branch were returned with twice the number of votes of each of their opponents. Branch was a Congregationalist deacon and a local employer of labour at his Bethnal Green Road boot manufactory, but Harrison was a wealthy West End solicitor, and the election result suggests that voters were not particularly bothered about having a local man to represent them. A classic Victorian work-obsessive, Harrison also found time to sail his yacht to far-off countries, as well as run his successful legal practice and represent Bethnal Green: 'What are the times and seasons at which Mr Charles Harrison takes food or sleep?' an LCC colleague once asked.[2]

While its many enemies declared the Progressive-dominated LCC to be a Socialist, or Collectivist, body – using the two words inter-changeably as terms of abuse – the Progressives did not consider themselves Socialist. Progressivism was a loose term, and under its umbrella huddled some disparate creeds and unlikely partnerships. The small so-called 'Labour bench' of twelve working men that emerged during the first council sought such measures as a fair wages policy, an eight-hour working day, the setting up of labour exchanges and free school meals, but nevertheless felt sure that these ideals could be achieved through the Radical wing of the Liberal Party. (The Independent Labour Party would have its first significant successes in the LCC election of 1913, although their first majority on a vestry was won as early as 1898.) The Social Democratic Federation had little impact on the early LCC, while the other major London Socialist organisation, the Fabians, sought to influence policy behind the scenes, by permeating the Liberals.

In these early years of the LCC, more important than any of these self-consciously 'leftist' groupings were the traditional London Radicals, many, or most, of whom wished for the eventual reunification of the Liberal Party, once Ireland's fate had been decided one way or another. In addition, a strong evangelical streak within many Progressives made them seek to improve the manners and mores, as well as the living and working conditions, of Londoners. The Progressives would later be disparaged as 'the dreamers of dreams',[3] seeking to make a utopia of the metropolis but lacking the political

An oil painting was commissioned to mark
the first meeting of the London County
Council on 21 March 1889, from which this
engraving was taken. Lord Rosebery is in
the chair, and in the doorway on the left
stands one of the three women elected to
the Council; until 1907, women could not
take their LCC seats, and were restricted
to sitting in on committee meetings.

heritage and experience to create long-lasting change. Certainly, the
first council was ambitious, with a raft of plans to make London
simply a fairer place in which to live and work.[4] But they would be
admonished both for moving too slowly and for rushing forward with
ill-thought-out plans, according to the political bias of the critic.

The first LCC elected as its chairman, by a huge majority, the
Liberal Lord Rosebery (who had been Foreign Secretary, and would
be again, before briefly becoming prime minister) – partly in order
not to alarm further the Salisbury government, and partly because
Rosebery was one of the few experienced politicians among the new
intake. Here was a figure with the *élan* that was largely missing from
the earnest unknowns at Spring Gardens and who might help to allay
fears of a municipal monster that would run amok with the ratepayers'
cash. Rosebery declined to be called 'My Lord' at the LCC and opted
instead for 'Mr Chairman', though someone called out at his first
meeting as chair, 'Why not Citizen Rosebery?' In a witty opening
address on 21 March 1889, Rosebery said he knew that they had 'been
stigmatised as an assembly of "Rads" and "Cads" and "Fads"' and were

being subjected to 'jealous scrutiny'[5], but said that they would set about the task that Londoners had given them with wisdom as well as vigour. He knew the Council as constituted by Salisbury did not have all the powers that it could wish and he foresaw a long campaign with parliament to gain the full range of responsibilities that was the due of a city council. The LCC had not been given control of the Metropolitan Police, or the gas, water and electricity supplies, while education remained with the London School Board. Each of the Council's actions had to be mandated by parliament.

Rosebery, who had stood for the LCC election as an independent, expressed the wish that national party politics would have no role in the council chamber; the task of modernising and reforming London was too important to allow factional disputes to hamper progress. On the one hand, an astonishing level of consensus would characterise the first four councils, from 1889 to 1898; but the triennial election campaigns would see the same old joustabouts, and by 1892 the mighty parties at Westminster were pulling their Spring Gardens cousins closer to heel.

But bliss was it in that dawn – sort of: the first councillors were determined to prove themselves a new kind of civic man for London, as far removed from the vestry, Corporation of London and Metropolitan Board types as could be imagined. In fact, although obscure, many of the LCC's 118 councillors and nineteen aldermen were top-quality folk – a highly unusual mix, for these quasi-democratic years, of self-educated working men and self-made businessmen with financiers, writers, clergymen, barristers and philanthropists. Their average age was forty-six, where the Board's had been sixty-one. There were even three women elected, but they would never be able to do more than sit in on committee meetings because Sir Walter de Souza, staunch Tory anti-feminist, claimed successfully in the courts that the wording of the Local Government Act did not allow for females to be elected as council members; not until 1907 and the passing of the Qualification of Women Act would this oversight be rectified.

The novelty of the first council's intake inspired a number of music-hall songs, such as the witless 'I'm a Member of the County Council', written and performed by Tom Bass, in the persona of a labouring man who has found himself elected to Spring Gardens:

The thirst for notoriety sends some men nearly mad,
At last my chance has come and I with joy and pride feel glad;
The name of Smith you soon will see in the 'Telegraph' each day,
I'm elected to the County Council, Hip, hip, hip, hooray!

CHORUS
I'm a Member of the County Council,
And as sure as dicky birds eat groundsel,
I'll make it jolly hot,
I'll upset the blessed lot,
Will this member of the County Council!

We can't be bigger duffers than the poor old Board of Works,
And, anyhow, our Council shan't become a 'Board of Perks'.
With Rosebery for Chairman (and the best one, under circs.)
We shall never have a chance of being called the Board of Shirks.

Now every meeting I'll attend and shout 'Hear hear' and 'Shame',
They curse and swear in Parliament, so I shall do the same;
I'll make a speech whene'er I like, whether I make friends or foes,
And if I can't catch the Chairman's eye, I'll punch the Chairman's nose.

It was the housing issue that secured the Council's immediate attention. Rosebery himself had stated that the LCC's 'great work' was to be its sanitary programme – 'its primary task will be the better housing of the poor'. The Housing Committee sought and obtained from parliament a new Housing of the Working Classes Act, passed in 1890, that consolidated and made easier to implement the Cross and Torrens Acts and also laid the legal foundations of the Council's later vast suburban 'cottage' estates, which still stand today. (*The Times* got the wrong end of the stick, concerned that the Act would lead to 'a London rebuilt by the benevolent despots of the County Council', and the newspaper insisted that, instead, landlords should be forced to rebuild their insanitary dens out of their own bulging pockets.)[6] In 1891 a new Public Health (London) Act increased the LCC's powers over the vestries and landlords on health and sanitation matters. The Council agreed to pay half the salaries of the vestries' medical officers and sanitary inspectors, in order to lessen the burden on the local ratepayer in poor districts and to encourage the appointment of more such officers (across London the number of inspectors rose from fifty-three to 208). The LCC's own medical officer of health – Dr Shirley Forster Murphy – was appointed in the first month of the Council's existence. Murphy, who lived near Regent's Park, had been the tireless medical officer of the dirty parish of St Pancras for six years and by 1888 he was lecturer on health and hygiene at St Mary's Hospital, Paddington, and an excellent health journalist, contributing to various influential journals. Murphy set extraordinarily high standards for new buildings' ventilation, sanitation and sunlight admission.

The Council invited Londoners to report any insanitary area, and within a year, 146 such places had been complained of to the Housing of the Working Classes Committee. The biggest offender? The Nichol. But its shortcomings had already been written up in a detailed report to the Committee by the indefatigable Dr Bate, who had seized the opportunity when the Council was just four months old to state that he had recently visited every single one of the Nichol's 730 houses

Punch magazine's cartoon 'Slaying the Slum Dragon', from its edition of 15 November 1890; the young County Council takes on Landlordism.

and considered 43 per cent of them incapable of being rendered fit for human habitation – no matter how much money were to be spent on repairs. Dr Murphy took his own tour of the Nichol, agreed with Bate and added his own statistical twist to Bate's data, after comparing death rates per 1,000 in respective areas. He put it to the Committee that ninety-four more people died in the Nichol every year than if they had lived elsewhere in Bethnal Green, and 114 more than if they had lived elsewhere in London.[7] The entire Committee went along to see for themselves and were struck by the narrowness of the streets (the widest measured 28ft), and the strange windows of many of the older houses – the legacy of the silk-weavers. The inhabitants exhibited 'a low standard of vitality', they decided. The clinching point for Lord Compton, chair of the Housing of the Working Classes Committee, was that he could not bear to have on his conscience a failure to act on an area 'where one person should only die [yet] two were actually dying . . . the means are in our hands of doing away with that'.[8] Attention-catching statistical data was coming into its own, and Murphy and Compton's dramatic way with figures was persuasive.

The Committee had been looking for a flagship – a mass clearance that would, like so many aspects of LCC work, prove an inspiration, a model of what was achievable; and on a vote of 72 members to 31, the Boundary Street Scheme became that flagship.

Rather than replace private enterprise, the Council saw itself as offering a role model to the Five Per Cent Philanthropists and other individuals and companies supplying cheap housing for the poor for a small profit. The LCC was not permitted by law to undertake rebuilding itself; parliament hadn't been that generous, and indeed the Council hadn't sought such powers, preferring to use its newly enforceable high standards to drive up the performance of the private companies. So the failed formula of demolition for resale of cleared land to private firms was adhered to, even though six of the old Metropolitan Board of Works' cleared sites remained unsold, proving unattractive to the private companies, and some 4,000 of the Board's evictees were thus still awaiting rehousing. When, in 1889, the LCC asked the Home Secretary for permission to build its own housing on an unsellable small plot in Deptford in south-east London, permission was refused; but a shift in policy arose in early 1892 for purely practical reasons. The LCC was about to start work on the Blackwall Tunnel project, running beneath the Thames in east London – a massive scheme that would require the demolition of hundreds of homes. The Blackwall Tunnel Act of parliament stipulated that no work could commence until those evicted had been rehoused, and it became apparent that no private builders were coming forward to supply these new homes. And so it was contingency that created London's first council housing – not so much a lurch towards Socialism as a sober, slightly reluctant admission on the part of council members that if a thing was worth doing, they would have to do it themselves.

As for Boundary Street, it was only when it became apparent, in July 1893, that no private builder was interested in its reconstruction that the Council asked the Home Secretary whether it could demolish and rebuild a small section in the north-east of the area, to give a lead and show private companies what could be achieved architecturally. The Home Secretary said a cautious yes.

The Boundary Street Shuffle

How was all this going down with the Bethnal Green Vestry, those brave battlers against modernity? As ever, their responses were dictated entirely by the pangs felt in the purse. Action on the Nichol under Part 1 (for large-scale sites) of the 1890 Housing of the Working Classes Act would be paid for by the entire city – and no extra cost would accrue to the ratepayers of Bethnal Green. This was good. The new LCC was desperate to show how unrevolutionary and trustworthy it was, and so compensation to Nichol landowners and leaseholders was likely to be on the generous side. This was also good. The LCC was now paying half of Dr Bate's salary. Good. Equalisation of the rates would help Bethnal Green. Good. The LCC-sponsored Public Health Act put strong pressure on them to appoint more inspectors (part funded by the rates) and pursue a vigorous attack on insanitary areas. This was bad – so bad, they weren't going to do it. It was this very attitude that had led to a fresh round of vilification in the national press, with *The Times*, in a leader of Friday 6 December 1891, accusing the Bethnal Green Vestry of not only 'simple indolent ignorance' but of 'culpable delay' which was quite clearly 'flagitious' (atrociously wicked).

On Wednesday 8 November 1893 the Sanitary Committee of the Vestry took a tour of the Nichol. They didn't know it but they were being shadowed by a newspaper reporter keen to overhear their comments and witness their reactions. There had been a complete turnaround in civic relations: the London County Council was now the landlord of the Nichol, having bought up – over the previous eighteen months – some 680 of the properties scheduled for demolition as part of the Boundary Street Scheme. The vestrymen took gleeful revenge in this reversal of roles, and swapping places with their accusers noted in detail the sanitary shortcomings of the 'Land of Desolation', as they dubbed the Nichol streets. Three thousand people had been evicted so far, but because of the shortage of suitable rooms to rent in neighbouring areas, the LCC had had to agree to allow hundreds to stay on as long as possible in the increasingly small number of Nichol buildings that were deemed still habitable.

Some of the previous owners had made an attempt at whitewashing and patching up in order to try for the additional 10 per cent that was to be paid by the LCC for properties deemed to be fit for human habitation; others had taken the opposite course, more or less abandoning their property to avoid any expense now that it was to be torn down. Some buildings were said to have become so ruinous that passers-by were in danger from collapsing walls. Ne'er-do-wells from across London had come to the Nichol to unboard the boarded-up insanitary houses and squat there as long as possible. The rat population ran amok. Mounted police patrolled after dark because of rumours that organised gangs of robbers had moved in from outside the area, intent on picking off pedestrians in the Bethnal Green Road. Wreckers had entered some semi-derelict homes and begun to strip them of fireplaces, lead and other resaleable materials. (For his part, Arthur Harding considered the Nichol in its final days as 'our ideal playground', with windows to smash with impunity and the excitement of scouring the houses for any goods that evictees might have left behind.)

The newspaper reporter followed the vestrymen and watched them reel and vomit and clutch at walls for support as they entered court after court; others smoked pipes or cigars continuously in order to ward off the evil fumes. This site visit allowed them to crow over the failures of the LCC, who were now realising, they insisted, that being responsible for such areas was not as easy as it might seem. While the LCC had got as far as tearing down the north-eastern section of the Nichol, the Sanitary Committee called for the immediate demolition of the entire area. They claimed to be toying with the idea of mounting a prosecution against the LCC for being landlords of insanitary property.

The reinvention of the Nichol had not so far been a happy story for any of the participants and had brought out the worst in everyone.

These fifteen acres of London's by now most squalid slumland were
the focus of equally squalid claims and counter-claims, with owners
attempting to squeeze every last farthing from the Council in compensation; and squatters and incomers keen to grab any cash that might
be forthcoming as pay-offs for weekly tenants. One fraudulent claim
by a timber tradesman led to a conviction for perjury at the Old
Bailey, and City solicitors touted among residents, urging them to
mount a joint action against the LCC for loss of trade. The high
ideals of the Progressives – that urge to do right, and to be seen to
be doing so – were being severely tested in their first ever dealings
with a slum. What's more, although the Council had received the
Home Secretary's permission to build the first of the new blocks in
the scheme, the rest of the site was still up for grabs for private
builders – and none had so far shown any interest in creating the
new Nichol.

The Council's challenges had started with calls from across London
for there to be no compensation at all for owners of such criminally
insanitary property. The initial budget for the scheme had suggested
that £508 per house would be pocketed by the owners (in the event,
that sum would average £250 per house). Why, it was asked – by such
organisations as the English Land Restoration League, the Strand
Liberal and Radical Association, the Holborn Gladstone Club, the
Plumstead Gasworkers' and General Labourers' Union – should the
Nichol's sixty-nine landlords be so amply rewarded, when anyone
caught adding water to milk, margarine to butter, alum to flour, or
chicory to coffee was prosecuted and fined under the well-enforced
food-adulteration laws? An insanitary house was potentially far more
deadly, and yet instead of being taken before the courts, the purveyors
of rotten property would receive public money. These Radical bodies
also called for the public naming of the sixty-nine owners (still largely
a mystery at this point), and the LCC wrote to the English Land
Restoration League sympathising with its point of view but equivo-
cating, stating that there was no precedent for publishing owners'
names and that such a move could lay the Council open to defama-
tion proceedings; and – more cravenly – asking who could be sure
that it wasn't the middlemen and the tenants who had rendered these
properties so unfit? This was a fudge – the first of many as Idealism
dipped its toe into Nichol reality.

In the event, the major Nichol owners had to come forward and identify themselves in order to claim compensation; and the fantastically detailed archives of the London County Council (a vivid contrast to the largely unwritten proceedings of the vestries) show the payments received by the largest property-owners. Baroness Kinloss received £8,400 for her thirty-eight properties; the Gwatkin family's massive holding earned them £35,000, while on behalf of George Woolley, deceased, £27,000 was paid to his trustees. These owners were among eighteen who had initially mounted an unsuccessful campaign against the scheme, contesting its legality and thereby contributing to the hold-up that led to the 1893 'desolation' denounced by the Vestry. The most problematic landlord, however, proved to be the Church of England, whose unseemly haggling over its dilapidated holdings in Calvert Avenue and Shoreditch High Street caused a long delay in what was originally to have been the earliest round of demolitions: to create a 180-yard-long tree-lined avenue into the new Nichol, from the High Street. The Ecclesiastical Commissioners had tried to wring £6,932 out of the LCC's valuer; the Council voted by a large majority in a full session not to give in to the Commissioners – whose claim added half as much again to the true market value of the freehold – and sought and won an Act of parliament to acquire the houses from the Church. However, with regard to London's wealthy breweries, the valuer allowed liberal amounts of compensation for the Nichol's seven pubs and four beershops, fearing litigation funded by the brewers' deep pockets. The LCC had decided that the new Nichol would be 'dry', and had to pay dear for this decision by buying out the remaining years on each of the licences.

The Council was torn in two directions on compensation. On the one hand, the 1890 Housing of the Working Classes Act had significantly lowered compensation calculations and added the 10 per cent bonus for all property deemed to be in a habitable condition; on the other, the LCC was keen not to be portrayed by a hostile press and parliament as mounting an unfair 'Socialistic' attack on property-owners. In virtually every case, the sum requested by the owner was reduced by the LCC valuer by around one-sixth; nevertheless, the Council did end up paying more than market value for Nichol land and property, and history has judged the payments to have been generous.[1] The four largest freeholders took almost half of the total

£266,000 (excluding legal costs) paid out in compensation. Weekly tenants were given thirteen weeks' notice to quit, and received sums that varied according to their length of tenure, level of rent and whether any loss of trade would be involved. Amounts ranged from the highly unusual £120 paid to Mrs S.A. Dennington, a toy dealer of 97 Church Street, to a few shillings. Most weekly tenants received between £1 and £2 if they had been in residence at least eighteen months. Chancers who had moved in after the announcement of the scheme managed to wangle five or six shillings each out of the Council.

The LCC had been assiduous in trying to soften the blow for the poor. They had decided to clear the Nichol in five separate sections, closing up and evicting only when one section's population had either found new homes or could be accommodated temporarily in the remaining sections. (This was what the Vestry failed to understand – that if the entire Nichol were demolished at one go, nearly 6,000 people would have been thrown simultaneously on to the accommodation market.) Meanwhile, rentals for remaining Nichol tenants were reduced by the LCC – sometimes by as much as half. The Council also set up a site office with an accommodation bureau at 3 Nichol Row, with details of any room vacancies within half a mile. Dr Shirley Forster Murphy insisted on visiting every new home that a Nichol-dweller moved to, and if he considered it to be insanitary, deductions were made from the weekly tenant's compensation payment. This type of officiousness by the 'Cahnty Cahncil' was greatly resented. Whenever Dr Murphy or another LCC official turned up in the Nichol, locals jeered them, making such comments as 'Taking away poor people's houses'; 'Ought to be ashamed of theirselves'; 'Call theirselves gentlemen'. There were also threats of violence. John Owen, a bottle-dealer of 8 Christopher Street (with three tons of empty bottles stored in his home), told one LCC officer, who had come to board up number 8, 'See those steps? If you come to the top, I'll throw you to the bottom of them', when he heard that deductions from his compensation would be made to recover his unpaid back rent.

A constable was posted outside the Nichol Row office, just in case, and in the evening two night-watchmen patrolled.

A letter was received at Spring Gardens:

Bethnal Green
September 92

Gentlemen,
We the inhabitants of Bethnal Green beg respectfully to know where the 'Dwellings' are which were promised us, before the people moved out of their houses, after some of us have been in them for 40 nay 50 years and more. We do not mind being 'turned' out if we did but know where to go too. If the 'Dwellings' had been erected in the 'Goldsmith Row' [off Hackney Road] as promised by Messrs Branch and Harrison in their meetings before they were elected (which, bye-the-bye, I do not think they will get in again) instead of 'Land to Lett Apply to LCC', the shoreing up men would not want constables to 'mind' them. We do not wish to be disrespectful, on the contrary, we only want a roof over our heads to earn an honest living instead of making criminals of us and putting us in the streets. We are still 'Rads' if put too, as will be seen if we do not get justice. We do not mean any hurt if only 'places' are found for us, we hope notice will be taken of our letter and not ignored as other letters have been.
Your obedient servants
R. Linette
S. Polo
J. Bow
J. Votes
X for A. Good
X for A. Francks
X for C. Shands
and a host of others if required.[2]

Others protested by withholding rent, and before long the LCC had an ever-expanding list of 'Contumacious Tenants', though internal memoranda between the LCC solicitor and the Housing of the Working Classes Committee reveal their uncertainty about how to proceed in recovering the money. Nothing could look less Progressive than hauling the poor and about-to-be-homeless in front of the magistrates for non-payment of rent; and the seizure of their pathetic worldly belongings smacked of the worst kind of rack-renter. The police had been called in on twelve occasions to evict the most contumacious, who would not comply with magistrates' orders to leave. This sort of thing did not look good as the nation looked on with interest at London's experiment in municipal landlordism.

James Shelton, a twenty-one-year-old of 12 Jacob Street, was upset to find himself on the Contumacious list, being £1 7s in rent arrears, and he wrote a letter to the LCC to say that he was blind and that his sister, with whom he lived, had lost the use of her limbs: 'I only get my living by an organ and I have been doing so very bad lately. I will do the best I can in the new year and will pay you some of the back rent. Gentlemen, I hope you will excuse it.'[3] The LCC men were ill equipped to tell to what extent tenants were trying it on and which were cases of genuine distress. They also admitted that they had not realised the extent to which Nichol houses could be customised to certain trades, and how hard it was to reconcile certain noxious, or animal-reliant, businesses with dwelling space. Proud of having discovered 591 rooms for let within one mile of the Nichol, the LCC valuer soon had it pointed out to him that most of these were entirely unsuitable for the evictees. Costers would have no place to stable their donkeys or store their barrows or carts, and most landlords would not allow foodstuffs, plants or birds to be kept on their premises. Bakers, fish-smokers, dog-breeders and all sorts of metal- and wood-workers could not be easily accommodated outside the Nichol.

Reverend Robert Loveridge of St Philip's, and one of his lay helpers, Miss Bertha Nicholson, made it their task to liaise between unhappy evictees and the inexperienced and increasingly nonplussed LCC offi-cers. (Father Jay – his new Holy Trinity immune from demolition, along with the Board Schools and the London City Mission Hall – took no part in easing the effects of the upheavals on residents.) A number of artisans and shopkeepers claimed via Loveridge and Nicholson (who embarked on a letter-writing campaign to the LCC, and even doorstepped councillors at Spring Gardens) that their tiny businesses had been ruined since shoppers and travellers from whole-sale firms refused to come into the neighbourhood in its devastated state. Among her small victories, Miss Nicholson obtained £6 from the LCC for an infirm mangler whose customers had all deserted; and she demanded that a cobbler of Turville Street be found a new room with sufficient light for him to be able to carry on his trade. But the LCC began to suspect that Loveridge's kind nature was being

The demolished Nichol, looking east, with the new estate under construction. In the distance is St Philip's, Mount Street; in the centre, the circular garden mound is taking shape, and the foundations of Shiplake Buildings are in place.

taken advantage of with a series of sob stories, and the Council found itself falling back on the sort of judgmentalism that Progressivism had been intended to supplant. As landlord, the LCC decided to evict one Mr Ellis, his wife, and four late-adolescent offspring from their one-room home at 77 Mount Street because of their 'noisy and riotous behaviour'. And the valuer scratched his head for weeks over the 'peculiar case' of Mrs Cox, a widow of seventy-seven, dependent on irregular handouts from her relatives but about to be evicted from 6 Half Nichol Street. 'She is a very respectable woman and has lived in the area all her life,' he wrote, fearing that the £2 gratuity she was about to be paid would only delay by a short while her application to the House. So because of her respectability Mrs Cox was allowed to stay in the Nichol rent-free as long as possible. Progressive policy was crumbling into a series of *ad hoc* moral judgements: there was the sound of ideals crashing to earth.

The Council had had high hopes that a private philanthropic housing scheme in Columbia Road, just north of the Nichol, would provide a pressure valve as the evictions got under way. The Guinness Trust was a new arrival in the working-class tenements business, and in 1892 was completing the Columbia Road development, to house 1,500 people in six-storey-high blocks on a small triangular site (of which Dr Murphy did not approve, as the height and closeness of the blocks threw shadows all round and made all the rooms extremely gloomy). The Guinness Trust rents were within range of Nichol residents (at 2s 6d for one small room; 2s 9d for a large; 4s 3d–4s 6d for two rooms; chimney-sweeping, hot water, blinds and baths cost extra), and indeed the rooms were only supposed to be let to those who earned less than the poverty-line wage; the Trust had even supplied thirteen sheds that costers could use for their donkeys. But the list of rules for the tenements was fearsome: no animals; no clothes-washing within rooms; no noise from children; no ball games; no disorderly or intemperate conduct; enforced cleaning of common space; regular room checks by Trust agents; all rents to be paid in advance and no arrears allowed. The Guinness Trust told the LCC that Nichol evictees were welcome to apply for these tenements, using the 'usual channel' of its application form plus interview. But when Mrs Dalla of 45 Jacob Street revealed that neither she nor her husband could write, and so could not manage the application form, the Trust superintendent refused them a place. The LCC became involved on behalf of the Dallas, asking the Trust to allow them to mark their form with an 'X' after an interview, but it is clear from the exchange of letters that the Trust simply did not want them on their estate, nor any applicants whose previous address was in the Nichol – not even if they were able to acquire a written testimonial from a 'respectable' member of society.

During all these delays, the LCC Architects Department had been reconsidering its plans. The Boundary Street Scheme was originally envisaged as a straightforward rebuilding of the Nichol streets on their existing grid system, with the new streets being much wider and with no courts or alleyways running between. But as the hitches in clearance continued, a much more imaginative and picturesque reconfiguration evolved on the drawing boards: a central ornamental garden upon a small hillock, from which would radiate seven 40–60ft-wide avenues, lined with stately apartment blocks in red brick with honey-coloured brick stripes, terracotta mouldings, soaring chimneys, large gables, and turrets with elegant little bay windows. Nothing like this

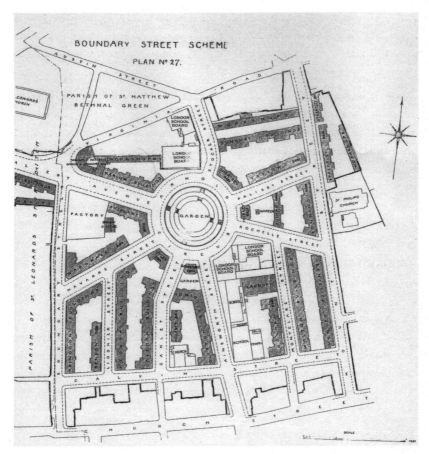

The reconfigured Nichol: seven broad, tree-lined avenues radiate from a raised garden. Streets are far wider, and surveillance and visibility are assured by the absence of courts and alleyways. The new estate was 'dry', reflecting the Council's temperance agenda.

had ever been contemplated for housing the poor. Too often, philanthropic housing looked like a punishment inflicted upon the poor – an unconscious carrying over of prison-like attributes to the design of tenement blocks. But these structures had more in common with Norman Shaw's exorbitantly priced Albert Hall Mansions apartments than with the barracks of Peabody and other charitable companies.

Comparing a map of the Nichol to the radial plan provides an idea of how reckless such generous amounts of open space between buildings may have looked in 1893: a squandering of land in an area where every inch had been rack-rented, and exhausted for decades by overuse. In fact, the new scheme would not cost more money than the original grid plan, despite its soaring aesthetic standard. However, the Home Secretary (by now the Liberal prime minister-to-be Herbert Asquith), whose personal approval had to be sought for every modification to the Boundary Street Scheme, thought that the circus looked 'hardly large enough to justify the inconvenience and the cost'.[4] But he gave his approval, nevertheless.

These new plans forced high on to the agenda a worrying matter that the Progressives had so far failed to address seriously: for whom was the estate being built? The 1891 Boundary Street Scheme Act of parliament stated that 5,100 'persons belonging to the working class' were to be rehoused in the new buildings: but which working class? It is clear from the September 1892 letter, on page 253, from R. Linette, S. Polo et al. that it was believed that whatever new buildings were erected would be homes for any Nichol locals who wanted to stay on – that this would be affordable, sanitary housing which simply replaced the hovels that were being torn down. Certainly, this is what local MP Pickersgill and LCC councillors Branch and Harrison had been trumpeting around the district. While minutes from the LCC's Housing of the Working Classes Committee show that it was hoped that as many Nichol people as possible would take advantage of the disruption to start a new life in the growing eastern and north-eastern London suburbs, it was expected – perhaps just assumed – that the majority of those displaced would resettle in the new Nichol. The LCC was committed to charging rents that were in line with those within the vicinity of the Nichol, in order to keep the new blocks affordable to the poor and to avoid the mistakes of the past, when 'a better class' of tenant had moved into new model dwellings built on the site of demolished rookeries. The LCC Architects Department and the Housing of the Working Classes Committee were fully aware of the dilemma of building for the very poorest. The arguments had been well rehearsed for years. The February 1875 parliamentary debate on the Cross Act had revealed that there was strong opposition to the fact that philanthropic companies built and accommodated only the 'respectable' poor, and that even the Peabody Trust – whose rents were the cheapest available – did not tend to house the very-poor. The Peabody chairman, Sir Curtis Lampson, admitted, 'Our trust does not deal with them at all.'[5]

The prevailing argument in the 1870s and 1880s had been that the 'worst class' of tenants would routinely effect the deterioration of new tenements; that their behaviour would drive out all other types of resident and that before long, colonies of the unruly would build up and a whole block would be morally and behaviourally beyond the pale. In any case, ran this argument, the 'worst' refused to enter housing that had rules and regulations and a resident superintendent. Supporters of this point of view (most notably flint-hearted philanthropist Octavia Hill, who provided housing to the poor, with her team of lady wardens keeping strict watch on residents) justified the demolition-and-rebuild programmes with the 'levelling-up' theory. Believers in levelling-up supposed that attracting a better class of working family into brand-new tenements would leave the rooms vacated by these people free to be taken up by the poorest, and so in this way, everybody obtained better homes – homes suitable to their station in life.

Boundary Street was supposed to be a new leaf, improving the conditions of the very people who originally occupied the land, instead of attracting those who could already afford to rent decent homes. The LCC Progressives believed that the physical and moral salvation of the poorest was possible through environmental change (the very opposite of the Jay/Morrison eugenicist view of the ineradicability of depravity). Surveyor Cubitt Nichols reported to Home Secretary Asquith that 'the object of the Council in altering the arrangement of streets [the radial plan] is in the hope of raising the character of the neighbouring occupants, by improving their surroundings, in planting trees in the streets and in the central open space reserved for that purpose. I think it an experiment well worth trying'.[6] Owen Fleming, the LCC architect-in-charge of the Boundary Street Scheme, envisaged happy couples promenading in the ornamental gardens after a hard day's artisanal toil by the head of the family, as music from a central bandstand played. Fresh air would sweep up the avenues; sunlight would pour into every home. Specially designed workshops sited to the rear of the northernmost blocks would mean that work no longer had to be undertaken within the home. A huge central laundry and a communal bakery took care of the old problem of clothes-washing and food preparation in residential space.

Each block was to be named after a town or village westwards along old Father Thames: Taplow, Sunbury, Marlow, Wargrave, and so forth. The radiating streets were to have Huguenot names, recalling

This drawing from the LCC Architects Department shows the Arts & Crafts and Queen Anne Revival influences of the Boundary Street apartment blocks. Detractors called it 'Stripeland'.

the noble artisan past of these fifteen acres before they were professionally and physically desolated by nineteenth-century market forces. More prosaically, the central garden would be called Arnold Circus, commemorating the new head of the LCC Main Drainage Committee, Arthur Arnold.

One of the early LCC's many initiatives was to increase the acreage of open spaces and gardens in poor districts (there was half as much open ground per inhabitant in East London as in West), and it allowed itself an annual budget of £4,000 for this purpose. This move was partly influenced by the temperance wing of the Progressives, who strongly believed that both wholesome surroundings (better homes, more parks) and 'rational' leisure pursuits (bicycling, football) would be key to keeping the poor out of the pub in their non-working hours. Arnold Circus would provide *rus in urbe* – but not the kind that already existed in the Nichol, the indiscriminate mixing of the outdoor (birds, animals, plants) with the indoor, and the vestiges of Romany wandering that the didicai had brought to this part of Bethnal Green when they settled, or semi-settled. The countryside would be brought to town in a pretty, polite, tame and whimsical way.

Owen Fleming (1867–1955) was an idealist who had lived for many years, by choice, in a working-class tenement on Stepney Green, having felt the need to study the poor close up. As a young man, Fleming had felt 'oppressed by the chain of circumstances that had compelled so many of the poor to live in insanitary dwellings. We were trying to get to the bottom of things'.[7] It was with this zeal that Fleming and his young and gifted team of nineteen architects set out to redraw the Nichol map, believing that in working-class housing 'some attention should be given to external appearance . . . the inhabitants would appreciate it . . . Take a walk from Hackney to Bethnal Green, Mile End, Poplar or Bow, and they would see just a long row of dreary monotony, all the houses being precisely the same, without any sort of architectural feeling at all.'[8] The central garden, with bandstand, was Fleming's way of showing that the estate should be a community, and not just a collection of squared-off blocks of flats with no relation to each other. The LCC architects, romantic–Socialist in outlook, peered into history to find a vocabulary of shapes, colours and textures that would express humanity in social building – English humanity. Of the Boundary Street designers, many had established, or would go on to establish, links with the restoration and recording of churches and old, vernacular buildings; some would interest themselves in the English folk movement.[9] Their new designs were a blending of the Arts & Crafts tradition of Ruskin, Morris and Philip Webb and the more urbane Queen Anne Revival, popularised at the upper end of the market by Norman Shaw and in poor districts by London School Board architect E.R. Robson, who saw his lofty, elegant red-brick school buildings as beacons of civility and aspiration sited right in the heart of London's slum areas. The Boundary Street flats could also be viewed in this light – as somewhere to aspire to. Their beauty would derive from simplicity, with ordinary, traditional local materials – such as the brick that gave Brick Lane its name – honestly used.

However, at no point in the Boundary Street story were the potential residents consulted about their needs or preferences; even the most sympathetic men (as typified by Fleming and his team) never thought to inquire directly what they felt about their homes, and so the long debates about self-containment, room sizes, utilities, maintenance and so on went on between designers, politicians and accountants. 'Mistakes' or the inappropriateness of buildings were detected only with hindsight.

Would the utopian workers' village that the Architects Department now had in mind be suited to the people of the Nichol? These did not look like homes for hawkers, washerwomen, charwomen or costers. (How on earth would you get a donkey up to the fourth floor?) When the very first LCC block was being finished off in July 1896 (Streatley Buildings, halfway up Mount Street, a comparatively severe affair and demolished in 1971), 140 selected people among the evicted were given first refusal on a tenement in the block, but only ten took up the Council's offer. Among their reasons for refusal were that the rent was higher than that charged for their old Nichol homes; they also felt that there were not enough yards, sheds and workshop facilities, and many stated that they preferred the freedom to come and go as they pleased rather than accept the rules and regulations that block life imposed. So while the Council was cherry-picking its potential residents from the evicted, the majority of the evicted were ruling themselves out of the new vision for Boundary Street, partly voluntarily and partly because it was simply too expensive.

So had the Council been speaking with a forked tongue in claiming that it was planning to rehouse the evicted? It seems that by the summer of 1896 the Progressives had backtracked. The American Academy of Political and Social Sciences had taken an interest in the scheme and had asked for further information. In the June of that year the LCC sent a report to the Academy, stating that

in consequence of the raising influence of the reconstruction of such a large area it is found difficult to let the dwellings to the class of persons who have been displaced. In many cases the people have been so long accustomed to live in dirty rooms that they can not be induced to keep these rooms clean, nor do they desire to live in rooms of this class. In fact, they very rarely apply for these dwellings and as many months must elapse between the time when they are turned out of the unwholesome dwellings and the time the new dwellings are ready, they have generally succeeded in establishing themselves in other houses of a description somewhat similar to those they have lived in.

The new dwellings are, however, always let to persons of the working class, and it is hoped that in course of time they will cause a marked improvement in the kind of accommodation provided for that class . . . Many of the inhabitants were of a very low type, but some were the honest working class, such as costermongers, machinists, market porters, toy-makers, warehousemen and others engaged in kindred occupations.[10]

This point of view was never circulated in Britain at the time, but it indicates that the LCC had already changed its mind about what it was attempting to achieve at Boundary Street.

Crucially, the financial implications of the scheme were by now becoming clearer, making it increasingly apparent that the affordability of accommodation could not be sustained. The Council had pledged never to subsidise the Boundary Street rents out of the local rates, yet needed to make enough profit at Boundary Street to cover debt repayment, which the Treasury had demanded be paid off within fifty-five years, rather than the 100 years that the Council had requested. Low rents, high-quality new buildings, and strict debt payment terms were irreconcilable. First to fall was the design standard: five storeys rather than a maximum of four were now factored in; and where self-containment had been key to the original plans – granting families privacy and dignity behind their own front door – more and more flats were downgraded to having shared WCs, baths and sculleries. (All these alterations had to be personally ratified by Asquith, who held the scheme up for weeks at a time, poring over and minutely debating with the LCC various designs for Boundary Street WCs, dustbins and fire escapes while the second Home Rule crisis raged around him.)

As building got under way, the costs of bricks (many of them hand-made, rather than the machine production so abhorred by Arts & Crafts devotees), steel, Portland cement, slate, York stone paving, smooth-grained oak for floorboards, lead, zinc and labour soared, and Fleming recalled days-long frosts and violent storms adding to the problems of creating 'the great structure'.[11] Because of complaints by the tenants in the earliest blocks to be completed, the Home Secretary (a new one by now) increased minimum room sizes, and so costs rose yet again. A new Building Act increased the thickness of walls; while another meant that more sinks had to be provided within tenements. Then the directly employed labour began to act up: the carpenters went on strike in the spring of 1896. Barely had they gone back to work when the plasterers and plasterers' labourers downed tools. Then the plumbers refused to work alongside plumbers from a rival union, and would hear no talk of work on the estate being given to local out-of-work Bethnal Green men. Dock Strike hero Ben Tillett (by now an LCC alderman) threatened to call in an outside contractor for Boundary Street if the plumbers would not end their calls for a closed shop. So much for solidarity.

On Saturday 3 March 1900, seven years after the first demolitions in the Nichol, the Prince of Wales with his princess, Alexandra, passed in their carriage along Calvert Avenue – decorated with Venetian masts, streamers and Union Jacks and lined with cheering crowds – into the new Nichol. They then proceeded to a large tented pavilion to the south of the circus, and the Prince spoke. He reprised Arthur Morrison's lies, emphasised his own long-standing fascination with the housing of the working classes, name-checked the Reverend Jay, urged the laying on of more workmen's cheap and early trains to the suburbs so that the poor would not need to huddle so close to town, and declared the Boundary Street Estate to be formally open. The band of the 4th East Surrey Rifle Volunteers (under Mr A.R. Spriggs) played 'Reminiscences of Offenbach', 'Cheer Up, Never Say Die!', 'Jolly Little Polly' and 'Chiko, Choko, Chikkori'. Ticket-holders were then free to go and nosy around the new flats, to see what all the fuss had been about all these years.

Epilogue

Around the Bandstand

Just eleven of the 5,719 evicted Nichol residents moved into 'Stripeland' – the nickname given to the new flats by the *British Architect* magazine.[1] While the LCC had indeed kept rents to the average charged in Bethnal Green and Shoreditch, only fifteen of the 1,069 new tenements were one-room dwellings, where the Nichol had had 752 single rooms housing nearly half its population. The strict overcrowding regulations that the Council as landlord applied to the Boundary Street Estate made the 900 or so two- and three-room flats unaffordable to those who had habitually had to pack tight together, sublet, and simply lie about the number of children in the family in order to be able to meet their weekly rent payments. Some 34 per cent of Nichol people could not have afforded even a single room on the estate, and a further 43 per cent could have managed to pay for one room only.[2]

As a rehousing scheme for the poor, Boundary Street was a red elephant – a very beautiful one: a role model for the latest in sanitary science and affordable aesthetics, but as an improvement to the lives of the locals, a disaster. As had happened during the preceding three decades with philanthropic housing, the fully employed, and even the lower-middle classes, put their names down for the new flats and were accepted by a delighted and relieved County Council, who would not now have to deal with 'the real thing' (Dr Bate's phrase) – the very-poor.

Where did *they* go? The Council made early attempts to keep track of the new addresses of the evicted but gave up its record-keeping in the summer of 1895. At that time it was stated that of 1,035 Nichol people whose movements were known, 56 per cent had moved within a quarter of a mile of their old home, 30 per cent between a quarter and half a mile, 9 per cent between half and one mile, and just 5 per cent had gone more than a mile away. This disappointed many observers, who disparaged the 'clannish' nature of the Nichol and the refusal to disperse to the suburbs – to cleaner air, wider streets, isolation behind the family front door. There was no understanding of how bound up small trades were with their established systems of credit and goodwill, proximity to employers, wholesale markets, ancillary workers and related trades – no realisation that in the terrifying bleakness of the East End labour market and the inadequacy of the Poor Law, kin and companions could mean the difference between life and death. These were not portable people, a crucial characteristic that had been entirely overlooked.

Beyond the 1895 LCC figures there is anecdotal evidence of the 'curious shuffling' (Charles Booth's description) that the new estate had caused among the populations of south-west Bethnal Green and eastern Shoreditch. As the Nichol-dwellers packed into the already overcrowded immediate vicinity they managed to oust many who decided they would prefer not to live amongst them, and so headed off to Hackney, Walthamstow and Dalston; some even decided to try block-living on the Boundary Street Estate. Various commentators swore that the Nichol people had contaminated their new environments – by thieving, being rowdy and simply poorer than their new neighbours. Charles Booth updated his Poverty Map for the 1902 reprint of *Life and Labour*, and the Boundary Street Estate was a very pretty pale pink, while Church Street had turned from pink to black, as had many of the streets into which the Nichol people had been condensed. Police Constable W. Ryeland, taking Booth investigator George Duckworth on a night walk on 10 May 1898, toured the black spots around the former Nichol, attributing these streets' darkening to 'deterioration due to immigration of thieves and housebreakers from the Boundary Street area'.[3]

The region's men of God had mixed feelings about all this: on the one hand, the arrivals from the Nichol brought new challenges – more *raisons d'être* for missionary work; but on the other, they feared the moral infection they might bring into their established congregations. Father Jay, Reverend Loveridge and the London City Mission's Robert Allinson all found their flocks severely depleted by the population movements, although many of their old Nichol faithful returned to visit them regularly. Allinson complained bitterly that the new flats

The Estate shortly before the erection of the central bandstand, looking eastwards.

were home to people who were 'better off, and think themselves above missions'.[4]

The estate was very popular with shopworkers, teachers, foremen, policemen and nurses (even a vicar or two moved in around the bandstand), who became the romanticised strollers of the leafy boulevards of Owen Fleming's imagination. There was widespread criticism that so much effort and money had gone into providing 'a nice little house at a very low rent, at the expense of the rates, to railway guards, clerks, teachers, clerks of works', as fellow of the Royal Institute of British Architects Henry Lovegrove put it, in 1900, 'while the people who were living from hand to mouth, getting a job where they could in the streets, had to crowd in miserable dwellings, because the buildings intended for them could not be designed for their needs'. Lovegrove claimed to have inspected some of the homes the evicted had moved into, and found one family of five inhabiting a scullery.[5]

Now on the defensive, Owen Fleming fell back on the old spurious 'levelling-up' argument and, once again, the Progressives found themselves closer than they might have liked in thought and deed to the old hierarchical and judgmental attitudes to the very-poor. Fleming

Residents in the Estate's large central laundry.

wriggled, and responded that it was 'theoretically unsound and prac-
tically impossible to build the new buildings down to the low standard of sanitation required by the displaced persons. Far more good
was done by providing accommodation at a higher standard.'[6]

At a Royal Commission convened at the start of the twentieth
century, the LCC's Dr Murphy was asked: 'You have got rid of an
unhealthy slum, and you have put up in its place artisans' dwellings,
so attractive as to provide for policemen, postmen, and men of a
higher class. Is that an advantage to the district do you think? Is it not
attracting that class from other districts?' Murphy replied, 'I dare say
it is attractive to people from outside.' It was the nature of these
'outsiders' that had prompted the Commission in the first place:
Murphy was actually testifying to the 1903 Royal Commission on Alien
Immigration, set up to explore the effects of foreign settlement on
the living and working conditions of the British labouring man. While
the true level of popularity of the Boundary Street flats among Jewish
families would never be firmly established, many of the 'anti-alien'
viewpoint were keen to exploit the apparent 'ousting' of the
British/London-Irish population by east European Jews. Father Jay
claimed the figure of 60 per cent Jewish tenancy in the new flats. A

map to accompany the 1900 book *The Jew in London,* by H.S. Lewis and C. Russell, contained a Booth-style colour-coded map, with Jewish populations featuring as dark blue to bright pink according to density; this suggests that the estate in some parts was 50 per cent Jewish, and in others was overwhelmingly gentile. The LCC's Stepney member A.T. Williams, giving evidence to the Royal Commission, had documentation that suggested the figure of 19 per cent, although he was not able to say whether these were recent arrivals or long-established English Jewry. Oddly, though, the LCC's Housing of the Working Classes Committee had come up with the higher figure of 27 per cent occupancy by people 'who would appear by their names to be foreigners', for the year ending 1902, in a minute dated 17 March 1903.[7] Williams was asked by the Royal Commission: 'Your point now is that these great building schemes that are prima facie for the native population are gradually benefiting in part at least the alien immigrants from abroad?' and he replied, 'Yes, that is my point.' 'And consequently that these great schemes form, and continue to form, one of the many attractions which would attract foreigners to this country?' 'Certainly.'[8]

Boundary Street had quite a starring role at the Royal Commission, and in February 1903 Bethnal Green South West Conservative & Unionist MP Samuel Forde Ridley – an anti-immigration campaigner – brought the subject of the estate up in parliament, stating that it was 'grotesque' that British workmen had been cast out so that 'alien families' could be 'comfortably ensconced in these dwellings'.[9] Ridley was keen to make use of the Boundary Street issue to press for restrictions on foreign immigration, a movement that was ultimately successful with the passing of the 1905 Aliens Act, Britain's first immigration legislation. Ridley's wild accusation was that the LCC built for the foreigner, and that he stood in parliament in an attempt 'to mitigate the national curse of this country – namely, that of being made the dumping ground of foreign criminals, from whatever country they may come'.[10] But the Jewish families were shown no special favour by the LCC, and they were as likely to be ejected for failure to keep the premises sanitary as any gentile family; there was no truth in the story that Ridley whipped up and made use of in parliament that Jews could afford to live on the estate because they habitually lived in overcrowded conditions and the LCC either failed to spot this or failed to act on it. Evictions in the early years of the estate were frequent and prompt, with no distinction made according to the ethnicity of the residents.

The anti-aliens also preferred to ignore the fact that block living had a longer heritage in Continental countries: the purpose-built flat was still a newish phenomenon in British cities in the dying years of the nineteenth century.[11] (Even today, in this country, the overwhelming stated preference of housing type is the bungalow and the cottage.) The presence of a resident superintendent and an agreed code of behaviour to adhere to were – to generalise – perhaps less irksome and less strange to newcomers to London than to the wilder-hearted native Londoner or didicai descendant.

The LCC went on to undertake eleven more slum clearance and rebuilding projects across London but the only one comparable in size and grandeur to Boundary Street was the Millbank Estate. The early-nineteenth-century 'Panopticon' prison, Millbank Penitentiary, was bought and demolished for the blocks that still stand today – magnificent, though a faint echo of glorious Boundary Street. Here, too, rents were too high for the local poor, and only two one-room flats were constructed.

Dr Bate and his team were disgusted with the LCC. The Council attempted no other major clearance in the increasingly overcrowded Bethnal Green, and Bate bitterly concluded that the Progressives had only been interested in constructing great show-off complexes: 'They [the LCC] form to a certain extent a mutual admiration society. They are not particularly anxious to clear areas in back slums, but prefer public improvement schemes in prominent positions to which they can refer for their own glorification.'[12] Bate and his deputy felt embattled by the LCC, who on the one hand were demanding the implementation of increasingly stringent regulations on overcrowding but on the other were failing to supply more affordable housing in the East End. By the turn of the century there were 8,000 more people than lodgings to house them in Bethnal Green, rents had soared by 26.9 per cent since the 1880s (the London average rise was 12 per cent), and Bate and his team cited the thousands made homeless from the Nichol as a major contributor to this latest crisis.

In the ten years before the Great War froze all endeavours and wrought such changes on the nation's social fabric, the LCC began a new policy of buying vacant land in the suburbs and creating cottage estates. These depended on cheaper offpeak train and tram fares for the working man to be able to get into town to his workplace, and parliament had to become involved to coerce the rail companies to keep to their legal requirement to run such services.

The Progressives stayed in power for the first eighteen years of the LCC's existence; but Boundary Street was symbolic of why they were ousted in 1907 by the Conservative faction – now renamed Municipal Reform – who would control the government of London for the next twenty-seven years. Under the Progressives, rates had risen by 160 per cent, while London property values had fallen some 40 per cent. The soaring rates were not all the LCC's fault: the national government had tinkered with its funding to the capital, and consistently failed to back the Council's ambitions, regardless of whether Whitehall was Tory or Liberal dominated. But that cut no ice with the London electorate, who saw their rates and rents rising for such projects as fine houses for new immigrants (as the right-wing press depicted it), and all sorts of interfering inspectorates. Increasingly, the puritan arm of Progressivism was making itself felt in London life: the charge of nosy-parkerism and red tape could with justification be levied against such activities as their interference in music hall performances; the fixing of shop opening hours; the fumigation of homes and people deemed to be verminous. All of these expensive intrusions into London life provided an open goal for a hostile Tory press, in particular the virulent attacks by the Harmsworth Press in its bestselling new newspaper, the *Daily Mail*, which persistently made an Aunt Sally of Progressivism. The newly invigorated and fantastically wealthy London Tory associations distributed 16 million pamphlets on the expense and wastefulness of the Progressives, while 369 different posters were designed to convey the same message. A fleet of thirty very expensive and barely used LCC steamboats on the Thames, with such heritage names as *King Alfred*, *Shakespeare*, *Charles Lamb* and *William Morris*, were launched in 1905; this seemed to be a utopian eccentricity too far, and Progressivism was scuppered for good. And the Progressives' failure to be more radical – more centralising; more willing to challenge the social and financial status quo – meant that they could not rely on the support of the emergent Labour faction,

THE MARQUIS AND THE MUNICIPAL MONSTER.

SALISBURY FRANKENSTEIN. "SORRY I EVER PUT YOU TOGETHER, YOU GREAT HULKING BOOBY! BUT
JUST YOU WAIT A BIT. I'LL SOON TAKE YOU TO PIECES AGAIN!"

The prime minister, Lord Salisbury, who had mistakenly thought that London was Conservative at heart, was alarmed at the Radical new administrative body that he had brought into being. In 1899 he created a strong new second-tier of London metropolitan boroughs, undermining the LCC and fragmenting London local government.

who felt that they should have gone much further to redress inequalities of income and ownership.

Tellingly, though, the Conservatives at the LCC were also unable to keep the rates down, and made a series of their own blunders, particularly with education and transport. (They also spent a small fortune on commissioning a coat of arms for the LCC.) When they had gained control of the Council, the Conservatives also reluctantly accepted the principle of municipal housing and buckled down to implementing Progressive-inspired policies on slum clearance and suburbanisation for East Enders.

The London of today has much to thank the early LCC for – not least some wonderful examples of the built environment. Boundary Street is holding up even better than its design team could have imagined, and there is no reason why the estate should not be good for at least another century. The Luftwaffe raid that did for Holy Trinity church – four years before Father Jay's death, at the age of eighty-seven – took out the top storeys of six of the tenement blocks, but they were restored. Today, the flats are home to three communities, the Bangladeshi, the traditional white Bethnal Greeners, and middle-class incomers, many of them connected to the art world that has found a home in neighbouring Shoreditch and Hoxton. Residents of the flats are repeatedly requested by Tower Hamlets Council to vote to transfer the stock into housing association ownership, which would relieve the local authority of the estate's high maintenance costs – the price of being Grade II* listed. They repeatedly refuse.

Nothing remains of the vanished world of the Nichol – save its ill-deserved reputation for evil, still talked of in some East London families. Its physical remains lie beneath the bandstand – the rubble was used to create the picturesque mound of Arnold Circus – and overhead, the LCC's saplings have grown into a vast canopy of green.

So what do we make of all this? This has been a voyeuristic book about voyeurism – an examination of who went into the slum, and why. What, if anything, did their various responses to late-nineteenth-century chronic poverty achieve? It's clear that philanthropic interventions from outside did not, could not, solve a problem like the Nichol. However, *not* to have intervened when the unfettered Market was wreaking such havoc would have been indefensible. A few individuals had their life prolonged, a medical condition eased or a horizon broadened, by one of the more imaginative philanthropists, such as Father Jay, or more State-linked interventionists, such as the dedicated and sympathetic schoolteachers and the officials of the NSPCC. The more significant achievement of the outsiders who came to the Nichol and to the other pockets of deep deprivation was the steady accumulation of data – both dry figures and startling anecdote – that eventually led to moves toward greater social justice at both local and national government level. Among the slum travellers to East London were William Beveridge (who had been a warden at Whitechapel's Toynbee Hall university settlement), whose authoritative reports on social and employment conditions were a keystone of the modern welfare state; and Clement Attlee – who ran the Stepney Mission for poor boys for fourteen years, from 1905. Many other less-well-known figures together slowly created a climate of informed and unhysterical discussion of poverty and class relations, permeating governmental committees and getting their views published by newspapers and periodicals of influence. The Nichol can take its place among the observation posts from which solutions of sorts began to be discovered by disparate individuals and groups pushing for change.

Along with a more humane welfarism, a huge machinery of State inspectorates and other forms of policing citizens' lives was created, and remains with us today. The extent to which the State may have undermined the poor's self-reliance and mutuality continues to be debated, with many commentators fingering the welfare state as the creator of an outcast underclass. I hope that if this book does anything, it will encourage those with such views to ponder the historical fact that outcasts were created in their hundreds of thousands in the nineteenth century precisely because individuals were left entirely to fend for themselves. Recent years have also seen a return to the pernicious, class-based social Darwinism of the late 1880s, with calls for the early detection of criminality and anti-social tendencies among the poorest; there are even hopes this can be undertaken *in utero*, so that the State can intervene to 'help' these pre-damned infants of our early-twenty-first-century underclass.

The desperate, extreme poverty seen in the Nichol in the late 1880s began to become less common in London by the turn of the century (London slum photographs taken after 1900 tend less often to feature the shoeless children of the previous three decades' pictures). This is not to say that deep, chronic distress was eradicated; but in relative terms (even during the Depressions of the 1920s and 1930s), Nichol-style destitution, and the scale of population affected by it, were history by the time of the outbreak of World War I. Grotesque levels of inequality characterise Britain – it's one of our traditions – and our own age is witnessing the ever more obscene widening of the gap between wealthy and otherwise, while our love affair with cheap

CENTRAL GARDEN · BOUNDARY STREET AREA

labour continues. Capitalism is as red in tooth and claw as it ever was in the nineteenth century. But on every available indicator, there has been no large-scale return to the deadly conditions described in this book – we have outsourced them offshore, to countries where the battles for fair wages and fair rents are just getting under way.

Who or what can we thank for the gradual improvement in the lives of the very-poor in Britain? Several intermingled factors suggest themselves. Trade improved from the mid-1890s, and real wages rose significantly at the same time that real prices began to fall. The Liberal Party was returned to power in a landslide general election victory in 1906, and was now dominated by its Radical wing and propped up by twenty-four members of the Labour Representation Committee (the forerunner of the Independent Labour Party). When Asquith became prime minister in 1908, a flurry of parliamentary activity saw the formation of a welfare state of sorts that slowly, slowly began to lift various sections of the community out of the Poor Law and charity loop. Old age pensions began in 1908, national insurance in 1911, a series of Rent Acts to limit exorbitant rises from 1915. The feeding and medical inspection of schoolchildren, shorter working hours, labour exchanges and sweated-labour wage-protection measures were put in place, while Lloyd George's controversial 'People's Budget' of 1909 raised taxes paid by the wealthy on their income and property. As Charles Booth had hoped, the limited form of 'Socialism' of 1906–14 did indeed reinvigorate British industry, with a more 'efficient' and healthier pool of labour, and just enough sops thrown to the poorest workers to deflate any talk of revolution.

The performance of the nation's working men in the Trenches (the class that suffered the overwhelming proportion of casualties in World War I) brought the lions led by donkeys a new-found confidence to challenge the status quo. What's more, the war demonstrated that the *lumpen* did not exist – the chronic labour shortages on the home front absorbed all those who had previously been considered unemployable.[13]

The increasing democratisation of the Poor Law Guardians and every tier of local government gave labouring-class men and women a greater say in the government of their own lives. This opening up of administrative structures was brought about by the combined efforts of the settlers and travellers in the slums and the Radical-leaning working men and women, determined to oust the shopocracies and reconnect local administration with those whose need was greatest.

Arthur Harding didn't approve of some of these cultural shifts. The consumerist aspirationalism and craving for 'respectability' arising from better wages, lower prices and the percolating through of thirty years of Board School education turned many of the poor into selfish show-offs, in his view. Sniffily, he noted his own mother's new mania, around 1902, for ornaments and knick-knacks (a china clock was her ultimate ambition), and recognised that a significant change in mentality was taking place among many who had shared his Nichol background. Let's give the final word to Arthur, our unreliable narrator: 'The poor were the salt of the earth, you know. There was nobody like the poor, I mean, they don't show off, you know. The blocks of flats have ruined them.'[14]

Appendix 1

Average Wages and Prices in the Poorest Parts of the East End, 1880s–90s

There were 12 pence (12d) in one shilling (1s). There were 20 shillings in £1.

WAGES

The 'Poverty Line': weekly subsistence wage for a family	18–21s
Hourly rate for building work	7d
Hourly rate for casual Dock work	4d
Weekly pay for female home-workers in small-manufacturing trades:	
learner	2s 6d–4s
'extra-clever' experienced hands	15–24s
Weekly pay for match-girl in a factory, mid-1890s	7s
Average parish 'out relief' per week for family of 5	9s 4d
Average 'out relief' per week for single person	2s 6d and two or three loaves

WEEKLY RENTS

A one-room home	2s 3d–3s
2 rooms	4s 4d
3 rooms	7s 6d

FOOD AND DRINK

Cup of tea or coffee	½d
Cake	2d a lb
Slice of bread and margarine	½d
Fish and chip supper	1 ½d–2d
Three-course lunch at a cheap restaurant	4d
Basin of soup	1d
Pint of beer	¾d
Bottle of whisky	7s 6d
Resale price of stolen bottle of whisky	2s 6d

OTHER

Man's suit	18s
Seat in the gallery of the music hall	3d
Doctor's appointment	6d
Home visit from a doctor (including prescription)	2s 6d
Omnibus fares: Bank of England to Hackney Road	2d
Bethnal Green to Trafalgar Square	4d
Child's funeral	30s
'Gates of Heaven' funeral wreath of best quality	50s
Fine for soliciting for prostitution	20s
Fine for failure to have child vaccinated	20s
A night with an East End street prostitute (indoors)	2s
A handgun	4–5s

Appendix 2

Table of Occupations of a Household's Main
Breadwinner in the Nichol, as surveyed by the London
County Council (working wives and other family
members do not figure in this data)

Box-makers	19	Labourers	149
Button-makers	5	Machinists	10
Cabinet-makers	120	Marble masons	23
Car-men	29	Market porters	31
Carpenters	10	Matchbox-makers	19
Cats'-meat sellers	2	Milkmen	3
Chair- and couch-makers	74	Mirror-makers	4
Chandlers' shops	10	Policemen	5
Charwomen	11	Sawyers	24
Coalmen	6	Shoemakers	74
Costers	23	Stick- and toy-makers	12
Dressmakers	9	Upholsterers	24
French polishers	22	Washerwomen	33
General dealers	119	Weavers	12
Hawkers	126	Wheelwrights	5
Ivory and wood turners	12	Various	27
Japanners and wire workers	5		

Source: London County Council *Minutes of Proceedings of the Council*,
July–December 1890, p. 911

Appendix 3

Poor Law data, 1887–88

On the first day of 1888, 831,353 people were receiving assistance nationally, of whom 206,134 were in the workhouse, while 625,067 were getting out-relief (152 people had received both within the same year). The total cost to the nation for the year to 1 January 1888 had been over £8 million, with £1,778,367 spent on workhouse accommodation; £2,528,250 on out-relief; £1,159,750 on insane asylums; and the remaining £2.7 million on staff salaries and loan repayments. These national figures were unremarkable, and showed that little change in numbers assisted and money spent had taken place since the start of the decade.

Of these 831,353 people who were 'on the parish', some 71,854 were insane; 5,844 were vagrants; and 268,369 were children under the age of sixteen. Some 372,905 men and women were ill, disabled or too old to work; and of the remaining adults, 19,206 men were 'able-bodied' males and 64,690 'able-bodied' females on outdoor relief. Of these men, 11,190 were described as suffering from a temporary disability; 204 had 'sudden and urgent necessity' (which was not explained further in the survey notes); 4,258 had suffered a family illness or funeral (an expensive item in a working-class budget); while 3,554 were described as 'unemployed'.

Of the 64,690 able-bodied women on outdoor relief in England and Wales, 41,318 were widows; 15,532 were wives of able-bodied men on parish relief; 3,556 had been abandoned by their husbands; 449 were 'the mothers of bastards'; 975 were wives of men in prison, and 125 were the wives of soldiers or sailors.

The regional figures showed that London had the country's highest rate of workhouse paupers per head of population (with 59,347 in the House at the end of 1887) and the lowest number on out-relief (44,750). In the previous July, London figures had been lower, with 52,656 in the workhouses and

34,480 on outdoor relief, making a total summer parish-assisted population of 87,136.

Source: *The Seventeenth Annual Report of the Local Government Board 1887–1888*, 1888, Volume XLIX [C 5526], p.xxxvii.

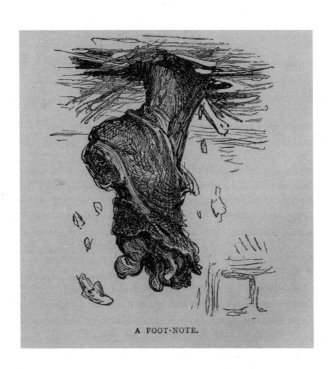

A FOOT-NOTE.

Notes

All items were published in London, unless otherwise stated.

The Empire of Hunger

1   *The Anarchists: A Picture of Civilization at the Close of the Nineteenth Century*
by John Henry Mackay, Boston, 1891, pp.161–9; reissued 1999 by
Autonomedia Black Triangle Anti-Authoritarian Classics, New York,
edited by Mark A. Sullivan.

   The Anarchists is a novelised semi-autobiography. Author Mackay
himself is the Anarchist who is taken to the Old Nichol by his friend,
who has been identified as Erich Otto Rinke (1853–99), known as 'Big
Otto'. Rinke was a German revolutionary who moved first to London
and then to the United States, unable to bear any longer the scrutiny
of London's police detectives. Rinke was on the Communist wing of
the international Anarchist movement, while Mackay had shifted to the
individualist libertarian end of the Anarchist spectrum of beliefs. *The
Anarchists* is in part concerned with the attempt by Mackay to win over
Rinke, and other Communists, to his way of thinking.

   Mackay was born in 1864 in Greenock, Scotland, to a Scottish father
and German mother, who, when widowed, took him to Hamburg,
where he was brought up in her wealthy family, with German as his
first language. Mackay first visited London in late spring 1887, the year
of Queen Victoria's Golden Jubilee and of mass demonstrations against
unemployment. This trip politicised Mackay, and he later wrote: 'It was
there, in London, where the great transformation in my seeing and
thinking took place, which was to give my life direction and my work
meaning' (p.viii of the 1999 reprint). He became an Anarchist but soon
split from the mainstream of the movement to embrace individualist
Anarchism, in which liberation of the self is the first and most important step towards dismantling the power structures of the State.

   Mackay was also a poet and lyricist and was called 'The First Singer
of Anarchy'; some of his songs were set to music by Richard Strauss.
From the early 1900s his 'Nameless Love' writings, published under the
pseudonym Sagitta, controversially celebrated homoerotic attractions
and relationships between adult men and teenage boys. Mackay died,
forgotten, in 1933 in Nazi Germany, possibly a suicide.

2   Source for Ann's Place bootmaker and family: *Later Leaves, Being Further Reminiscences of Montagu Williams QC* by Montagu Williams, 1891, pp.297–8.

Matchbox-making: *Recollections of a School Attendance Officer* by John Reeves, *c.* 1915, pp.55–7; *East End Underworld: Chapters in the Life of Arthur Harding* by Raphael Samuel, 1981, p.21; Charles Booth, *Life and Labour of the People in London,* Third Series: Religious Influences, Volume 2, *London North of the Thames: The Inner Ring,* 1902, Chapter V, 'Illustrations', p.238.

Coffin: Reeves's *Recollections,* p.57.

Collingwood Place overcrowding: *Eastern Argus,* 22 December 1883. The newspaper actually states '7 feet 3 inches by 4 feet square' – which must surely be a typographical error, since twelve individuals would be hard pushed even to stand upright in a room of such dimensions.

Livestock in living quarters: *Eastern Argus,* 7 December 1889; Williams's, *Later Leaves,* p.301.

Fish-smoking: Minute Books of the Bethnal Green Vestry Sanitary Committee in the Tower Hamlets Local History Library and Archive, L/MBG/B/4/9 [BG/574], Book no. 9, 1886–88, entry dated 6 April 1887.

The wool-trimming weavers: *Daily Telegraph,* 19 November 1889.

The former governess and the baronet's brother: *The Man with the Book; or, The Bible among the People* by John Matthias Weylland, 1872, pp.68–9.

Box, the dog-dealer: the London County Council's *Minutes of Proceedings of the Council,* January–December 1895, p.629; and the Booth Archives at the London School of Economics, Book A2, Rupert St Leger's survey of Half Nichol Street.

Bobby the chanter's son: Weylland's *The Man with the Book,* pp.9–10.

Charles Mowbray: *The Slow-Burning Fuse: The Lost History of the British Anarchists* by John Quail, 1978, p.38. Mowbray at this time considered himself to be an Anarchist–Communist, and knew Big Otto Rinke.

3   Death rates given in *The Housing Question in London, 1855–1900* by C.J. Stewart, 1900, p.192. London's death rate tended to be slightly lower than that of Britain's other major centres of population, and the capital's surprisingly average mortality figures were partly attributable to the creation of large specialist institutions for some of the most lethal afflictions, and perhaps also to the constant influx of rural migrants.

Bethnal Green had double the London rate of deaths from respiratory diseases, excluding TB; 26 per cent of all deaths in the parish were attributed to chest, lung and throat problems.

2006 England and Wales deaths per 1,000 data supplied by the Vital Statistics Output branch of the government's National Statistics Office. 5.95 was the 'age-standardised mortality rate' used by the Office's statisticians; the non-age-standardised calculation puts the figure at 9 per 1,000.

The 2006 death rate per 1,000 for the under-ones in England and Wales was 5.

4   Lady Mary Jeune, *Lesser Questions*, 1894, pp.228–9.

5   West End rental comparison source: *Daily Telegraph*, 4 November 1889. John Galt, a London City Mission missionary, reported in his unpublished memoirs, *A Providence That Shapes* (c. 1933, p.138), that Nichol rents were four times those for the equivalent cubic footage in Belgravia.

The 'vampyres' metaphor belongs to Henry Lazarus, in his book *Landlordism*, 1892, p.6.

6   Issue dated 16 October 1883.

7   The Royal Commission on the Housing of the Working Classes, 1884–85, heard evidence of 150 per cent profits, as well as the staggering proportions of income paid out as rent.

8   *Life and Labour of the People in London*, First Series, Volume 2: *London Continued*, 1891, Chapter IV, 'Influx of Population', by Hubert Llewellyn Smith, pp.446–7.

In the 1881 census, of a total Bethnal Green population of 126,961, 872 people described themselves as Irish, and just 925 as 'foreigners'.

9   Arthur Harding in Samuel's *East End Underworld*, p.2; and from taped conversations with Raphael Samuel, housed in the Museum of London, tape II, transcript p.31.

How to Create a Slum

1   *The Victoria History of the Counties of England: A History of the County of Middlesex*, Volume 11, *Early Stepney with Bethnal Green*, Oxford, 1998, edited by T.F.T. Baker, pp.162 and 203.

2   *Romano Lavo-Lil, Word-Book of the Romany; or, English Gypsy Language* by George Borrow, 1874; p.317 of the 1982 paperback edition.

3   A map of 1643 showing the twenty-three redoubts is reproduced on pp.26–7 of *The History of London in Maps* by Felix Barker and Peter Jackson, 1990.

4   According to Peter Guillery of English Heritage, there are no survivors among the late-seventeenth/early-eighteenth-century buildings in the Nichol. *Another Georgian Spitalfields: 18th-Century Houses in Bethnal Green's Silk-Weaving District*, English Heritage Survey Report, July 2000, pp. 18–19 and 24.

5   After the onset of the decline in the English silk industry from the 1820s, these weavers' skills became increasingly rare. East End weavers were sourced by Pope Pius IX in the 1870s for a particular fabric for a vestment, and they continued to be commissioned to create cloth for ceremonial garments for the British royal family until the early twentieth century.

6   Many a Nichol pub was similarly named, including the Lord Nelson at 49 Half Nichol Street, the Victory in Nelson Street and the Admiral Vernon in New Nichol Street; other Great Men were also incarnated as Nichol watering holes – the Gladstone was in Boundary Street, and there were at least two Prince of Waleses.

7   Quoted in the *Times* obituary for Lord Shaftesbury, whose measure the bill was, in the issue of 2 October 1885.

8   Under the Torrens Act of 1868, and its subsequent amendments, a vestry's medical officer of health was required (not merely allowed) to report to the vestry any house he considered to be 'unfit for human habitation'. In a bold move against the rights of property-owners, the medical officer was now entitled to request entry to any suspect house without having to apply for a magistrate's order. The Torrens Act also set out in detail how the vestry could ensure that a property-owner brought a house up to an acceptable standard; and if s/he would not, an 1879 amendment permitted the vestry to undertake the work itself and then to bill the owner for these improvements. The vestry could even demolish the house and pay cash compensation to the owner; or the owner could require the vestry to purchase the property and demolish, with its site being set aside solely for new working-class dwellings. Ultimately, under the Torrens Act, if the local authority would not rouse itself, Whitehall was empowered to intervene, if it so chose.

9   *Hansard*, 1867, Volume 189, column 754, quoted in Anthony S. Wohl, *The Eternal Slum: Housing and Social Policy in Victorian London*, 1977, p.87.

10   Robert Walker, district surveyor of the parish of St Martin's in the Fields, reported in the *Daily Telegraph*, 15 November 1889.

11   Under the Cross Act, the vestry medical officer of health was now compelled to report to the Board any district which he believed to be 'unhealthy'. The Board was required to consider such a declaration, and permitted to clear the buildings and make the site available for private-sector redevelopment for working-class housing, if Whitehall agreed. A vestry was also allowed to undertake such rebuilding, but had to dispose of the properties on to the open market within ten years of completion. Under the Cross Act, at least as many people who were made homeless by clearances were to be rehoused in any new buildings, in order not to exacerbate London overcrowding.

12   More radical suggestions that were made to the Select Committee included the imposition of progressively higher rates upon owners of insanitary property, and the prohibition on landowners' rebuilding anything but working-class housing on cleared land; all were firmly rejected.

13 'Labourers' and Artisans' Dwellings', *Fortnightly Review*, December 1883.
14 John Valentine Jones, quoted in the *Eastern Argus*, 20 October 1883.

Dr Bate's Dilemma

1   Radical–Liberal MP for Stoke, Henry Broadhurst, *Report & Evidence of the Royal Commission on the Housing of the Working Classes*, 1884–85 [C4402], Part 2, p.29.
2   Although a smart residential street, King Edward Road was also known locally as the Monkey Parade, because on Sunday afternoons a crowd of around 300 adolescent boys and girls, sons and daughters of middle-class Hackney professionals, would parade up and down the road, insulting passers-by and pushing them into the roadway: *Eastern Argus*, 30 August 1890 and 22 November 1890.
       Bate's appearance and demeanour: Notebook B/381, District 9, ff.3–37, in the Booth Archives at the London School of Economics.
3   Bate's evidence to the Public Inquiry into the Sanitary Condition of Bethnal Green, reported in the Mansion House Council on the Dwellings of the Poor *Report for the Year ending 31 December 1887*, p.33.
4   *Eastern Argus*, 19 December 1885.
5   All details taken from the report by Bate dated December 1883, in *Reports &c from Medical Officers of Health Relative to the Artisans' Dwellings Acts* in *Accounts and Papers (21) Local Government, Local Taxation*, 1883, Volume LVII, pp.14–16. In this series of London medical officer of health returns to the Local Government Board, Bate's report was the longest and most exhaustive.
6   Bate, writing in the journal *Public Health*, March 1889.
       Minutes of the Bethnal Green Vestry Sanitary Committee give glimpses of some of the Nichol landlords' brinkmanship. (It was Bate's view that a landlord was being 'obstructive' if s/he took any longer than two months to address a sanitary problem.) Samuel Crews, the owner of 65 to 67 Old Nichol Street, 6 and 7 Turville Street and George Terrace, was summonsed by Worship Street magistrates on 28 February, 1 March, 9 April and 19 May 1887. Each time Crews pleaded that works were under way, and each time he was believed. Only by late May had all the improvements been made and checked by the Bethnal Green sanitary inspectors, but even then, water had not been fully laid on to the WCs, as required in law. In the summer of 1889, Crews would be equally uncooperative, failing to meet the Sanitary Committee, as requested, to discuss his properties and falsely claiming that the remedial work demanded for 65 to 67 Old Nichol Street could not be undertaken because the existing drain was too near the surface of his cellars – a point that the vestry surveyor easily refuted.

At 17 and 19 Church Street, at the southernmost end of the Nichol, it was found that the drains were connected to those of neighbouring Devonshire Place, and not to the main sewer in Church Street, as legally required. The drains of 17 and 19 were constantly backing up and causing the most appalling stench. (At the coroner's hearing into the death of a baby in Church Street in September 1887, a doctor said, tactlessly, and most unscientifically, that he was surprised that the child had lived as long as it had, considering the 'horrible smells' of that street (reported in the *Eastern Argus* of 3 September 1887). The magistrate served notice on owner William Green Brighten, of Bishopsgate, and then fined him 14s 6d for failing to act on this notice. Brighten refused to pay up, claiming he would take the case to a higher court. Eventually, though, he did acknowledge liability, and paid for the work to be done.

On 18 October 1887 Lydia Allder, owner of the foetid Devonshire Place, wrote to the vestry five weeks after her premises had been declared unfit for human habitation: 'I beg to inform you that I have arranged with all the tenants to leave the above houses. I am quite willing to do all the committee may require.' Perfectly charming; quite reasonable. By 2 November nothing had been done, and Allder was fined 14s 6d, plus costs, and was ordered to close the premises. By the end of the year she had emptied and boarded up Devonshire Place, asking the vestry if she could please allow one tenant to stay on at number 9, in order to 'protect the property'. In July 1888, she asked the vestry if she could now begin to make her repairs, and the vestry agreed. (Lydia was one of three Allders owning Nichol slum property – there was even an Allders Buildings in Nichol's Row.)

The owner of 74 Virginia Road, one Mr Woolf, was less fortunate. He was served with a notice on 5 October 1888 for works to be done; they were not done, and he was then summonsed on 13 December, and again on 18 December, with the requirement that the work be done within fourteen days. Woolf claimed that he had started the work right away but had had to evict his tenants before it could be continued. He was believed, and the summons was withdrawn, but three months later, when the work had still not been completed, he was forced to pay his fines and costs to date, which, in the six months, had come to total £25 10s and 4d. (Costs to magistrates rose by 10s for each day they went unpaid.) This was a steep sum, and punishments for negligent landlords of the Nichol rarely reached this level. I have found no higher fine for negligent Nichol property-owners than this.

All cases taken from the Minute Books of the Bethnal Green Vestry Sanitary Committee, L/MBG/B/4/9 [BG/574], Book no. 9, 1886–88, and [BG/575], Book no. 10, 1888–89.

7   Letter dated 9 March 1887, reprinted in Mansion House Council, *Report*,
     p.66.
8   Reverend Hansard had personal experience of Bethnal Green's dilapi-
     dation, complaining in a letter reprinted in *The Times* on 18 August 1885
     of the eight tumbles he had taken into old graves as he made his way
     across St Matthew's poorly maintained burial ground. Hansard chose
     to live in Kensington, because of his 'love of clean air', as he put it (*The
     Idea of the Victorian Church – A Study of the Church of England, 1833–1889*
     by Desmond Bowen, Montreal, 1968, p.324).
9   Mansion House Council, *Report*, p.33.
10   Meakin's testimony also made public the embarrassing fact that the
     vestry had given the Gwatkin Estate the benefit of the doubt when the
     estate's solicitors had explained that the very short leases remaining on
     the Gwatkins' Mount Street property would soon run out, and that
     they would be happy to demolish or improve this property as soon as
     that happened and before new leaseholds were arranged. The vestry
     then had to admit at the inquiry that other freeholders had successfully
     duped them by promising that demolitions or comprehensive repairs
     would happen immediately the leases ran out. The vestry had taken
     these landlords at their word and had issued no summonses against
     them for 'nuisance', only to discover that when the leases did eventu-
     ally expire, new, long leases had been legally pre-arranged by the free-
     holder, with no improvement or demolition taking place.

The Old Circular Cowpath

1   *Eastern Argus*, 23 April 1887.
2   *Ibid.*, 21 February 1885.
3   *Ibid.*, editorial, 22 May 1886.
4   Report dated 6 August 1888 in the Local Government Board papers in
     the Public Record Office/National Archives at MH 12/6880.
5   Figure quoted in *The Government of Victorian London, 1855–1889: The
     Metropolitan Board of Works, the Vestries and the City Corporation* by David
     Owen, Harvard, 1982, p.220.
6   *Eastern Argus*, 15 May 1886.
         Some publicans even induced children to visit pubs by offering them
     sweets and toys. One survey of the time showed that in certain districts
     of London, between 10 and 16 per cent of pubs' clientele were chil-
     dren; statistics given in *Child Abuse and Moral Reform in England, 1870–1908*
     by George K. Behlmer, Stanford, 1982, p.177.
7   Mansion House Council, *Report*, pp.49–50.
8   The higher the rateable value of a property, the more votes its owner

was allowed when voting for the board of guardians: a property rated at between £50 and £100 permitted two votes, and so on in scale up to the £250-rated house, which brought its lucky owner six votes. Female householders were allowed to vote for both the vestry and guardians if they were the ratepayer, which tended to exclude married women. An estimated 15 per cent of local-government voters before World War I were women, the majority being widows and single women.

Women had been allowed to stand in elections to the national boards of guardians since 1834, but none was elected in London until 1875, in Kensington. They had a far higher profile on the nation's school boards, on which they had been entitled both to vote and to sit since the Education Act of 1870.

The parliamentary franchise, on the other hand, extended by the 1884 Reform Act and the 1885 Redistribution Act, added 1,762,441 males to the nation's electoral roll, meaning that around four million men – or 58 per cent of adult males – could vote. Women continued to be excluded from voting for members of parliament until 1918, when females over the age of thirty who were householders, or the wives of householders, were enfranchised.

9   Quoted in G.R. Searle, *A New England? Peace and War 1886–1914*, Oxford, 2004, p.228.

10   This would particularly be the case with the Liberal Party, following the January 1887 formation of the London Liberal and Radical Union. By this point, Gladstone's Liberals had undergone their (eventually fatal) split over the issue of Home Rule for Ireland; at the same time the emergent Socialist movement was attracting more and more consideration from moderately progressive people who might otherwise have drifted towards Radical Liberalism.

11   Figures given in *The Victoria History of the County of Middlesex*, Volume II, p.128.

12   This type of action had been made easier by 1870s legislation that facilitated loans to vestries for municipal development, at low interest and with long repayment terms.

Whether this willingness to borrow was foolhardy or far-sighted was an issue that made Shoreditch local politics particularly fiery; but after loud, sometimes physically violent, debates, the Shoreditch Vestry voted to borrow in order to build a new workhouse and infirmary (completed in 1866 and still standing, in Kingsland Road) and town hall (built 1865–67, also still standing and still magnificent). These building projects had a secondary benefit in giving building-site employment to local men, so lowering the rate of male unemployment in the district. Loans paid, too, for major paving and sewer works between 1858 and 1863; in 1877

Shoreditch became the first London parish to ensure a constant water supply to its inhabitants, while at the end of the century the Shoreditch Dust Destructor, on the north side of Hoxton Market, burned household refuse and used the steam generated by the heat to supply electric light to the borough – Britain's first such waste / electricity project.

13   Citywide dissatisfaction with the vestry system of local government had been growing: in 1885, just one in thirty men who were eligible to vote in London's vestry elections chose to do so, indicating that many other parishes were just as moribund as St Matthew's Bethnal Green. The London Municipal Reform League was founded in 1881 and by 1884 had over 1,000 members. Harcourt's London Government Bill of that year had proposed the abolition of the vestries and the Metropolitan Board of Works and the substitution of a single, citywide council that would include local representatives elected on a more democratic franchise. Harcourt told the House of Commons during debate on the bill that he was aware that London municipal reform was a sea 'strewn with many wrecks, and whose shores are whitened with the bones of many previous adventurers'. The bill was met with extreme hostility from the Corporation of London, the medieval local authority for the Square Mile, which was determined to see no central government incursion into its ancient rights. The Corporation had the ear of many an MP and newspaper editor, plus a huge slush fund with which to wage battle against modernity. A parliamentary Select Committee later heard evidence of 'malversation' by the Corporation in its campaigns against local government reform, and was told of the organised heckling and breaking up of Municipal Reform League meetings; the creation of anti-reform petitions with phantom signatories; the planting of newspaper stories smearing the reformists, and the formation of the largely bogus Metropolitan Ratepayers' Protection Association to protest at Harcourt's bill. But an even worse enemy of the bill was parliamentary apathy – an average of fifteen MPs attended the debates on reform of London government, and Harcourt withdrew the motion.

Owners

1   The Mansion House Council on the Dwellings of the Poor, *Report for the Year ending 31 December 1890*, pp.6 and 8.

2   Of such salon nights, it was said that 'if by any chance her house caught fire, and her guests had been burned, half the most famous names would have disappeared from the peerage. The Royal Academy would have been decimated. The theatres would have been obliged to close.

The most eloquent pulpits would have been dumb. Science would have been at a standstill.' Quoted in *Some Victorian Women, Good, Bad and Indifferent* by Harry Furniss, 1923, p.189.

3   The letter, dated 23 December 1890, was written to John Reeves of the London School Board; it is printed in Reeves's *Recollections of a School Attendance Officer*, p.55.

4   Williams, *Later Leaves*, pp.294–5.

5   Issue dated 5 December 1889.

6   The Duke of Buckingham and Chandos (1823–89) had been a Tory MP from 1846 to 1859, later becoming a Privy Councillor, then Lord President of the Council, Colonial Secretary, and Governor-General in Madras. In 1886 he became chair of the Committees of the House of Lords. He was a strong supporter of the Church of England and a keen opponent of women's suffrage. His dissolute father had died in debt, and the third Duke undertook one of the largest land and property sell-offs of the nineteenth century, but his Nichol portfolio was not among his dispersals (*The Rise and Fall of the Grenvilles: Dukes of Buckingham and Chandos, 1710 to 1921* by John Beckett, Manchester, 1994).

7   *Eastern Argus*, 16 November 1889.

Prince Arthur

1   Samuel's tapes were published in book form by Routledge in 1981 as *East End Underworld: Chapters in the Life of Arthur Harding.* All direct quotations by Arthur are taken from Samuel's book and supplemented by extracts from the transcripts of the original tapes now housed in the Museum of London. Extracts from *East End Underworld* are reproduced here by courtesy of Alison Light for the Raphael Samuel Estate, while extracts from the tapes are by permission of the Museum of London's Oral History Department and Alison Light.

2   In *The Times* of 28 February 1890 it is reported that Arthur (Lark) and James Harding were prosecuted at Worship Street magistrates' court by the Inland Revenue for evading excise with illicit Sunday morning sales of beer and spirits at their beershop at number 2 Sarah Street, off Half Nichol Street. Police Inspector Babbington claimed in court that the brothers had been doing this for five years. The magistrate fined the pair, but they were jailed for three months because they did not have the money with which to pay.

Lark was said by Arthur to have been very good-looking. He was one of the short-lived Hardings, not making the age of forty, as a result of cancer, Arthur believed.

3   Reeves's *Recollections*, p.36.

4   At the age of fourteen, in 1896, Mighty got herself a job cleaning the head office of Lipton's the grocers, earning 7s 6d a week, working from 7 to 9 a.m., and then 5.30 to 7.30 p.m. In the hours between, she sold lemons in Roman Road Market; she would get to Spitalfields Market at about 5 a.m. and buy 300 lemons for very little money, selling them on for three or four a penny.

    Mighty lived into her mid-nineties.

5   Information taken from the taped conversations with Raphael Samuel, housed in the Museum of London; tape DD, transcript p.26.

6   Mary C. Tabor, 'Elementary Education', in Charles Booth's *Life and Labour of the People in London*, First Series, Volume 2: *London Continued*, 1891, p.506. Hereafter cited as *Life and Labour*.

7   Reeves's *Recollections*, p.34.

8   Tape DD, transcript p.1.

9   Tape II, transcript pp.11–12.

10   *Life and Labour*, First Series, Volume 1: *East London*, 1889, p.117.

11   *Eastern Argus*, 9 February 1889. Booth's investigations, *Life and Labour*, First Series, Volume 2, 1891, p.174, and Notebooks B/77 and B/80 in the Booth Archives.

12   The phrase was coined by journalist Henry Morley, writing mid-century about the non-criminal, non-begging, non-workhouse poor of Bethnal Green. 'The Quiet Poor', *Household Words*, Volume 9, 1854, pp.201–6.

13   Tape DD, transcript p.43.

Help

1   Figures quoted in *The Relief of Poverty, 1834–1914* by Michael E. Rose, 1986, p.17.

2   Those in a skilled trade unaffected by imports or mechanisation, and who did not change their job, saw their real wages rise by as much as 50 per cent between 1850 and 1900. However, many artisans in such businesses as tailoring and shoemaking saw their trade degenerate into mass 'slop' work, and their wages undercut by the unskilled.

    The wages of the unskilled did not rise significantly during the century, while the cost of their outgoings – notably rent – did.

3   Coroner's hearing into the case of Sophia Nation reported in the *Eastern Argus*, 16 January 1886; that of the elderly man reported in the *Eastern Argus*, 4 July 1885. Sophia Nation and Annie Maria Rogers cases also detailed in *Return of the Number of all Deaths in the Metropolitan District in the Year 1886, upon which a Coroner's Jury have returned a Verdict of Death from Starvation or Death accelerated by Privation*, in Parliamentary Papers, Accounts and Papers (23), 1887, Volume LXXI.

4 *Eastern Argus*, 7 January 1888.

5 It was the lack of the 4d fee for a bed for the night in a common lodging-house that threw Polly Nichols and Annie Chapman into the path of Jack the Ripper the following summer. Warren's letter to the Bethnal Green guardians was written in November 1887, ten months before the Ripper killings began. It is interesting that it was the much-maligned Warren (blamed in 1888 for failing to capture the Whitechapel Fiend, and scorned by most twentieth-century armchair Ripper-hunters) who made such a practical request; but charitable feeling had little to do with it, in fact – his was a pragmatic attempt to clear the streets of the burgeoning street-sleeper population who were becoming so visible.

6 Parliamentary Papers, 1834, Volume XXVII, p.127.

7 H.G.C. Allgood in *The History of Bethnal Green*, 1894, p.139.

8 Appendix B to the *Sixteenth Annual Report of the Local Government Board*, 1887, Volume XXXVI [C5131 and C5171], p.55.

9 *Eastern Argus*, 16 August 1890.

10 Paupers on poor relief in England and Wales per 1,000 head of population on 1 January 1888, by region: table on p.xiv of the *Seventeenth Annual Report of the Local Government Board 1887–1888*, 1888, Volume XLIX [C5526].

Region	In Workhouse	Outdoor Relief	All Paupers
The South West	6	36.2	42.2
Eastern Counties	7.5	31.6	39.1
Wales	4.2	33.8	38
South Midlands	6.6	28.1	34.7
The South East	8.3	24.4	32.7
West Midlands	7	24.7	31.7
North Midlands	4.9	23	27.9
London	14.4	13.4	27.8
The North	4.6	20	24.6
Yorkshire	4.3	19.4	23.7
The North West	6.4	14.4	20.8
Average	7.3	22.1	29.4

11 Report dated 18 February 1888 in the *Seventeenth Annual Report*, Appendix B, Reports and Inquiries no. 15.

12 Hubert Llewellyn Smith's deduction in his essay 'Influx of Population' in *Life and Labour*, First Series, Volume 2, *London Continued*, 1891, p.468.

13 Corbett, writing in *The Universities and the Social Problem: An Account of the University Settlements in East London*, edited by John M. Knapp, 1895, p.114.

14   Reported in the *Eastern Argus*, 4 September 1886.

15   Issue of 4 April 1891.

16   The clash between playwright and journalist George Sims and his ques-
      tioner Samuel Morley – a hosiery magnate – as the former gave evidence
      on 22 April 1884 at the Royal Commission on the Housing of the Working
      Classes typifies the dispute about the role of drink in the lives of the
      poor: 'Mr Samuel Morley tried to make me say that drink was the cause
      of poverty, and pounded away at me like an Old Bailey cross-examiner
      until Lord Salisbury came to my rescue and contended that I had fully
      answered the question when I said that drink was one of the causes of
      poverty, but that poverty was one of the causes of drink.' *My Life: Sixty
      Years' Recollections of Bohemian London* by George R. Sims, 1917, p.137.
          The interchange is reported verbatim in the *First Report of Her
      Majesty's Commissioners for Inquiring into the Housing of the Working Classes*,
      1884–85 [C4402], Q5788.

17   Undated interview with Bailward in Notebook B/225, District 9, f.133,
      in the Booth Archives. The interview is likely to have occurred in 1898.

18   The Reverend James Davies of St Andrew's Congregationalist church
      in Bethnal Green Road; Notebook B/229, District 9, f.95, in the Booth
      Archives.

Phantoms in the Fog

1   Contemporary estimates put the number of London 'street arabs' at
      30,000.

2   Quotation from the taped conversations with Raphael Samuel; tape LL,
      transcript p.31.

3   Evidence given to the *Royal Commission on the Duties of the Metropolitan
      Police*, 1908 [Cd 4156], p.330.

4   *Old Bailey Sessions Papers*, Volume 144, p.299; trial date 6 April 1906.
          'Long Hymie' Eisenberg's family had arrived in London from
      Argentina. Arthur alleged that Eisenberg went on to attempt to murder
      a police officer in Enfield and that he was eventually deported back to
      Argentina.

5   Evidence given to the *Royal Commission on the Duties of the Metropolitan
      Police*, pp.330 and 377. Arthur appeared before the Commission as a result
      of a complaint he had lodged about police persecution following his
      acquittal on a charge of assaulting one PC Michael Cann in Bacon
      Street in 1906.

6   To 'squeak' was to grass; a 'slit' was a detective.

7   Marx, 'The 18th Brumaire of Louis Bonaparte', 1852, in *Selected Works*,
      Volume 1, quoted in *Campbell Bunk: The Worst Street in North London*,

2003, by Jerry White. White describes *lumpenproletariat* as 'a more-than-usually contentious term . . . an ugly word, more often one of political abuse than theoretical explication', p.31.

8   Tape 9, transcript p.5.

9   Tape II, transcript p.37.

10 Tape AA2, transcript p.12. Arthur said he liked Edward Heath, but distrusted Harold Wilson.

11 *Eastern Argus*, 11 October 1890.

12 Report dated 9 October 1890, presented to the London County Council's Housing of the Working Classes Committee, papers held in the London Metropolitan Archives.

13 Nurse's testimony, *Life and Labour*, Third Series, Religious Influences, Volume 2, 1902, p.97; the brotherhood's physical safety, 'A Shoreditch Club', article in the *Daily Telegraph* of 22 October 1887, by James Greenwood; J.F. Barnard of the Penny Bank, *The New Fiction and Other Essays on Literary Subjects* by H.D. [Henry Duff] Traill, 1897.

14 Roderick Macdonald was, from June 1888, coroner for north-east Middlesex and was gaining a reputation for hastiness in closing inquests, and for brusqueness and high-handedness with coroners' juries and witnesses. On 12 November 1888, Macdonald brought the inquiry into the death of final Ripper victim Mary Kelly to an indecently swift end; the newspapers of the day noted that his refusal to field any questions from a confused jury at the Kelly inquest was very strange and unhelpful behaviour.

15 I am grateful to Stewart P. Evans for telling me that Donald McCormick was the source of the Old Nichol Gang 'theory', which Evans details in his 2006 book, co-authored with Donald Rumbelow, *Jack the Ripper, Scotland Yard Investigates*, pp.258–9. My own researches in newspaper and court archives failed to supply any suggestion of males extorting money from street prostitutes, but *The Blackest Streets* assumes that the written records of crime are but a faint trace of its actuality. For what it's worth, the groups of street-robbers (who may not even have considered themselves to be gangs) that *are* on record as operating in the Whitechapel area in the late 1880s and early 1890s selected male victims, presumably because they were more likely to have significant sums of cash or valuables about their person.

16 The 'High Rip Gang' had made their appearance in a Liverpool newspaper in 1886. It was a journalistic name that bundled together what were, in fact, a number of crimes with different perpetrators; but once created, the Liverpool 'High Rips' took on a life of their own in the minds of the public, according to Sir William Nott-Bower, a former Liverpool police officer, in his 1926 memoirs *52 Years a Policeman*.

17 *Life in Darkest London: A Hint to General Booth* by the Reverend Arthur Osborne Jay, 1891, p.105.

18 *A Story of Shoreditch* by the Reverend Arthur Osborne Jay, 1896, pp.54–5.

19 The murder of Emma Smith on 3 April 1888 provides a dramatic illustration of how the police view of a quiet night in Whitechapel contrasts with the point of view of street prostitutes working in the same area. Smith lived long enough after her attack – which happened at 1.30 a.m. on the corner of Wentworth Street and Osborn Street, the southern continuation of Brick Lane – to say that she had been robbed and attacked by two or three men, one of whom was no more than nineteen years old. Smith had been raped with a blunt instrument (which ruptured her peritoneum and would cause her death two days later from peritonitis) and had had part of her right ear torn away. She would have walked past several police constables on her way, first, back to her lodging, and then on the half-mile walk, assisted by two female friends, to the London Hospital; but, as Chief Inspector John West of H (Whitechapel) Division reported, 'Witnesses stated that they didn't think it necessary to report the circumstances to the police. Whole of police on duty deny all knowledge of the occurrence.'

At the 7 April inquest into the death of Emma Smith, Margaret Hames, a friend of Smith's, who also worked the streets, revealed that she had met Smith on the night of her death much further east, at the Limehouse end of Burdett Road. Hames was rushing to get away from the area because she had just been violently assaulted by two men. 'There had been some rough work that night,' said Hames, who had been hospitalised for a fortnight four months earlier when two men attacked her in the same part of Limehouse, causing multiple injuries to her face and chest. She reported neither attack to the officers she passed on the way home.

20 *Pictures and Politics: A Book of Reminiscences* by Arthur Pillans Laurie, 1934, p.76.

21 Memo dated 3 August 1889, reprinted in *The Ultimate Jack the Ripper Sourcebook* by Stewart P. Evans and Keith Skinner, 2000, p.470.

22 Interview with Jay in the Booth Archives, Notebook B/228, District 9, ff.37–59.

23 Similarly disbelieved was Constable 396H – in fact, he was accused outright of lying by a Worship Street magistrate when he claimed that he had been assaulted with a stick by William Jones in Half Nichol Street in September 1891. The constable contradicted himself in his account of events leading up to the assault, was told to shut up and sit down by the clerk of court and by his own police inspector, and the magistrate accepted instead the version given by the defendant's mother

and sister – that the constable had been drinking alcohol in a court off Half Nichol Street and had struck a child who was staring at him, with Jones coming to rescue the child.

The Cruelty Men

1 *Old Bailey Sessions Papers*, Volume 15, pp.462–7; trial date 11 February 1892.

Sullivan made a living of sorts from taking in ironing, but admitted to Selina Lewis that she could fit all her belongings into a handkerchief, apart from her bonnet.

On hearing his guilty verdict, Muir shouted to 'Old Joe' Norton in the Old Bailey public gallery, 'You can have my tools, mate', as he put his hands around his neck, gesturing the noose.

2 *Life and Labour*, Third Series: Religious Influences, Volume 2, 1902, p.67; and Reeves's *Recollections*, p.34.

3 *Eastern Argus*, 18 October 1890.

4 Montagu Williams, *Round London: Down East and Up West*, 1896, p.51.

5 Quoted by Maeve E. Doggett in *Marriage, Wife-Beating and the Law in Victorian England*, 1992, p.120.

Unfortunately, the Associate Institute could do little to protect families after a jailed man had served his sentence until the Matrimonial Causes Act (known colloquially as 'The Poor Person's Divorce') of 1878 permitted a woman legally to refuse to live with a husband who had a proven record of violence and to claim weekly maintenance from him. Later amendments would allow mothers additionally to claim sole custody of their children. In common law, a husband who had not been proven to be violent still had custody rights over his wife's body, until an Appeal Court decision of 1891. (In Britain, a man could legally rape his wife until 1991.)

Only around 8,000 Poor Person's Divorces were requested and granted each year in England and Wales, and in many of these cases the separation tended to be temporary, indicating that reconciliation of some kind was overwhelmingly preferred by warring spouses. In fact, what most wives who came to the magistrates' court sought was the enforcement of maintenance payments, or an increase in the level of maintenance, without separation.

6 Weylland's *The Man with the Book*, p.45.

7 *Ibid.*, pp.103–4.

8 Tape LL, transcript p.20.

9 The National Vigilance Association would campaign for many years for changes to the various laws on the admissibility of evidence, in order to try to make children's evidence more acceptable to courts, and to

make the judicial process less daunting for junior plaintiffs, particularly for those who were accusing their parents or relations of sexual assault.

10 In 1978 Anthony S. Wohl, in his essay 'Sex and the Single Room', surveyed the evidence on incest in poor families in the late-Victorian city and found it to be 'fragile and unquantifiable'. Wohl writes: 'Unfortunately, for the historian, the various committees and commissions failed to press for more, or more precise, information.' 'Sex and the Single Room', in *The Victorian Family: Structure and Stresses*, edited by Anthony S. Wohl, 1978.

11 Samuel, *East End Underworld*, p.55 and p.239.

12 *First Report of Her Majesty's Commissioners for Inquiring into the Housing of the Working Classes* [C4402], Q19.

13 *Ibid.*, Q3690.

14 *Ibid.*, Q1951.

15 *Ibid.*, Q5872 and Q5873.

16 Beatrice Webb, *My Apprenticeship*, 1926, p.310.

17 *Second Annual Report of the East London Branch of the National Society for the Prevention of Cruelty to Children*, 1890–91, in the archives of the NSPCC; pp.1–5.

The following year's report gave these figures for the Society's East London branch: 415 cases dealt with, of which 143 were of starvation, desertion or neglect; 64 cruel exposure to excite sympathy; 86 injurious assaults; 90 of 'unnecessary suffering'; 32 immoralities against girl children. Of these cases, 84 went to court; two cases were still pending as the report was compiled; 234 led to warnings to the parents; 95 cases were dropped, transferred or 'otherwise dealt with'; and 616 children were stated to have 'benefited' from the branch's intervention.

18 The comparative paucity of prosecutions of sexual assaults upon boys is cited in *Child Sexual Abuse in Victorian England* by Louise A. Jackson, 2000, p.5.

19 *Second Annual Report*, p.5.

20 Behlmer, *Child Abuse and Moral Reform in England, 1870–1908*, p.83. Behlmer reveals that of 10,169 cases investigated by the NSPCC between May 1889 and April 1891, only 396 instances were found of abusive families with weekly incomes below the 'poverty line' level of 18s–21s. Over 3,000 of the investigated parents earned more than 27s a week. Behlmer writes that what the NSPCC deduced from its fact-finding missions prefigured current conclusions about child cruelty – namely, that it is 'multi-causal'.

21 *Eastern Argus* editorial, 31 December 1887.

Today, an estimated 300 babies a year die in the UK because exhausted parents take them into their own beds and accidentally roll on to them.

22 Figure quoted in *The Victorian Town Child* by Pamela Horn, Stroud, 1997.

23 Notebook B/80 in the Booth Archives.

24 The following August, the coroner praised Mary Ann and Thomas Stalman of 12 Half Nichol Street for having reared nine healthy children of ten in such appalling surroundings. Mary Ann had awoken to find their two-month-old baby lying dead alongside them, which the coroner's jury decided was accidental. The jury was less sympathetic to John Smith, a costermonger, of 2 Orange Court, Old Nichol Street. The jury foreman said that Smith had been 'very culpable' in the suffocation death of his two-day-old baby: since his wife had given birth so recently, Smith, the foreman felt, should not have been anywhere near the marital bed. 'But I kept my clothes on,' the bereaved father protested. The coroner intervened to criticise the (female) property-owner who profited by allowing such a high level of overcrowding in her tenements; these conditions, he said, contributed to baby-suffocation deaths, and the jury brought in a verdict of accidental death.

At the inquest in November 1890 into the death of eleven-month-old George Thomas Gosford, at 26 Jacob Street, the coroner became increasingly astonished as his mother, Mary, and her neighbour and character witness, Mary Besson, revealed their living conditions and income. Mary Gosford was a washerwoman earning just 6–7s a week, but she had never once missed her weekly rental payment of 2s 6d; the coroner couldn't see how she managed this. She had gone to bed at midnight – sober, she was keen to point out to the coroner, but exhausted from a whole day spent washing. Baby George and her two other children slept between her and the wall of her one-room home. When she awoke, George was dead. Mary was unmarried but all three children had the same father, who gave her 2s a week. The coroner demanded that she present to the court her four-year-old, which she did, and the jury and spectators noted that while it was inadequately dressed it did not look badly fed, which was 'most extraordinary' in the circumstances, said the coroner. The verdict was accidental suffocation.

Sources for overlaying cases: *Eastern Argus*, 5 December 1885, 7 January 1893, 28 August 1886, 15 October 1887 and 15 November 1890.

25 *Eastern Argus*, 16 January 1892.

26 The follow-up Prevention of Cruelty Act of 1894 allowed the police to take suspected victims from their homes without a court order, and, among this Act's other requirements, parents were, for the first time, legally obliged to call in a doctor if their child became ill or injured. Fines and prison terms for neglect and cruelty were increased yet further, while ten years later the law was again amended in an attempt to make court proceedings in neglect/cruelty cases easier for child plaintiffs, and

to allow NSPCC inspectors to 'rescue' children from their homes without police, magistrate or Poor Law presence.

27   *Second Annual Report*, p.4.

28   Figures quoted in *Child Welfare in England, 1872–1914* by Harry Hendrick, 1994, p.56. The breakdown of this figure was 112 'cruel immoralities and other wrongs', 112 starvation cases, 523 assaults, 219 cases of 'dangerous neglect', 66 of desertion, and 87 of insufficient clothing.

29   Behlmer, *Child Abuse and Moral Reform*, p.172.

30   Quoted *ibid.*, p.167.

Tickling the Elephant

1   Kitz's exhortation was made at the Revolutionary Conference that took place in London on 3 August 1890, quoted in E.P. Thompson, *William Morris: Romantic to Revolutionary*, 1955, p.568.

2   *London City Mission Magazine*, 1 September 1893, pp.223 and 225. Allinson was described as 'a man of character and originality' when interviewed for Charles Booth's *Life and Labour* survey; he stood out in the Nichol's streets, in his black frock coat and silk top hat. Notebook B/229, District 9, ff.155–71, in the Booth Archives.

3   *Freedom: A Journal of Anarchist Communism*, April 1912. Kitz's memoirs appear as the monthly column 'Recollections and Reflections' in the issues from January to July 1912.

4   Overheard by London City Mission worker John Galt and reported in his memoirs *A Providence That Shapes*, p.139.

5   Lady Emilia Dilke, 'Trades Unionism among Women', *Fortnightly Review*, May 1891.

6   *Lady Dilke, A Biography* by Betty Askwith, 1969.

7   John Bruce Glasier, *William Morris and the Early Days of the Socialist Movement*, 1921, p.128.

8   Kitz's obituary, unsigned, in *Justice* magazine, 18 January 1923.

9   Weylland, *The Man with the Book*, pp.70–1 and 87–90.

10   Unnamed contemporary quoted in *Anarchist Portraits* by Paul Avrich, Princeton, 1988, p.159.

11   'A Review of Twelve Years' Work in the Nichol Street District, Shoreditch', *London City Mission Magazine*, 1 September 1894, p.224.

12   Peter Latouche, *Anarchy! An Authentic Exposition of the Methods of Anarchists and the Aims of Anarchism*, 1908, p.63.

13   Quoted in Kropotkin's essay 'Mutual Aid among Animals', *Nineteenth Century* magazine, September 1890.

14   Letter dated 24 July 1884 in *The Collected Letters of William Morris, Volume 2, 1881–1884*, edited by Norman Kelvin, Princeton, 1987, p.307.

15   Letter dated 3 February 1885, *ibid.*, p.385.

16   Diary entries dated 26 January 1887 and 21 March 1887, in *The Socialist Diary of William Morris*, edited by Florence Boos, 1981, pp.4 and 23.

17   'The Problem of the Slums' by Frank Kitz in the *Voice of Labour* journal, Volume 1, no. 1, 18 January 1907.

18   Kropotkin quoted in *The International Anarchist Movement in Late-Victorian London* by Hermia Oliver, 1983, p.17.
      Marx and Engels had been similarly baffled by the English working man, fifteen years earlier. Marx considered that the proletariat of Britain had gone down with a 'bourgeois infection', and Engels, regretting the passing of mid-century Owenite Utopian Socialism, and the death – in 1848 – of the Chartist movement, wrote to Marx that 'the revolutionary energy of the English proletariat has to all intents and purposes completely evaporated, and the English proletarian is declaring his complete agreement with the rule of the bourgeoisie'. For Engels's letter dated 8 April 1863 and Marx's reply, written the following day, see: *Karl Marx and Friedrich Engels, Correspondence 1846–1895, A Selection with Commentary and Notes*, edited by Marx's son, Carl, 1934, p.147.

19   Diary entry dated 23 February 1887, in *The Socialist Diary of William Morris*, p.14.

20   Issue dated Monday 14 November 1887.

21   Letter dated 4 October 1886, quoted in Avrich's *Anarchist Portraits*, p.157.

22   Mowbray writing in *Commonweal*, the Socialist League journal, originally edited by William Morris but subsequently the organ of the Anarchist wing of the League; issue dated 29 November 1890.

23   Lincoln Springfield, *Some Piquant People*, 1924, p.134.

24   Latouche's *Anarchy!* p.65.

25   Springfield's, *Some Piquant People*, p. 34.

26   Bourdin – a Parisian émigré living at 30 Fitzroy Street, a solitary but well-liked member of Club Autonomie – was found at 4.40 p.m. in a kneeling position in Greenwich Park, his left hand blown off and with appalling abdominal injuries, of which he died soon afterwards. He had been carrying a bomb in a brown paper parcel.
      The Greenwich Park Mystery (no one has ever discovered if the bomb was intended for a genuine Anarchist London outrage, or to be sent off to Paris by an intermediary; or whether Bourdin was a *mouchard à la* Verloc) gave Joseph Conrad the germ of the story that he would develop into *The Secret Agent*, published in 1907. Conrad considered the event 'a blood-stained inanity of so fatuous a kind that it was impossible to fathom its origin by any reasonable or even unreasonable process of thought' (Author's Note to *The Secret Agent*).

For what it's worth, David Nicoll had an interesting explanation of the Mystery, which he wrote in 1897 and which is reprinted in full in Norman Sherry's *Conrad's Western World*, Cambridge, 1971, pp.379–394. He believed that H.B. Samuels, seemingly an Anarchist but in fact an infiltrator for Scotland Yard, had sent Bourdin, his own brother-in-law, to the Park with the bomb, with the intention that Bourdin would be arrested in possession of the explosive device and the London Anarchists tarnished by association with him; the plot failed because Bourdin's device went off too soon. Nicoll in his later years gained a reputation for paranoid outbursts, suspecting police plots and treachery amongst his comrades; in the circumstances, though, this behaviour seems to have been justifiable, and needn't necessarily have indicated mental instability. The Anarchists *had* been infiltrated; there were police spies; got-up cases did result in prison sentences. The lucidity of this article – even if one does not agree with its argument – suggests that Nicoll was still in command of his faculties in 1897.

The Houndsditch Murders of 1910, and the subsequent Sidney Street siege, were not the work of Anarchists but of Latvian Social Democrats.

27   Glasier, *William Morris and the Early Days of the Socialist Movement*, p.124.
28   *Freedom*, April 1912.

A Voice of Their Own

1   *A Catalogue of Anti-Vaccination Literature*, 1894.
2   'Homes in the East of London: A Fresh Visit to Bethnal Green', in *The Builder* magazine, 28 January 1871.
3   *Eastern Argus*, 27 April 1889.
4   Reeves, *Recollections*, p.35.
5   Quoted in *The London Years* by Rudolf Rocker, 1956, p.80.
6   This rumour does not make a great deal of sense. As Liberal MP for Ross-shire, Macdonald – from June 1888 the coroner for north-east Middlesex – would have had little reason to try to protect Jacobs, a Conservative.
7   Jacobs quoted in the *Eastern Argus*, 6 March 1887.
8   *Life and Labour*, First Series, Volume 1, *East London*, 1889, pp.99 and 118.
9   Noted by Marc Brodie in *The Politics of the Poor: the East End of London 1885–1914*, Oxford, 2004, pp.38–9.
10   *Ibid.*, p.63.
11   Calculations arrived at by Duncan Tanner and John Davis, by comparison of census data and electoral roll addresses for the Nichol, published in John Davis, 'The Enfranchisement of the Urban Poor in Late-Victorian Britain', in *Politics and Culture in Victorian Britain: Essays in Memory of*

Colin Matthew, edited by Peter Ghosh and Lawrence Goldman, Oxford, 2006.

12　*Ibid.*, p.103.

13　Marc Brodie points out that only four of the eleven East End parliamentary constituencies voted Conservative consistently, and of these, two (Mile End and Stepney) were the wealthiest in the area: 'Extreme East End poverty seems to have been the least likely reason for Conservatism in these seats,' *The Politics of the Poor*, p.199.

The Scientific Slum

1　*Life and Labour*, First Series, Volume 1, *East London*, 1889, pp.67–8.

2　Laurie, *Pictures and Politics*, p.73.

3　*Victorian Aspirations: The Life and Labour of Charles and Mary Booth* by Belinda Norman-Butler, 1972, p.105.

4　Quoted in *Mr Charles Booth's Inquiry: Life and Labour of the People in London Reconsidered* by David Englander and Rosemary O'Day, 1993, p.144.

5　*Academy*, 29 June 1889.

6　*Life and Labour*, Volume 1, 1889, p.6.

7　*Charles Booth, A Memoir* by Mary Booth, 1918, p.23.
　　In 1908, the old age pension became a reality, with legislation passed under David Lloyd George's chancellorship.

8　Other more minor aspects of working-class life that perplexed and perturbed Booth's investigators and many other slummers included late rising in the morning; women 'gossiping', and other forms of female boisterousness; the ill-kempt hair, slatternly garments, bare arms and bonnetless-ness of middle-aged women, and the loud, showy hats of the younger ones.

9　Volume 2, *London Continued*, 1891, p.81.

10　Volume 1, 1889, p.39.

11　*Ibid.*, p.155.

12　*Ibid.*, p.42.

13　*Ibid.*, p.38.

14　Booth's Summary of Classes B to G are found on pp. 42–60 of Volume 2, 1891.

15　Volume 2, 1891, pp.41–43.

16　*Ibid.*, p.172.

17　Third Series, 'Religious Influences', Volume 2, *London North of the Thames: The Inner Ring*, 1902, p.104.

18　Interview with Loveridge in the Booth Archives, Notebook B/228, District 9, ff.155–65.

19   Reported in *A Story of Shoreditch* by the Reverend Arthur Osborne Jay, p.41.

20   Rupert St Leger's notebook, dated 16 January 1891, in the Booth Archives, Booth Papers A2. NB: real names, taken from Notebooks A2, B/77 and B/80, rather than the printed *Life and Labour* false names, have been used for the Nichol individuals in these paragraphs.

21   Notebooks B/77 and B/80.

22   *Life and Labour*, Volume 2, 1891, p.96.

23   Third Series, Volume 2, 1902, p.68.

24   Volume 1, 1889, p.162.

25   *Ibid.*, p.154.

26   *Ibid.*, pp.174–5.

27   *Ibid.*, p.168.

28   The *Saturday Review*, 20 April 1889; and the *Spectator* of the same date.

29   A pencilled note from 30 April 1898, in Booth Papers A39, box 5, p.4.

30   *Life and Labour*, Volume 1, 1889, p.133.

Our Father

1   Arthur Baxter's interview with Jay on 10 February 1898 in Notebook B/228, District 9, ff.37–59 in the Booth Archives.

2   Jay's letter to the Bishop of London dated 28 January 1887, in the Fulham Papers at the Lambeth Palace Library, Temple, Volume 35, ff.263–4.

3   *A Story of Shoreditch*, p.70.

4   *Life in Darkest London: A Hint to General Booth* by Jay, p.13. Jay's title for this, his first work, was chosen to reference the famous book, published one year earlier, by William Booth (co-founder of the Salvation Army), *In Darkest England and the Way Out*. Jay abhorred the Salvation Army on the grounds of over-centralisation (in place of parish-based pastoral care); and the 'blood and fire' of the Army's rhetoric, which worked the listener 'up to a red-hot pitch of ignorant excitement' (*Life in Darkest London*, p.9).

5   Novelist Arthur Morrison, interviewed by the *Daily News*, Saturday 12 December 1896.

6   Notebook B/228 in the Booth Archives.

7   Melvin Richter, *The Politics of Conscience: T.H. Green and his Age*, New York, 1964, p.129.

8   The phrase is that of Henry Scott Holland, Canon of St Paul's.

9   'Working Men's Clubs' in *The Universities and the Social Problem*, edited by John M. Knapp, 1895.

Winnington-Ingram's predecessor, Herbert Hensley Henson, had been even more keen to exclude women, describing his delight when the decision was made to keep evening lectures and debates all-male affairs: *Retrospect of an Unimportant Life*, 1942, Volume 1, p.27.

10   *C.R. Ashbee: Architect, Designer and Romantic Socialist* by Alan Crawford, Yale, 1985, p.20; Ashbee was describing openly homosexual poet Edward Carpenter, who set up home with a working-class man in 1885.

Seth Koven's 2004 book *Slumming: Sexual and Social Politics in Victorian London*, Princeton, provides a thorough and persuasive exploration of the complex interconnections between sexuality/gender and philanthropy in these years.

11   Henry Scott Holland, *Memoir and Letters*, edited by Stephen Paget, 1921, p.88.

12   Quoted in *Father Adderley* by T.P. Stevens, 1943, p.14.

13   Interview with Bate and his deputy in 1898, in Notebook B/381, District 9, f.35, in the Booth Archives. Bate thought that the Roman Catholics and the Salvation Army were both able to connect to the poorest of the poor, but that within East End Anglicanism, only Jay was 'doing excellent work, though hardly in a religious way'.

14   *London at the End of the Century: A Book of Gossip*, 1900, Chapter 24, 'Entertaining the Working Man', p.209.

15   *A Story of Shoreditch*, pp.56–7.

16   *Ibid.*, p.27.

17   Seth Koven's *Slumming* explores this theme in depth; see Chapter 1.

18   Jay claimed that Miss MacPherson expressed herself coarsely and was highly combative. He said that upon one of her returns from a visit to Canada, she told her Mothers' Meeting: 'Now, you deceitful old bitches, I know what you've been doing while I've been away – you've been going to Father Jay, so losing the chance not only of the relief I should give you in this life, but at the same time imperilling your immortal souls': Arthur Baxter's 1898 interview with Jay, Notebook B/228, District 9, ff.37–59 in the Booth Archives. A pencil note in the margin of Booth's own written-up notes of this interview describes this story of Jay's as a 'fabrication': Booth Papers, A39, p.39.

Tainted Blood

1   Exchange of letters in the Fulham Papers, Temple, Volume 35, ff.334–7.

Rupert St Leger, in his investigations for Charles Booth, was also told by several of the people he visited that they objected to the 'sparring' at Jay's club.

2
> Ho, my comrades, see the signal,
> Waving in the sky!
> Reinforcements now appearing,
> Victory is nigh.
>
> 'Hold the fort, for I am coming,'
> Jesus signals still;
> Wave the answer back to heaven,
> 'By thy grace we will.'

3   Letter from Loveridge dated 18 November 1886 in the Fulham Papers, Temple, Volume 35, ff.244–8.

4   St Peter's, Hackney Road, for instance, had a congregation of 286 in the morning and 284 in the evening; and St Thomas's, Baroness Road, 140 and 220. The vast parish church of Shoreditch – St Leonard's – seated 1,000 but rarely attracted more than 200 on Sunday evenings. As for the Noncons, the Adelphi Chapel in Hackney Road got 271 worshippers in the morning and 570 in the evening; the Methodist Middlesex Chapel nearby in Hackney Road had 232 and 383 respectively; while the Bethnal Green Congregationalists were seating 323 and 567. The 1886 church and chapel attendance figures are found in *The Victoria History of the County of Middlesex*, Volume 11, pp.217–40.

5   Edward Smith, Booth Notebook B/229, District 9, f.187; 'old woman' description, Booth 'secretary' Arthur Baxter, Booth Notebook B/228, District 9, ff.155–65.

6   *A Story of Shoreditch*, p.41.

7   Jay, *The Social Problem: Its Possible Solution*, 1893, p.35.

8   Whelk-cooker, 'Strology Woman and tiny Catholic chapel, Weylland's *The Man with the Book*, p.14, pp.70–1 and pp.101–2; Old Joe Lee, Borrow's *Romano Lavo-Lil*, p.318.

9   Booth Notebook, B/227, District 9, f.140.

10   The church snooper was working for Charles Booth's *Life and Labour* 'Religious Influences' series; Notebook B/387, District 9, 'A Sunday Walk', dated 6 March 1898.

11   Letter from Scott Holland to fellow Christian Social Union member Harold Anson, written in 1913, in *Memoir and Letters*, p.286.

12   *The Reverend William Cuff in Shoreditch: Realistic Sketches of East London Life and Work* by A Travelling Correspondent, 1878, pp.92–3.

13   'The Ritualistic Kilburn Sisters', *c.* 1896.

14   *A Valiant Victorian: The Life and Times of Mother Emily Ayckbowm, 1836–1900, of the Community of the Sisters of the Church,* an anonymous biography published in 1964, p.152.

15   Quoted in a later pamphlet published to highlight the organised nature of the smear campaign against the sisterhood, *The Kilburn Sisters and their Accusers: A Full Account of the Investigation into the Charges brought against the Kilburn Sisters, together with a Detailed Description of the Methods of the Attack,* 1896.

16   Jay, *The Social Problem,* pp.84–5.

17   Issue dated 12 March 1896.

18   *The Descent of Man,* second edition, 1875, p.140.

19   In the Old Nichol girls' school logbook, 1884–88, in the London Metropolitan Archives, at CC/EO/DIV5/NIC/LB/1, are lists of exemptions from examinations, of which these two are typical samples. In some cases, the same girl has had two different conditions attributed to her.

January 1887 (65.2 per cent attendance at classes)

Annie Eagle	Defective intellect
Bella Wilson	"
Caroline Currie	"
Eliza Wilkins	"
Margaret Berry	"
Esther Wilson	"
Emily Brown	"
Charlotte Brown	"
Sarah Middleton	"
Charlotte Hutchings	"
Kate Bourne	Delicate health
Rebecca Isaacs	"
Kate Leversuch	"
Eliza Mott	"
Sarah Thomas	Defective sight
Maggie Thomas	"
Jane Mason	"
Louisa Braham	Subject to fits
Martha Braham	"

Teacher Mrs Shea suffering from 'bad eyes'.

July 1887

Emily Brown	Defective intellect
Charlotte Brown	"
Maria Payne	"
Hannah Harvey	"
Annie Farrell	"
Annie Bennett	"
Sarah Middleton	Unable to learn through starvation
Charlotte Hutchings	"
Eliza Mott	Delicate health
Eliza Griffiths	"
Louisa Dodd	"
Martha Carter	"
Eliza Hudson	"
Caro Currie	"
Alice Thomas	"
Sarah Thomas	Ophthalmia
Hannah Wood	Cataract

20   Highly entertaining in the Report of the Committee is the seeing-off
      of eugenicist/racial theorist J. Gray, secretary to the Anthropometric
      Committee of the British Association, who was repeatedly presented
      with data that contradicted his assertion that Jews are a 'degenerate'
      race. The committee also pointed out that the British are a racially
      mixed people, which greatly affronted Mr Gray. Source: the *Report of
      the Inter-Departmental Committee on Physical Deterioration*, 1904 [Cd 2175,
      2186 & 2210] Volume XXXII, pp.140–3 and pp.147–8.
          During conscription for World War I, only three out of nine men
      were fit for active service in the army or navy; four were deemed wholly
      unfit.

21   *The Social Problem*, pp.84–5.

22   Jerry White, in *Campbell Bunk*, p.112, points out that hereditarian language
      remained a characteristic of British social and medical discourse from
      around 1912 until the Holocaust – the event that showed where such
      genetic determinism could lead us. As late as 1929, the report of the
      Wood Committee on 'social problem groups' stated that the first country
      to be able to eradicate its most 'deficient' 10 per cent of population by
      preventive breeding would gain an advantage over other nations. Those
      that would not, the report suggested, risked 'the racial disaster of mental
      deficiency'.

23   'To Check the Survival of the Unfit: A New Scheme by the Rev. Osborne
      Jay, a Militant Bethnal Green Parson, for Sending the Submerged to a
      Penal Settlement', *London* magazine, 12 March 1896.

Telling Tales

1   I am indebted to Seth Koven's *Slumming* for alerting me to the works
      of L.T. Meade, and in particular to *A Princess of the Gutter*.
2   Another, less plot-alluring, manner in which Joan could have acted was
      to take the case before a magistrate under the existing sanitary legisla-
      tion – anyone was entitled to report such property. No JP in London
      would have failed to enforce improvement or closure on her say-so. Or
      she could have opted to shoulder the lessee's loss on lower rental income.
3   Arthur Osborne Jay angrily denied critic H.D. Traill's claim that Weech
      was intended to be a portrayal of a Jewish fence; letter to the *Fortnightly
      Review*, February 1897.
          Weech, in fact, comes across as a blend of Fagin, Uriah Heep and
      Bleak House rag- and bottle-dealer Krook.
4   Jay's 'shipwrecks', *The Social Problem*, p.62, and 'shoals', *Darkest London*,
      p.110; the master of the workhouse, R. Bushell, was interviewed (by a
      panel that included Charles Booth) for the *Royal Commission on the Poor
      Laws and Relief of Distress*, 1909, Volume XXXVII [Cd 4499] Appendix
      Volume II, Minutes of Evidence, p.325.
5   'The New Realism' in the *Fortnightly Review*, January 1897, reprinted in
      The New Fiction by Traill.
6   'What is a Realist?' by Arthur Morrison, *New Review*, Volume 16, March
      1897; reprinted from Morrison's preface to the third edition of *A Child
      of the Jago*, dated February 1897.
7   Traill, *The New Fiction*, p.25.
8   Allinson repeated and augmented his claims of Morrison and Jay's
      grotesque distortion in the 1898 interview he gave to Booth *Life and
      Labour* interviewer George Arkell, Notebook B/229, ff.155–71 in the
      Booth Archives. In Notebook B/225, f.35, the headmaster of the Nichol
      Street Board School, Mr Jackson, also expressed his indignation with
      Morrison's exaggeration.
9   'A Novel of the Lowest Life', review in the *British Review of Politics,
      Economics, Literature, Science and Art*, 9 January 1897.
10   'A Slum Novel', review in the *Saturday Review*, 28 November 1896. Wells's
      view here is all the more extraordinary since he would go on to become
      an ardent eugenicist.
11   *Daily News*, 12 December 1896.
12   *A Story of Shoreditch*, p.79.

13   *Daily News*, 12 December 1896.

14   *Eastern Post & City Chronicle*, 10 March 1890.

The Dreamers of Dreams

1   From the Board and the Justices of the Peace the LCC inherited control of main drainage, street improvement, bridge maintenance, fire protection, parks and open spaces, contagious diseases, public building safety/control, pauper lunatic asylums, reformatories, baby-farm and dairy-farm inspection, the licensing of places of entertainment, technical education, weights and measures, shop hours, the sale and storage of explosives and petrol, and various other 'health and safety' style administrative duties.

2   Quoted in the biography of his brother, *Frederic Harrison: The Vocations of a Positivist* by Martha S. Vogeler, Oxford, 1984.

3   The famous opening lines of the ode by Arthur O'Shaughnessy (1844–81):

> We are the music-makers,
> And we are the dreamers of dreams,
> Wandering by lone sea-breakers,
> And sitting by desolate streams . . .

4   The Progressives' main aims were to secure the total unification of London by absorbing the Corporation. There were also vigorous campaigns in these early years to have ground landlords' rental receipts taxed, and for greater financial contribution to local improvements to come from these landowners, rather than from the rate-paying occupiers. In addition, the chronic under-assessment of rateable properties on the part of vestries (an attempt to lift the rates burden on the middle classes) was to be tackled, while moves towards further equalisation of the rates – to help ease the burdens on poor districts – were to be successful in 1894. Powers over the police and the utilities were high on the agenda, too, while the LCC's own huge Works Department was supposed to act as a model to employers with regard to pay and conditions.

5   Quoted in William Saunders, *History of the First London County Council, 1889–1891*, 1892, p.48.

6   Issue of 9 December 1890.

7   Housing of the Working Classes Sub-Committee Presented Papers, Bundle A3, May 1890–31 December 1892, report dated 5 June 1890, at the London Metropolitan Archives at LCC/MIN/7320.

8   Quoted in Saunders, *History of the First London County Council*, p.353.

The Boundary Street Shuffle

1   The considered verdicts of J.A. Yelling in *Slums and Slum Clearance in Victorian London*, 1986, and Richard Vladimir Steffel in 'Housing for the Working Classes in the East End of London, 1890–1907', Ph.D. thesis, Ohio State University, 1969.

2   Found in the Presented Papers of the LCC Housing of the Working Classes Sub-Committee, Bundle A3, May 1890–31 December 1892. Goldsmith's Row was known locally as Piggy's Island.

3   *Ibid.*

4   Memo in the Ministry of Health file HLG1/17/5 in the Public Record Office/National Archives.

5   Quoted in C.J. Stewart's *The Housing Question in London, 1855–1900*, p.44.

6   Memo dated 28 August 1893 in HLG1/17/5.

7   Fleming writing in the *London County Council Staff Gazette*, June 1901, p.71. Fleming shared his Stepney Green flat with Lionel Curtis (1872–1955), a Church of England evangelical, and later a mover and shaker in Commonwealth affairs, particularly with regard to South Africa. Curtis was, in the 1890s, head of the Haileybury public school mission at Stepney, and Fleming recalled him explaining to 'the collarless boys of the district ... that strawberries did not grow on trees, and that Haileybury School ... was not a reformatory'.

8   Quoted in *A Revolution in London Housing: LCC Housing Architects and their Work, 1893–1914* by Susan Beattie, 1980, p.22.

9   The team included the following men, who cited a variety of Arts & Crafts influences and connections.

Charles Canning Winmill (who designed Boundary Street's Molesey block, along with Clifton, Laleham and Hedsor, and possibly also Sonning, Culham, Taplow and Sunbury) was a protégé and friend of influential architect Philip Webb. Winmill also became a member of William Morris's Society for the Protection of Ancient Buildings (SPAB) and the Art Workers' Guild. Winmill went on to restore faithfully the ruined Old Chingford church, and helped in the restoration of many Essex and Kent churches. Perhaps more significantly for Londoners, in 1900 he and Owen Fleming took over the LCC Fire Brigades department and their legacy of Arts & Crafts influenced fire stations can still be seen in the city.

Reginald Minton Taylor (responsible for Cookham, Cleeve, Marlow, Shiplake, Chertsey, Hurley and Sandford blocks) made special studies of brick architecture in Holland and the eastern counties of England, and became a SPAB member.

Arthur Maxwell Philips (Iffley and Abingdon) also joined SPAB and had professional links to the London School Board architect and Queen Anne Revivalist E.R. Robson.

For those with time to wander, interesting comparisons can be made between Boundary Street and Philip Webb's number 1 Palace Green, Kensington Palace Gardens (1868–70), controversial in its day, designed for the ninth Earl of Carlisle. Also, 47 Palace Court, Bayswater (1888), by Winmill's one-time boss Leonard Stokes; the Euston Road Fire Station (1901–2), designed by the LCC department that Fleming and Winmill headed up; and Norman Shaw's New Scotland Yard (1886–90) on the Embankment.

10   Found in the Housing of the Working Classes Committee Papers, March 1896–December 1896, LCC/MIN/7353.

11   'The Rebuilding of the Boundary Street Estate', a talk by Owen Fleming, published in the *Journal of the Royal Institute of British Architects*, 7 April 1900, which reported the debate about the estate.

Epilogue: Around the Bandstand

1   Issue dated February 1897. While admiring the blocks' 'restraint' and 'simplicity' and high standard of sanitary fittings, the journal deplored 'this workman's paradise': the British worker, the magazine writer stated, was nothing more than 'a pampered pet' who would now no doubt be contemplating when the government 'really meant to allow him to pass from the partly useful to the wholly ornamental'.

2   The findings of J.A. Yelling in *Slums and Slum Clearance*, p.147.

3   Notebook B/352, ff.107, in the Booth Archives.

4   Booth Notebook B/229, ff.155–171.

5   Lovegrove was responding to Owen Fleming's talk 'The Rebuilding of the Boundary Street Estate', in the *Journal of the Royal Institute of British Architects*, 7 April 1900.

6   *Ibid.*

7   London County Council's *Minutes of Proceedings of the Council*, 17 March 1903, p.422.

8   Report of the Royal Commission on Alien Immigration, 1903, IX, Minutes of Evidence, Q1617–Q1621.

9   *Hansard*, 1903, Volume 118, column 953, 26 February.

10   *Ibid.*, column 197, 18 February.

11   Lew Grade, showbusiness impresario and uncle of Michael Grade, recalled in his 1987 memoir *Still Dancing: My Story* moving into 11 Henley Buildings on the Boundary Street Estate in 1913, when he was eight years old. His family, the Winogradskys, had fled anti-Semitic persecution in Odessa, arrived in London and originally taken lodgings

in Brick Lane; a relative who lived on the estate told them of a flat that was to let. Grade recalled a great spirit of community at Boundary Street.

12   *Report on the Sanitary Condition of Bethnal Green*, 1905, p.66.

13   Sidney and Beatrice Webb, *English Poor Law History*, Part II, Volume 2, 1927, p.669.

14   Samuel, *East End Underworld*, p.25.

Bibliography

All items were published in London, unless otherwise stated.

Unpublished Papers

THE CHARLES BOOTH ARCHIVES, LONDON SCHOOL OF ECONOMICS
Notebooks B/77, B/80, B/225, B/227, B/228, B/229, B/352, B/381, B/387
Papers, A2, A39

LONDON METROPOLITAN ARCHIVES
Old Nichol girls' school logbook, 1884–88, CC/EO/DIV5/NIC/LB/1
Housing of the Working Classes Sub-Committee Presented Papers, Bundle
 A3, May 1890–31 December 1892, LCC/MIN/7320
Housing of the Working Classes Committee Papers, March 1896–December
 1896, LCC/MIN/7353

TOWER HAMLETS LOCAL HISTORY LIBRARY AND ARCHIVE
Minute Books of the Bethnal Green Vestry Sanitary Committee,
 L/MBG/B/4/9 [BG/574], Book no. 9, 1886–88; and [BG/575],
 Book no. 10, 1888–89

NATIONAL ARCHIVES/THE PUBLIC RECORD OFFICE
MH 12/6880, Local Government Board papers
HLG1/17/5, Ministry of Health papers

LAMBETH PALACE LIBRARY
The Fulham Papers, Bishop of London's correspondence and archive, Temple,
 Volume 35

NSPCC ARCHIVES
'Second and Third Annual Report of the East London Branch of the National
 Society for the Prevention of Cruelty to Children', 1890–91

Parliamentary Papers

PP 1834, XXVII *Report of the First Poor Law Commissioners*

PP 1883, LVII *Reports &c from Medical Officers of Health Relative to the Artisans' Dwellings Acts* in *Accounts and Papers (21) Local Government, Local Taxation*

PP 1884–85 [C4402] *Report and Evidence of Her Majesty's Commissioners for Inquiring into the Housing of the Working Classes*

PP 1887, LXXI *Return of the Number of all Deaths in the Metropolitan District in the Year 1886, upon which a Coroner's Jury have returned a Verdict of Death from Starvation or Death accelerated by Privation* in *Accounts and Papers (23)*

PP 1887, XXXVI [C5131 and C5171] *Sixteenth Annual Report of the Local Government Board*

PP 1888, XLIX [C5526] *Seventeenth Annual Report of the Local Government Board*

PP 1903, IX *Royal Commission on Alien Immigration*

PP 1904, XXXII [Cd 2175, 2186 & 2210] *Report of the Interdepartmental Committee on Physical Deterioration*

PP 1908, I [Cd 4156] *Royal Commission on the Duties of the Metropolitan Police*

PP 1909, XXXVII [Cd 4499] *Royal Commission on the Poor Laws and Relief of Distress*

Hansard Parliamentary Debates, 1867, Volume 189; and 1903, Volume 118

Newspapers and Periodicals

Academy
British Architect
The British Review of Politics, Economics, Literature, Science and Art
The Builder
Commonweal
Daily News
Daily Telegraph
Eastern Argus
Eastern Post & City Chronicle
East London Observer
Fortnightly Review
Freedom: A Journal of Anarchist Communism
Home magazine
Household Words
Journal of the Royal Institute of British Architects
Justice
London magazine
London City Mission Magazine
London County Council Staff Gazette

New Review
Nineteenth Century
Pall Mall Gazette
Public Health, The Journal of the Society of Medical Officers of Health
Saturday Review
Spectator
The *Star*
Temple magazine
The Times
Voice of Labour

Books, Articles and Pamphlets

À Beckett, William, *London at the End of the Century: A Book of Gossip*, 1900

Allgood, H.G.C., *The History of Bethnal Green*, 1894

Allinson, Robert, 'A Review of Twelve Years' Work in the Nichol Street District, Shoreditch', *London City Mission Magazine*, 1 September 1894

Askwith, Betty, *Lady Dilke, A Biography*, 1969

'A Travelling Correspondent' (anon.), *The Reverend William Cuff in Shoreditch: Realistic Sketches of East London Life and Work*, 1878

Avrich, Paul, *Anarchist Portraits*, Princeton, 1988

Barker, Felix, and Jackson, Peter, *The History of London in Maps*, 1990

Beattie, Susan, *A Revolution in London Housing: LCC Housing Architects and their Work, 1893–1914*, 1980

Beckett, John, *The Rise and Fall of the Grenvilles: Dukes of Buckingham and Chandos, 1710 to 1921*, Manchester, 1994

Behlmer, George K., *Child Abuse and Moral Reform in England, 1870–1908*, Stanford, 1982

Booth, Charles, *Life and Labour of the People in London* (17 volumes), 1889–1903

Booth, Mary, *Charles Booth, A Memoir*, 1918

Booth, William, *In Darkest England and the Way Out*, 1890

Borrow, George, *Romano Lavo-Lil, Word-Book of the Romany or, English Gypsy Language*, 1874; reissued in paperback, 1982

Boulton, Harold, 'A Novel of the Lowest Life' in *The British Review of Politics, Economics, Literature, Science and Art*, 9 January 1897

Bowen, Desmond, *The Idea of the Victorian Church – A Study of the Church of England, 1833–1889*, Montreal, 1968

Brodie, Marc, *The Politics of the Poor: the East End of London 1885–1914*, Oxford, 2004

Caine, T.H. Hall, *The Christian*, 1898; and 'The Son: Arthur Osborne Montgomery Jay, Vicar of Holy Trinity, Shoreditch', 1910, in *Father and Son: A Study in Heredity*, compiled by 'DN'

Chamberlain, Joseph, 'Labourers' and Artisans' Dwellings', in *Fortnightly Review*, December 1883

Conrad, Joseph, *The Secret Agent*, 1907

Crawford, Alan, *C.R. Ashbee: Architect, Designer and Romantic Socialist*, Yale, 1985

Darwin, Charles, *Origin of Species*, 1859; and *The Descent of Man, and Selection in Relation to Sex*, 1871, second edition, 1875

Davis, John, 'The Enfranchisement of the Urban Poor in Late-Victorian Britain', in *Politics and Culture in Victorian Britain: Essays in Memory of Colin Matthew*, ed. Peter Ghosh and Lawrence Goldman, Oxford, 2006; and 'Slums and the Vote', in *Historical Research*, Volume 64, 1991

Dilke, Emilia, 'Trades Unionism among Women', in *Fortnightly Review*, May 1891

Doggett, Maeve E., *Marriage, Wife-Beating and the Law in Victorian England*, 1992

Ellis, Havelock, *The Criminal*, 1890

Englander, David, and O'Day, Rosemary, *Mr Charles Booth's Inquiry: Life and Labour of the People in London Reconsidered*, 1993

Evans, Stewart P., and Rumbelow, Donald, *Jack the Ripper, Scotland Yard Investigates*, 2006

Evans, Stewart P., and Skinner, Keith, *The Ultimate Jack the Ripper Sourcebook*, 2000

Furniss, Harry, *Some Victorian Women, Good, Bad and Indifferent*, 1923

Galt, John, *A Providence That Shapes*, unpublished memoirs, written *c.* 1933

Galton, Francis, *Hereditary Genius*, 1869; *Hereditary Improvement*, 1873; and *Natural Inheritance*, 1889

Glasier, John Bruce, *William Morris and the Early Days of the Socialist Movement*, 1921

Grade, Lew, *Still Dancing: My Story*, 1987

Greenwood, James, *The Seven Curses of London*, 1869; *Low-Life Deeps, An Account of the Strange Fish to be Found There*, 1876; and 'A Shoreditch Club', in the *Daily Telegraph*, 22 October 1887

Guillery, Peter, 'Another Georgian Spitalfields: 18th-Century Houses in Bethnal Green's Silk-Weaving District', English Heritage Survey Report, July 2000; and *The Small House in Eighteenth-Century London*, 2004

Hendrick, Harry, *Child Welfare in England, 1872–1914*, 1994

Hensley Henson, Herbert, *Retrospect of an Unimportant Life* (three volumes), 1942

Horn, Pamela, *The Victorian Town Child*, Stroud, 1997

Jackson, Louise A., *Child Sexual Abuse in Victorian England*, 2000

Jay, Reverend Arthur Osborne, *Life in Darkest London: A Hint to General Booth*, 1891; *The Social Problem: Its Possible Solution*, 1893; and *A Story of Shoreditch*,

Being a Sequel to Life in Darkest London, 1896; 'To Check the Survival of the Unfit: A New Scheme by the Rev. Osborne Jay, a Militant Bethnal Green Parson, for Sending the Submerged to a Penal Settlement', in *London* magazine, 12 March 1896

Jeune, (Lady) Mary, *Lesser Questions*, 1894

The Kilburn Sisters and Their Accusers: A Full Account of the Investigation into the Charges brought against the Kilburn Sisters, together with a Detailed Description of the Methods of the Attack, anon., 1896

Kitz, Frank, 'The Problem of the Slums', in the *Voice of Labour* journal, Volume 1, no. 1, 18 January 1907

Knapp, John M. (ed.), *The Universities and the Social Problem: An Account of the University Settlements in East London*, 1895

Koven, Seth, *Slumming: Sexual and Social Politics in Victorian London*, Princeton, 2004

Kropotkin, (Prince) Peter, 'Mutual Aid among Animals', in *Nineteenth Century* magazine, September 1890

Latouche, Peter, *Anarchy! An Authentic Exposition of the Methods of Anarchists and the Aims of Anarchism*, 1908

Laurie, Arthur Pillans, *Pictures and Politics: A Book of Reminiscences*, 1934

Lazarus, Henry, *Landlordism*, 1892

Lewis, H.S., and Russell, C., *The Jew in London*, 1900

London County Council Minutes of Proceedings, July–December 1890; January–December 1895; and January–December 1903

London Society for the Abolition of Compulsory Vaccination, *A Catalogue of Anti-Vaccination Literature*, 1894

Mackay, John Henry, *The Anarchists: A Picture of Civilization at the Close of the Nineteenth Century*, Boston, 1891

Mansion House Council on the Dwellings of the Poor, *Report for the Year ending 31 December 1887*; and *Report for the Year ending 31 December 1890*

Marx, Carl (ed.), *Karl Marx and Friedrich Engels, Correspondence 1846–1895, A Selection with Commentary and Notes*, 1934

McCormick, Donald, *The Identity of Jack the Ripper*, 1959

Meade, L.T., *A Princess of the Gutter*, 1895

Mearns, Andrew, *The Bitter Cry of Outcast London*, 1883

Morley, Henry, 'The Quiet Poor', in *Household Words*, Volume 9, 1854

Morris, William, *The Socialist Diary of William Morris*, ed. Florence Boos, 1981; and *The Collected Letters of William Morris*, ed. Norman Kelvin (three volumes), Princeton, 1984–96

Morrison, Arthur, *A Child of the Jago*, 1896; *Tales of Mean Streets*, 1894; and 'What is a Realist?' in *New Review*, Volume 16, March 1897

Norman-Butler, Belinda, *Victorian Aspirations: The Life and Labour of Charles and Mary Booth*, 1972

Nott-Bower, William, *52 Years a Policeman*, 1926

Old Bailey Sessions Papers, 1892 and 1906

Oliver, Hermia, *The International Anarchist Movement in Late-Victorian London*, 1983

Owen, David, *The Government of Victorian London, 1855–1889: The Metropolitan Board of Works, the Vestries and the City Corporation*, Harvard, 1982

Protestant Association, *The Ritualistic Kilburn Sisters*, c. 1896

Quail, John, *The Slow-Burning Fuse: The Lost History of the British Anarchists*, 1978

Reeves, John, *Recollections of a School Attendance Officer*, c. 1915

Report on the Sanitary Condition of Bethnal Green, 1905

Richter, Melvin, *The Politics of Conscience: T.H. Green and his Age*, New York, 1964

Rocker, Rudolf, *The London Years*, 1956

Rose, Michael E., *The Relief of Poverty, 1834–1914*, 1986

Samuel, Raphael, *East End Underworld: Chapters in the Life of Arthur Harding*, 1981

Saunders, William, *History of the First London County Council, 1889–1891*, 1892

Scott Holland, Henry, *Memoir and Letters*, ed. Stephen Paget, 1921

Searle, G.R., *A New England? Peace and War 1886–1914*, Oxford, 2004

Sherry, Norman, *Conrad's Western World*, Cambridge, 1971

Sims, George R., *How the Poor Live*, 1883; *Horrible London*, 1889; and *My Life: Sixty Years' Recollections of Bohemian London*, 1917

Springfield, Lincoln, *Some Piquant People*, 1924

Steffel, Richard Vladimir, 'Housing for the Working Classes in the East End of London, 1890–1907', Ph.D. thesis, Ohio State University, 1969

Stevens, T.P., *Father Adderley*, 1943

Stewart, C.J., *The Housing Question in London, 1855–1900*, 1900

Thompson, E.P., *William Morris: Romantic to Revolutionary*, 1955

Traill, H.D. (Henry Duff), *The New Fiction and Other Essays on Literary Subjects*, 1897

A Valiant Victorian: The Life and Times of Mother Emily Ayckbowm, 1836–1900, of the Community of the Sisters of the Church, 1964 (anon.)

The Victoria History of the Counties of England: A History of the County of Middlesex, Volume 11, *Early Stepney with Bethnal Green*, Oxford, 1998

Vogeler, Martha S., *Frederic Harrison: The Vocations of a Positivist*, Oxford, 1984

Webb, Beatrice, *My Apprenticeship*, 1926; and with Sidney Webb, *English Poor Law History*, Part II, Volume 2, 1927

Wells, H.G., 'A Slum Novel', review in the *Saturday Review*, 28 November 1896

Weylland, John Matthias, *The Man with the Book; or, The Bible among the People*, 1872

White, Jerry, *Campbell Bunk: The Worst Street in North London*, 2003

Williams, Montagu, *Later Leaves, Being Further Reminiscences of Montagu Williams QC*, 1891; *Round London: Down East and Up West*, 1896

Wohl, Anthony S., *The Eternal Slum: Housing and Social Policy in Victorian London*, 1977; and 'Sex and the Single Room', in *The Victorian Family: Structure and Stresses*, ed. Anthony S. Wohl, 1978

Yelling, J.A., *Slums and Slum Clearance in Victorian London*, 1986

Note

Additionally, my understanding of Vestrydom, the parish/county franchise and London local government has been informed by the following books and essays: *Reforming London: The London Government Problem 1855–1900* by John Davis, 1988; *Socialists, Liberals and Labour, The Struggle for London 1885–1914* by Paul Thomson, 1967; 'The Millennium by Return of Post: Reconsidering London Progressivism, 1889–1907' by Susan Pennybacker, in *Metropolis London: Histories and Representations since 1800*, ed. David Feldman and Gareth Stedman Jones, 1989, and Pennybacker's *A Vision for London, 1889–1914*, New York, 1995; *Metropolitan London: Politics and Urban Change, 1837–1981* by Ken Young and Patricia L. Garside, 1982.

Picture Credits

Index

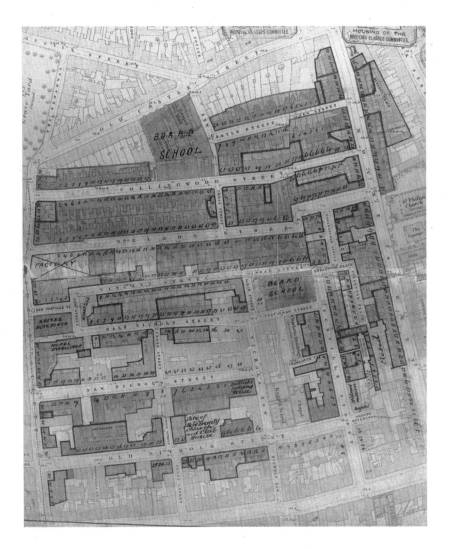

Map courtesy of London Metropolitan Archives. The areas shaded pink were to be demolished as hopelessly insanitary; the blue areas were deemed to be habitable but were nevertheless scheduled for demolition; the brown regions were reserved for institutional buildings, such as schools, church premises, mission houses etc.